PRACTICE

Practice Of BHAKTI YOGA

Sri Swami Sivananda

Published by

THE DIVINE LIFE SOCIETY

P.O. SHIVANANDANAGAR—249 192

Distt. Tehri-Garhwal, Uttarakhand, Himalayas, India

Price | **2007**   [**Rs. 120/-**

First Edition:	1937
Second Edition:	1961
Third Edition:	2000
Fourth Edition:	2007

[1,000 Copies]

ISBN 81-7052-158-0

ES 300

Published by Swami Vimalananda for
The Divine Life Society, Shivanandanagar, and printed by him
at the Yoga-Vedanta Forest Academy Press, P.O.
Shivanandanagar, Distt. Tehri-Garhwal, Uttarakhand,
Himalayas, India

OM
Dedicated to
The Brahma-Kumara
Deva Rishi Narada
Who Still Roams About
In the Three Worlds
With His Tambura
Singing Sriman Narayana
Narayana Narayana
OM

SRI SWAMI SIVANANDA

Born on the 8th September, 1887, in the illustrious family of Sage Appayya Dikshitar and several other renowned saints and savants, Sri Swami Sivananda had a natural flair for a life devoted to the study and practice of Vedanta. Added to this was an inborn eagerness to serve all and an innate feeling of unity with all mankind.

His passion for service drew him to the medical career; and soon he gravitated to where he thought that his service was most needed. Malaya claimed him. He had earlier been editing a health journal and wrote extensively on health problems. He discovered that people needed right knowledge most of all; dissemination of that knowledge he espoused as his own mission.

It was divine dispensation and the blessing of God upon mankind that the doctor of body and mind renounced his career and took to a life of renunciation to qualify for ministering to the soul of man. He settled down at Rishikesh in 1924, practised intense austerities and shone as a great Yogi, saint, sage and Jivanmukta.

In 1932 Swami Sivananda started the Sivanandashram. In 1936 was born The Divine Life Society. In 1948 the Yoga-Vedanta Forest Academy was organised. Dissemination of spiritual knowledge and training of people in Yoga and Vedanta were their aim and object. In 1950 Swamiji undertook a lightning tour of India and Ceylon. In 1953 Swamiji convened a 'World Parliament of Religions'. Swamiji is the author of over 300 volumes and has disciples all over the world, belonging to all nationalities, religions and creeds. To read Swamiji's works is to drink at the Fountain of Wisdom Supreme. On 14th July, 1963 Swamiji entered Mahasamadhi.

SECRET OF RENUNCIATION

1. Renounce (the desires of) this world.
2. Renounce (the desires of) the other world.
3. Renounce egoism, selfishness, Dehadhyasa (body-idea).
4. Renounce the desire for liberation
5. Renounce the renunciation itself (Tyaga-abhimana).

FOUR SPIRITUAL GEMS

1. REMEMBER THE PAINS OF SAMSARA.
2. REMEMBER DEATH.
3. REMEMBER THE SAINTS.
4. REMEMBER GOD.

*1 and 2 will produce Vairagya. 3 will bring inspiration.
4 will cause Darshan of God or attainment of
God-consciousness.*

HARI STOTRA

शान्ताकारं भुजगशयनं पद्मनाभं सुरेशं
विश्वाधारं गगनसदृशं मेघवर्णं शुभाङ्गम् ।
लक्ष्मीकान्तं कमलनयनं योगिहृद्ध्यानगम्यं
वन्दे विष्णुं भवभयहरं सर्वलोकैकनाथम् ।

Santakaram bhujagasayanam padmanabham suresam,
Visvadharam gaganasadrisam meghavarnam subhangam,
Lakshmikantam kamalanayanam yogihriddhyanagamyam,
Vande Vishnum bhavabhayaharam sarvalokaikanatham.

I bow to that Lord Vishnu Whose form is Peace, Who is sleeping on the bed of snake, Who has Lotus in the navel, Who is Lord of the gods, Who is the support for this world, Who is like ether, Whose colour is like cloud, Whose limbs are beautiful, Who is the husband of the Goddess Lakshmi, Whose eyes are like lotuses, Who is obtainable by Yogins by meditation, Who destroys the fear of Samsara, and Who is the One Lord of all the worlds!

SURYA-NAMASKARA

ॐ सूर्यं सुन्दरलोकनाथममृतं वेदान्तसारं शिवं,
ज्ञानं ब्रह्ममयं सुरेशममलं लोकैकचित्तं स्वयं ।
इन्द्रादित्यनराधिपं सुरगुरुं त्रैलोक्यचूडामणिं,
ब्रह्माविष्णुशिवस्वरूपहृदयं वन्दे सदा भास्करं ।

I always adore Surya, the Sun, the beautiful Lord of the world, the immortal, the quintessence of the Vedanta, the auspicious, the absolute knowledge, of the form of Brahman, the Lord of the gods, ever-pure, the one true consciousness of the world itself, the Lord of Indra, the gods and men, the preceptor of the gods, the crest-jewel of the three-worlds, the very heart of the forms of Brahma, Vishnu and Siva, the giver of light.

ॐ मित्राय नमः ।	Om Mitraya Namah
ॐ रवये नमः ।	Om Ravaye Namah
ॐ सूर्याय नमः ।	Om Suryaya Namah
ॐ भानवे नमः ।	Om Bhanave Namah
ॐ खगाय नमः ।	Om Khagaya Namah
ॐ पूष्णे नमः ।	Om Pushne Namah
ॐ हिरण्यगर्भाय नमः ।	Om Hiranyagarbhaya Namah
ॐ मरीचये नमः ।	Om Mareechaye Namah
ॐ सवित्रे नमः ।	Om Savitre Namah
ॐ अर्काय नमः ।	Om Arkaya Namah
ॐ आदित्याय नमः ।	Om Adityaya Namah
ॐ भास्कराय नमः ।	Om Bhaskaraya Namah

He who repeats these names early in the morning before sunrise will possess wonderful health, vigour and vitality. He will be free from any kind of disease of the eye. He will have powerful eye-sight.

ESSENCE OF FOUR YOGAS

(Triplets)

1. Karma Yoga

Grow	Expand	Sacrifice
Serve	Give	Purify

2. Bhakti Yoga

Love	Sing	Surrender
Remember	Weep	Worship
		(Ram Ram Ram)

3. Raja Yoga

Control	Subdue	Restrain

4. Jnana Yoga

Hear	Reflect	Meditate
Enquire	Investigate	Ratiocinate
Assert	Know	Feel
Search	Understand	Realise
		(Om Om Om)

SAGUNA MEDITATION

(Meditation on form with attributes)

Twelve Formulae

1. God is one.

2. God exists.

3. God is Love. He is All-merciful.

4. He is omniscient (Sarvajna).

5. He is omnipotent (Sarva Saktiman).

6. He is omnipresent (Sarva Vyapak).

7. He is Sarva-Antaryamin (Inner ruler of all).

8. He is the support for everything (Sarva-adhara).

9. He is endless (Ananta).

10. He is imperishable (Avinasi).

11. He is indivisible (Akhanda).

12. He is light of lights (Jyotis-Swaroop). He gives light to sun, moon, stars, lightning and fire.

Fix the mind on the image of your Ishta-Devata. Keep the image in the heart or in the space between the two eye-brows by closing the eyes or in front of you. Meditate on the above ideas. Repeat mentally Om or your Ishta Mantra or Sri Ram, Hari Om, Sitaram, Om Namah Sivaya, Om Namo Narayanaya or Om Namo Bhjagavate Vaasudevaya or Maha Mantra. Select any formula you like best. If the mind runs about, bring it back to the image and rotate the mind from one formula to another and finally fix it on one formula. Keep the image of your Ishta also before your mind. After some practice, the mind will get concentrated. Meditation and Samadhi will result eventually. You will have eternal infinite Peace, Bliss and Immortality.

UNIVERSAL PRAYER

O All-pervading, hidden and homogeneous Essence! O adorable Lord of the universe! Thou art witnessing the drama of this world from behind the screen. Thou dwellest in the hearts of all beings. Thou art self-luminous. Thou art the basis for all these names and forms. Thou art one without a second. Thy glory is ineffable. Thou art the source of all sciences, knowledge and beauty.

I do not know how to worship Thee. I have no strength to do any kind of Sadhana. I am full of weaknesses and Doshas. My mind is wavering. Indriyas are powerful and restless. Some say: "Thou art Sakara and Saguna." Others say: "Thou art Nirakara and Nirguna." I don't want to indulge in fighting, discussions and debates. Give me peace and devotion. Give me strength to resist temptations and to control this enemy and thief—mind. Let me utilise my body in Thy service. Let me remember Thee always. Let me be ever looking at Thy sweet, loving face. Grant me this prayer, O Ocean of Love!

Give me true Viveka and lasting Vairagya. The Vairagya cometh and goeth. Let me be established in Para Vairagya. My self-surrender is not perfect and sincere too. I admit my faults. Not a drop of tear comes out of my eyes. Make me weep for Thee. But make me weep in solitude, when I am alone. Let me not shed crocodile tears. Then only I can see Thee in my tears. My heart is harder than flint, steel and diamond. How can I make it as soft as butter? Give me the heart of Prahlada or Gouranga. This is my fervent prayer. O Lord of Love! Grant me this humble prayer of mine. I am suppliant to Thee. I am Thy disciple, Thou art my Guru.

LORD KRISHNA

There the Yamuna shines brilliantly,
Where the blue waters move swiftly.
He plays upon the Flute,
And lo! Radha hastens from Barsana.
He plays with cow-boys under the Kadamba tree,
He does Rasa-Lila in Seva Kunj;
He roams in the forests of Brindavan,
And moves sometimes to Nandgopa.
He perambulates round Govardhan,
And lo! He sits quietly in Gokul.
He enters the houses of Gopis,
Breaks the pots and eats the butter.
There Yasoda brings a rope to tie Him,
Thither He jumps vehemently and smiles!
There stands my Brij Raj, Shyam Sundar,
The Lord of the three worlds and the joy of Devaki.
His Mantra is Om Namo Bhagavate Vaasudevaya.
Repeat it constantly and obtain His Grace.
Do total self-surrender and sit at your ease.
This is the way to real Blessedness.
Bhaktas proclaim it with marked boldness.

BHAJA GOVINDAM

(Of Sri Sankaracharya)

भज गोविन्दं भज गोविन्दं भज गोविन्दं मूढमते ।
संप्राप्ते संनिहिते काले न हि न हि रक्षति डुकृञ्करणे ॥१॥

O thou ignorant one! Sing Govind, the Name of the Lord, sing Govind, Govind! Worship Govind. When you are in the dying condition, the study of grammar will not protect you. Therefore, take refuge in the Lord and sing Govind, Govind! (1)

बालस्तावत्क्रीडासक्तस्तरुणस्तावत्तरुणीसक्तः ।
वृद्धस्तावच्चिन्तासक्तः परे ब्रह्मणि कोऽपि न सक्तः ॥२॥

In childhood you are absorbed in play. In adolescence you are a slave of lust. In old age you groan under the burden of family cares. When will you find time to think of God? (2)

अङ्गं गलितं पलितं मुण्डं दशनविहीनं जातं तुण्डम् ।
वृद्धो याति गृहीत्वा दण्डं तदपि न मुञ्चत्याशापिण्डम् ॥३॥

Man has grown weak. All his organs have become old. Hairs have become grey. All teeth have fallen. The old man walks with the help of a stick. Yet desire has not left him. (3)

पुनरपि जननं पुनरपि मरणं पुनरपि जननीजठरे शयनम् ।
इह संसारे बहु दुस्तारे कृपयापारे पाहि मुरारे ॥४॥

Birth, then death; then lying in the mother's womb, then birth, then death—in this way goes on the endless ocean of births and deaths. Pray to Lord Krishna, the Ocean of Mercy to cross this ocean of births and deaths. (4)

दिनमपि रजनी सायं प्रातः शिशिरवसन्तौ पुनरायातः ।
कालः क्रीडति गच्छत्यायुस्तदपि न मुञ्चत्याशावायुः ॥५॥

Days and nights roll on. Mornings and evenings come and go. Seasons rotate. Time plays. Life decays. But alas! the greed of man never leaves him. Therefore take refuge in the Lord. Sing Govind, Govind! (5)

जटिलो मुण्डी लुञ्छितकेशः काषायाम्बरबहुकृतवेषः ।
पश्यन्नपि च न पश्यति मूढः उदरनिमित्तं बहुकृतवेषः ॥६॥

For the sake of this belly, what sort of disguise man puts on? One grows Jata on the head, another shaves his head, another puts on orange-coloured robe. Ignorant sees not though he sees. Therefore sing Govind, Govind! (6)

वयसि गते कः कामविकारः शुष्के नीरे कः कासारः ।
क्षीणे वित्ते कः परिवारो ज्ञाते तत्त्वे कः संसारः ॥७॥

If you become old, lust will vanish (there will be no attraction for sensual enjoyment). Just as a tank is left when the waters dry up, so also you will be deserted by your relatives when you become poor. If you get the knowledge of the Self, the Samsara will vanish (you will be free from bondage). Therefore sing Govind, Govind! (7)

अग्रे वह्निः पृष्ठे भानू रात्रौ चुबुकसमर्पितजानुः ।
करतलभिक्षस्तरुतलवासस्तदपि न मुंचत्याशापाशः ॥८॥

In front there is fire, in back there is sun. In night he suffers from cold and sleeps by placing his face between the knees. He uses his hands as the begging bowl. He sleeps underneath the tree. Yet the desire has not left him. (8)

यावद्वित्तोपार्जनसक्तस्तावन्निजपरिवारो रक्तः ।
पश्चाज्जीवति जर्जरदेहे वार्तां कोऽपि न पृच्छति गेहे ॥९॥

As long as you earn money, so long will your wife, sons

and other relatives love you. When there is no income, when you are afflicted by disease and old age, nobody will ask you: "Are you all right? How do you do?" Therefore, take refuge in the Lord and sing Govind, Govind! (9)

रथ्याचर्परटविरचितकन्थः पुण्यापुण्यविवर्जितपन्थः ।
योगी योगनियोजितचित्तो रमते बालोन्मत्तवदेव ॥१०॥

Having clad himself in the rags that are found in the streets, having gone beyond good and evil and having fixed the mind in Yoga, the Yogi rejoices like a child and a mad man. (10)

नारीस्तनभरनाभीदेशं मिथ्यामायामोहावेशम् ।
एतन्मांसवसादिविकारं मनसि विचारय वारं वारम् ॥११॥

Do not be infatuated by looking at the breasts of fair ladies. Whenever its memory flashes in your mind, think that it is nothing but a mass of flesh. Therefore, take refuge in the Lord and sing Govind, Govind! (11)

गेयं गीतानामसहस्रं ध्येयं श्रीपतिरूपमजस्रम् ।
नेयं सज्जनसङ्घे चित्तं देयं दीनजनाय च वित्तम् ॥१२॥

Sing Gita and Vishnu Sahasranama. Meditate always on Vishnu. Seek the company of the wise. Distribute your wealth to the poor. (12)

भगवद्गीता किंचिदधीता गङ्गाजललवकणिका पीता ।
सकृदपि येन मुरारिसमर्चा क्रियते तस्य यमेन न चर्चा ॥१३

What can Yama do for that man who has studied a little of Bhagavad Gita, who has drunk a little of Ganga water and who has worshipped Murari at least once? He will not fight with you. (13)

कस्त्वं कोऽहं कुत आयातः का मे जननी को मे तातः ।
इति परिभावय सर्वमसारं विश्वं त्यक्त्वा स्वप्नविचारम् ॥१४॥

(17)

Who are you? Who am I? Wherefrom did we come? Who is mother? Who is father? Enquire like this. Renounce this world which is like a dream. Take this world of names and forms as worthless. (14)

का ते कान्ता कस्ते पुत्रः संसारोऽयमतीव विचित्रः ।
कस्य त्वं कः कुत आयातस्तत्त्वं चिन्तय तदिदं भ्रातः ॥१५

Who is your wife? Who is your son? Who are you? Whence have you come? Oh! This is mysterious world! Think well. Reflect on Truth. Therefore sing Govind, Govind! (15)

सुरमन्दिरतरुमूलनिवासः शय्या भूतलमजिनं वासः ।
सर्वपरिग्रहभोगत्यागः कस्य सुखं न करोति विरागः ॥१६ ॥

The temple or the tree is the dwelling-abode. The earth is the bed. Deer skin is the garment. There is no attachment for anything, any place or person. If there is such a kind of Vairagya, who will not get the supreme bliss of Atman? (16)

यावत्पवनो निवसति देहे तावत्पृच्छति कुशलं गेहे ।
गतवति वायौ देहापाये भार्या बिभ्यति तस्मिन्काये ॥१७ ॥

As long as you breathe or Prana remains in your physical body, so long those in the house will enquire of you. But when the breath goes away, even the wife is frightened to look at the corpse. (17)

कुरुते गङ्गासागरगमनं व्रतपरिपालनमथवा दानम् ।
ज्ञानविहीनः सर्वमतेन मुक्तिं न भवति जन्मशतेन ॥१८ ॥

One can take bath in the Ganga. He can do charity. Even if he does all these in thousand births, he cannot attain Moksha without Jnana or Knowledge of the Self. (18)

EMOTION NEEDS CULTURING

Devotion is ingrained in every being. Even an atheist is devoted to his atheism. Love dwells in the heart of every creature. Without love, life itself cannot exist. Even the most cruel-hearted men love something or other.

As everything else, this love also needs culturing. What is the difference between gardens and forests? In forests, too, there are flowerbeds, there are fruit-bearing trees. Yet, man is afraid to enter the forest. The earth is strewn with thorns; there are ominous-looking bushes here and there that hide wild animals. The trees also grow haphazardly and a violent storm produces a forest-fire which destroys the entire forest. Not so is the case of a garden. The plants are beautifully and artistically laid out. There are order, harmony and pruning. The ground is swept clean and you take delight in walking over the lawns. All foul-smelling things are removed from the garden and the sweet fragrance of the flowers wafts around.

Similar is the case with love. Love grows wildly in the ignorant man's heart. There is the luscious fruit of love in a corner of the heart; but the entire heart is strewn with thorns of hatred, jealousy and so many other vicious qualities that the charm of love is marred. There are bushes of lust, anger and greed which hide within them the wildest animals. Love lies hidden far beneath and far beyond reach. It is as good as non-existent. But, in the case of a true devotee of the Lord, this love has been cultured, and the garden of his heart is cleared of the thorns of vicious qualities, of the bushes of lust, anger and greed. Love of God which is the sweetest of fragrances wafts from such a heart.

Turn your gaze within. Look into your own heart. Find out your love. Take firm hold of this love. Cultivate it consciously and deliberately. Find out the thorns and the bushes. By intelligent methods, throw them out. They have no place in the beautiful garden of your heart where the Lord dwells. See what great preparations you make for the reception of a king, a Governor or a big leader! How nicely you sweep the roads, how beautifully you decorate your houses! How much more preparation is necessary for receiving in the temple of your heart the Lord of the Universe, the Governor of the Universe?

When you eradicate the vices that lurk within and cultivate virtues, you will more fully manifest the hidden love. The great Masters of Bhakti have classified Bhakti into five Bhavas. You can adopt any one of these Bhavas or attitudes towards God. These Bhavas are the natural sublimated human attitudes of love. You love your child; correspondingly there is the Vatsalya Bhava towards God where you treat Him as your child. You love your friend; there is the Sakhya Bhava or attitude of friendship towards God. You love your master; there is the Dasya Bhava where you serve the Lord as your Master. You love your husband or wife; there is the Madhurya Bhava where you take the Lord as your Supreme lover. Some people are loving by nature and their love is distributed on all; they have no particular love-attitude; corresponding to this there is the Santa Bhava where the devotee loves the Lord in his heart, in peaceful contemplation.

Find out where your love lies, whom you love most in the world. Adopt the same love-attitude towards God, your Indweller, your Lord, your real Friend, who resides within your heart. Love for your friends and relations is Moha or deluded attachment. It binds you faster to the wheel of Samsara. It is fleeting and it is fraught with all sorts of unpleasant consequences. Love of God is liberating. It will lead you to perennial bliss and immortality. It is Bhakti which will bring about an Eternal Union between you and the Supreme Lord of the Universe. It will enable you to realise your identity with Him.

(20)

CONTENTS

Chapter 1

GOSPEL OF BHAKTI

Chapter V

OBSTACLES IN GOD-REALISATION

Chapter VI

SAMADHI OR COSMIC CONSCIOUSNESS

Chapter VII

BHAKTI SUTRAS OF NARADA

Chapter VIII
INSPIRING SONGS OF SIVA

Chapter IX

LIVES OF BHAKTAS

APPENDIX

Practice of
BHAKTI YOGA

Chapter 1

GOSPEL OF BHAKTI

1. Who Is God?

God is Truth. God is love. God is Light of lights. He is an embodiment of eternal bliss, supreme peace and wisdom. He is all-merciful, omniscient, omnipotent and omnipresent. He has neither beginning nor end. He is the Supreme Being or Paramatma. The Gita styles Him as Purushottama or Supreme Purusha or Mahesvara. He knows everything in detail (Sarva-vit). He is the support for this world, body, mind, Indriyas and Prana. Without Him not an atom can move. He is the womb for the Vedas. Indra, Agni, Varuna, Vayu and Yama are His assistants. Earth, water, fire, air and ether are His five powers. Maya is His illusive Sakti.

Brahma, Vishnu and Siva are the three aspects of God. Brahma is the creative aspect; Vishnu is the preservative aspect; and Siva is the destructive aspect. There are three other aspects: Virat is the manifested aspect; Hiranyagarbha is the immanent aspect; and Isvara is the causal aspect. Virat is the sum total of all physical bodies; Hiranyagarbha is the sum total of all minds – He is the cosmic mind; and Isvara is the sum total of all causal bodies (Karana Sarira).

Srishti (creation), Sthiti (preservation), Samhara (destruction), Tirodhana or Tirobhava (veiling), and Anugraha (grace) are the five kinds of activities of God.

God is the exquisite taste in vimto. He is the sweetness in the words of a beautiful, young lady. He is the strength in a Pahilvan (wrestler). He is the beauty in the Himalayan landscape. He is the thrilling melody in music. He is the fragrance in jasmine and Champaka. He is the softness in a velvety cushion and silk-cotton. He is the Prana in body, and intelligence in Antahkarana.

Earth denotes His all-supporting nature. Water proclaims the message of His purity and sanctity. Fire indicates His self-luminous nature. Air signifies His omnipotence. Ether heralds His all-pervading nature. Maya is under His perfect control. This is the Upadhi or subtle body of Isvara.

He has the six attributes of divine wisdom (Jnana), dispassion (Viragya), powers (Aisvarya), strength (Bala), wealth (Sri) and fame (Kirti). Hence He is called Bhagavan. He is the absentee landlord of this world. He is the wire-puller (Sutradhara) of all these physical bodies of beings. He is the inner Ruler (Antaryamin) of all beings.

He dwells in your heart. He is in you and you are in Him. He is quite close to you. You were thinking in the beginning that He could be found only in Mount Kailasa, Ramesvaram, Mecca, Jerusalem, sky or Heaven. You had very vague ideas. This body is His moving temple. The *sanctum sanctorum* is the chambers of your own heart. Close your eyes. Withdraw your Indriyas from the sensual objects. Search Him there with one-pointed mind, devotion and pure love. You will surely find Him. He is waiting there with outstretched arms to embrace you. If you cannot find Him there, you cannot find Him anywhere else.

God-realisation alone can put an end to the Samsaric wheel of birth and death with its concomitant evils such as birth, growth, disease, death, sorrow, pain etc. Eternal happiness can be had only in God. That is the reason why sages and saints, scriptures and Srutis make a very emphatic statement and lay great stress on the importance and necessity of God-realisation. Bhakti or devotion can help one in the attainment of this God-realisation. So I have described in this book the various methods to cultivate Bhakti and come face to face with God, taste the nectar of God-consciousness which alone is the *summum bonum* of human life and human endeavour. Purify. Control the Indriyas. Sing His Name. Feel His Presence everywhere.

Repeat His Mantra. Meditate on His form. Realise Him. Rejoice in Him. Attain peace, bliss and immortality.

2. God Exists

There is a display of intelligence in every inch of creation. Who pumps blood in the arteries? Who converts food into chyle and red-coloured blood? Who does the peristalsis in the bowels and stomach and sends the faecal matter to the rectum and anus? Who closes and shuts the eye-lids to prevent dust from falling into the delicate eyes? Who gave intelligence to the cells and glands to secrete semen, milk, bile, saliva, gastric juice etc., from the blood? Who gave intelligence and power to spermatozoa to move, unite with the ovum in the womb and then develop into a foetus? Wherefrom does this minutest, subtlest substance Jiva as nice as the ten-thousandth part of the point of a hair derive the capacity to assume gradually the features, complexion and shape of its parents? What is the power which sustains it and helps its growth in the mother's womb? Who arranges for milk in the mother's breast before the child is born? Who provides food for the little frog living hidden in between the strata of rocks? Who clothed the fruits with skin to prevent contamination from outside? Who divided seasons and Ritus? Who made the water hot beneath the ice to enable fish to live comfortably in the icy regions of the Himalayas in Gauri Kund and other places? Who has combined four parts of inert nitrogen with the combustible oxygen gas?

At whose command does the sun rise punctually in the morning and set in the evening? The sun is miles and miles away from the earth. What a great wonder it is that from such a long distance the sun is able to send light, heat, energy and vitality to all living beings inhabiting this fair earth? There are countless millions of suns much larger than the one that we see but which appear to us as tiny stars on account of their being remoter than the sun with which we are acquainted. It takes millions of years for the light to reach this earth from these stars. Velocity of light is 1,86,000 miles per second. Light from distant stars has not yet reached us even now. What a marvel it is! All these stars, planets and satellites are revolving in the sky in fixed orbits from day to day, month to month and year to year under immutable definite laws.

Now the question arises whether all this organisation is the work of some intelligent Creator behind or is the product of a fortuitous combination of particles of matter, Anus, Parama Anus, Dvi Anus, atoms and molecules? It is the former hypothesis that appeals to our intellect. The Vedas also quite endorse the verdict of our reason. They emphatically declare that the sun and the moon, heaven and earth were created by God.

Who supplies water to the trees, flowers, various shrubs etc., that are found in the forests? Who is this unseen, untiring gardener who works without wages or any sort of remuneration? Who gives nourishment in time to tigers, lions, birds, fishes, plants, insects and worms? How is it that only human beings are born of human beings, birds of birds, beasts of beasts, tigers of tigers, dogs of dogs, horses of horses, elephants of elephants, ants of ants, bears of bears, mules of mules, an exact copy of their parents in every respect? From a tiny seed there springs a huge banyan tree that can give shelter to thousands of persons! From a tiny seed there comes out a big mango tree that gives abundance of luscious fruits! What is that power that supports and nourishes these trees? What is that hidden and miraculous power that brings out a huge form with hair, fingers, toes, nose, teeth, ears, legs, thighs etc., out of one drop of semen? What is that power that brings a mighty tree with foliage, flowers, twigs and fruits out of a tiny seed?

Again how wonderful is the human machine! How harmoniously all the organs work in unison in the economy of nature! In the Gita this body is known as "the nine-gated city" (*Navadvarapura*). In summer the skin works energetically to throw off all impurities of the body. In winter the kidneys work hard to eliminate the impurities of the blood and to relieve the over-worked skin. The endocrine glands, pituitary, pineal, adrenals work in perfect harmony in manufacturing the internal secretions to help the metabolic process of the body and its growth and structure.

It is a great marvel to see the working of the nervous system under the control of the brain and the movement of the afferent and efferent impulses through the spinal cord. There is magnificent electric battery within, with switch-board and wires. The operator is the Inner Ruler (Antaryamin), who controls and supervises everything. He is the supervisor (Upadrashta), permitter (Anumanta) and the great Lord (Mahesvara). Look again at the heart and lungs which work under the direct control of the brain! How wonderful are these vital organs of life? Can any scientist manufacture any of these organs, tissues, fibres, tendons or cells in his boasted laboratory with his boasted intellect? How harmoniously the different systems of the body work without any rest, murmur or grumble! How very beautifully the different centres in the brain such as the vision-centre, the auditory-centre, the centre for smell and so on do their functions! One is struck with awe and amazement as he begins to think seriously on the working of this delicate human machinery. To think that this most wonderful mechanism is the result and product of a fortuitous combination of particles of matter or atoms is simply absurd and illogical indeed! It has been doubtless, moulded and fashioned by some architect who is infinitely more skilful, more intelligent and more powerful than these ordinary architects who build mansions, palaces and bungalows. Remember this point well. That architect is God or Isvara or Creator. Call Him by whatever name you may please. It does not matter much.

Then again look at the miraculous powers of the mind! In the Kena Upanishad the first verse begins: "Who is the Director of the mind?"

There is the play of Divine Hand here also. Can my brother psychologist manufacture a mind in his boasted laboratory? Look at the various faculties of the mind — power of discrimination, power of judgement, power of reasoning, retentive power, power of imagination, cogitative faculty, power of reflection, and so on and so forth! No one but God can create such a powerful and miraculous mind.

Karma or action is non-sentient. Who is the dispenser of fruits of actions? Who fixes the span of life? Some live for 120 years while some others live for only 10 years. How do you explain these variegated appearances of this universe? Some are born decrepits. Some are sandows. Some are kings, earls and millionaires whereas some others are peasants and beggars. Some are born blind, deaf and dumb. Some are beautiful. Some are ugly. Some are fools, some are intellectual giants and sages. Some are rogues and dacoits. Some are martyrs and honest men. The theory of Karma and the presence of God who awards fruits of actions with justice to everybody can alone satisfy these above questions.

It is obvious that ever since the beginning of creation some miraculous power has been at work in every clime and at every age and that it will continue to work forever. You can call this "Mysterious Power", the all-pervading Intelligence or by any name you choose. Call Him "Father in Heaven", "Jehovah", "Allah", "Substance", "Essence", "Brahman", "Ahur-Mazda". It is all the same.

This Intelligence is Truth. This Intelligence is pure love or God. He is Jnana Svaroopa or embodiment of wisdom. He is Jnanamaya or full of knowledge. He is Svayam Jyotis or self-luminous. He is Svayambhu or self-existent. He is Svatantra or independent. He exists in the past, present and future. He is unchanging or Nirvikara. He is *Avang-Mano-Gochara* or beyond speech and mind. He is Sat-Chit-Ananda or Existence-Knowledge-Bliss Absolute. He is Omniscient, Omnipresent, Omnipotent, Supreme Being.

He can be realised by meditation with a pure, one-pointed heart. O my dear friends, will you still remain sceptics, materialists and atheists or spiritual giants? Bow your head with humility and sincerity at the lotus-feet of the All-Wise Creator. You will get His Grace. Do not delay even a second to approach Him. Purify. Pray. Sing. Meditate. Realise.

3. God Is Immanent

As I have said already, God is an absentee landlord of this world. He is hiding Himself within these objects. He is remaining within these objects. He is the Indweller and inter-penetrating Presence or Essence or Substance, the intelligent and creative principle of the universe itself. This is a fundamental conception of pantheism. You will find in the Svetasvatara Upanishad:

एको देवः सर्वभूतेषु गूढः सर्वव्यापी सर्वभूतान्तरात्मा ।
कर्माध्यक्षः सर्वभूताधिवासः साक्षी चेताः केवलो निर्गुणश्च ॥

"One shining Being sits hidden in every creature, pervading all, the Inner Self of all beings, the watcher of all acts, abiding in all created things, the witness, the heart, the absolute, free of all attributes."

Just as oil is hidden in seed, butter in milk, mind in brain, foetus in the womb, sun behind the clouds, fire in wood, sugar or salt in water, scent in buds, sound in the gramophonic records, gold in quarts, microbes in blood, so also God is hidden in all these beings and forms. Just as you see the bacilli of cholera, typhoid fever, consumption or any other disease as for that matter through the powerful lens of microscope, so also you can see God through the eye of intuition (Jnana Chakshus).

The first Sloka of the Isavasya Upanishad begins with: "*Isa-vasyam-idam sarvam* – All these movable and immovable objects are indwelt by the Lord." In the Katha Upanishad (I-iii-12) you will find: "*Esha sarveshu bhuteshu gudho-atma...* – This Atman is hidden in all beings." He who has a sharp, subtle, pure intellect can see Him.

God is full of mercy, love and compassion. He has been described as "Ocean of Mercy." His mercy flows like the streams of the Ganga and the Yamuna. He is depicted as having sold Himself to His devotees, so to say. He willingly suffers endless pain in the eyes of the world in order to alleviate the sufferings of His devotees. He bears the scar left on His chest by the kick of Bhrigu as an ornament. He wears the skulls of His devotees as a garland round His neck. He ran with lightning speed to save the modesty of Draupadi from being outraged.

He apologised and begged pardon of Prahlada in the following words:

"O dear, you were too tender of age and too delicate of body to stand the terrible tortures inflicted on your person by your hot-headed father. A parallel of his atrocious deed I have never seen. Pray, therefore excuse me if I was late in coming to your rescue."

You are all aware of the dying Jatayu in the lap of Sri Rama, who caressed the bird which was mortally wounded in its heroic efforts to rescue Sita from the clutches of the demon king, Ravana. He wiped off the dust on its body with the trusses of His hair. Mark here the unique, tender affection of Sri Rama towards His devotees!

God becomes a slave of His devotees. Lord Krishna says:

"I am not in My control. I am under the complete control of My Bhaktas. They have taken entire possession of My heart. How can I leave them when they have renounced everything for My sake only?"

Lord Rama carried the palanquin of His devotee, Sri Tyagaraja of Tiruvayur, the late reputed songster-Bhakta. He carried water in a vessel for His ablution. He is ever waiting for a chance to serve you in the same way. May His blessings be upon us all!

4. What Is Bhakti?

Bhakti is the slender thread of Prem or love that binds the heart of a devotee with the lotus feet of the Lord. Bhakti is intense devotion and supreme attachment to God. Bhakti is supreme love for God. It is the spontaneous outpouring of Prem towards the Beloved. It is pure, unselfish, divine love or Suddha Prem. It is love for love's sake. There is not a bit of bargaining or expectation of anything here. This higher feeling is indescribable in words. It has to be sincerely experienced by the devotee. Bhakti is a sacred, higher emotion with sublime sentiments that unites the devotees with the Lord.

Sandilya defines Para Bhakti or preliminary devotion as supreme attachment to God. *"Sa paranuraktir ishvare."* "Para Anurakti" is intense attachment or love for God. The Narada Pancharatna defines it as realisation of God alone as "mine" accompanied by deep love for Him without attachment to any other object in the world. It is undivided love for God in which He alone is felt as "mine".

A distinction is drawn by some later devotional literature between Bhakti and Prem. Bhakti is spontaneous attachment to God. The devotee is entirely possessed by Him. He is absorbed in Him. Prem is the crowning consummation of Bhakti. It is the most concentrated love for God which is full of the most intense attachment and

...s the heart thoroughly. Love of God is the ...letion and perfection of devotion.

...ve between husband and wife is physical, selfish and hypocritical. It is not constant. It is carnal passion only. It is sexual appetite. It is tinged with lower emotions. It is of a bestial nature. It is finite. But Divine Love is infinite, pure, all-pervading and everlasting. There is no question of divorce here. There is no internal union between husband and wife in reality in the vast majority of cases. Savitri and Satyavan, Atri and Anasuya are very, very rare in these days. As husbands and wives are extremely united only for selfish ends there is only some show of smile and external love, it is all mere show only. As there is no real union in their heart of hearts, there are always some kind of friction, rupture, wry faces and hot words in every house. If the husband does not supply his wife with the necklace and silk sari she demands and take her to the cinema, there will be regular tug-of-war and fighting in the house. Can you call this real love? It is mercenary, commercial, business. On account of lust men have lost their integrity, independence and dignity. They have become slaves of women. What a pitiable spectacle you see! The key is with the wife and even for few rupees the husband has to stretch his hands to her. Still he says under delusion and intoxication of passion: "I have a sweet, loving wife. She is really a Mira. She can be really worshipped."

Robert J. Ingersoll, the great philosopher defines Love as follows:

"Love is the only bow on life's dark cloud. It is the Morning and the Evening Star. It shines upon the cradle of the babe and sheds its radiance upon the quiet tomb. It is the mother of art, inspirer of poet, patriot and philosopher. It was the first to dream of immortality. It fills the world with melody, for Music is the voice of Love. It is the perfume of the wondrous flower—the heart. Without it we are less than beasts but with it earth is heaven and we are gods in embryo."

5. Fruits of Bhakti

Bhakti softens the heart and removes jealousy, hatred, lust, anger, egoism, pride and arrogance. It infuses joy, divine ecstasy, bliss, peace and knowledge. All cares, worries and anxieties, fears, mental torments and tribulations entirely vanish. The devotee is freed from the Samsaric wheel of births and deaths. He attains the immortal abode of everlasting peace, bliss and knowledge. Love for God is as sweet as nectar by tasting which one becomes immortal. One who lives, moves and has his being in God becomes immortal.

"That unmanifested, the Indestructible, It is called; It is named the highest path. They who reach It return not. That is My Supreme Abode" (Gita: VIII-21). "By His grace thou shalt obtain supreme peace, the everlasting dwelling place" (XVIII-62). "The devotees, liberated from the bonds of birth, go to the blissful seat" (II-51). Param Dhama (Supreme abode), Anandamaya Pada (Blissful seat), Sasvata Pada (everlasting abode), Parama Gati (highest path) are all synonymous terms.

6. Six Classifications of Bhakti

There are the following six classifications in Bhakti:

1. Apara (lower) and Para (higher) Bhakti.
2. Ragatmika and Vidhi Bhakti.
3. Sakamya and Nishkamya Bhakti.
4. Vyabhicharini and Avyabhicharini Bhakti.
5. Mukhya (primary) and Gauna (secondary) Bhakti.
6. Sattvic, Rajasic and Tamasic Bhakti.

Ragatmika Bhakti is otherwise known as Mukhya or primary Bhakti. Para Bhakti is also primary devotion. Sakamya Bhakti is Gauna or secondary devotion. Nishkamya

Bhakti, Avyabhicharini Bhakti or Para Bhakti is otherwise known as Ananya Bhakti.

In Apara Bhakti the devotee is a neophyte. He observes rituals and ceremonies. He rings bells, applies sandal-paste to the Murti and offers flowers, Arghya, Naivedya, etc. He has no expanded heart. He is sectarian. He dislikes other kinds of Bhaktas who worship other Devatas.

Para Bhakti is Nirguna Bhakti which is free from the three Gunas. It is the spontaneous, unbroken flow of pure love towards God. It is Ahaituki (free from any sort of motive) altogether. It is Avyavahita or unmeditated devotion towards God. This type of devotee does not care for divine Vibhutis even if they are offered. He wants the lotus feet of the Lord. He does not want even Kaivalya Mukti or absolute independence. He wants to serve God. He wants to see His face always. He wants pure divine love. God is the be-all and end-all of the devotee of Para Bhakti.

A devotee of Para Bhakti type is all-embracing and all-inclusive. He has cosmic love or Visva Prem. The whole world is Vrindavana for him. He does not visit temples for worship. He sees his Ishtam everywhere. He has equal vision. He has no hatred for any object. He welcomes snakes, pain, disease and suffering as messengers of God. His mind is ever fixed at the lotus feet of the Lord. His Prem flows like oil in one continuous current. Para Bhakti is Jnana only. This is the highest culminating point in devotion. Nama Dev, Tukaram, Rama Das, Tulasidas and Hafiz had Para Bhakti.

In Ragatmika Bhakti there are no fetters, shackles or barriers of customs or rules of society. There is no binding of any sort. There is an absolutely free flow of divine Prem. The devotee cares not a jot for public opinion. He is above public criticisms. He is as simple as a child. He pours forth exuberantly his love towards his Beloved. The devotee is intoxicated with divine Prem. Whereas in Vaidhi Bhakti the devotee observes rules and ceremonies and has certain restrictions. The simple-hearted cow-maids of Vrindavana and Mira had Ragatmika Bhakti. Though Mira was a Rani, she never cared for the opinion of the public and her relations and husband. When she was under intoxication of Krishna Prem she danced in the streets and open places amidst men and ordinary people. Ordinary people were not able to gauge the depths of her heart. Even Bhaktas were not able to fathom out the recesses of her innermost chambers of heart, the depth of her unbounded love for Lord Krishna. Her thrilling devotional songs which bring tears from the eyes of the hearers bespeak clearly the exalted state of her heart that was deeply saturated with the nectar of devotion towards Lord Krishna. She says: "I have none else for me besides my Giridhar Gopal." Can anyone fully understand the God-intoxicated Mira?

Showing devotion to God for getting riches or son or removal of sufferings from diseases is Sakamya Bhakti. Sakamya Bhakti will eventually terminate in Nishkamya Bhakti. Prahlada only had Nishkamya Bhakti from the very beginning. Even the boy Dhruva had only Sakamya Bhakti. It was for getting dominion that he retired into the forest on the advice of his mother in the beginning. It was only later on that he developed Nishkamya Bhakti after he had Darshan of Hari. All his desires melted away.

To love God for sometime and then wife, children and property for sometime is Vyabhicharini Bhakti. To love God and God alone for ever and ever is Avyabhicharini Bhakti. Mark this carefully!

In Sattvic Bhakti the quality of Sattva predominates in the Bhakta. He worships God to please Him, to destroy Vasanas etc. All these three types of Bhakti are secondary devotion only.

In Rajasic Bhakti the quality of Rajas predominates in the

devotee. He worships God to get estates, wealth, name and fame.

In Tamasic Bhakti the quality of Tamas predominates in the devotee. He is actuated by wrath, arrogance, jealousy and malice in showing devotion to God. To worship God for destroying one's enemy and for getting success in an enterprise through unlawful means is Tamasic Bhakti. The thief prays to God: "O God Ganesha! Let me get something tonight. I will offer Thee 100 cocoanuts." This is Tamasic Bhakti.

Sandilya also mentions of primary Bhakti and secondary Bhakti. The primary devotion is the attachment to the Lord. It is single-minded devotion. It is one-pointed, whole-hearted devotion to God (Ekanta Bhava). Primary devotion is the principal, because others are subservient to it.

According to the Gita (VII-16), there are four kinds of Bhaktas. "Fourfold in division are the righteous ones who worship Me, O Arjuna! The distressed, the seeker for knowledge, the selfish and the wise." The devotion of the distressed, the seeker for knowledge and the selfish man is after all secondary as they have ulterior, selfish motives in view. But the devotion of the wise is pure and absolutely unselfish. It is Para Bhakti or primary devotion. He has undivided love and whole-hearted devotion to the Lord. He is eternally united with Him. God is the dearest to him and he is the dearest to God. Lord Krishna says: "Noble are all these but I hold the wise as verily Myself; he self-united is fixed on Me, the highest path" (Gita: VII-18).

Prahalada later on meditated on his own Self as Lord Hari. This is Abheda Bhakti. This is the advanced stage of devotion.

When a devotee has devotion for Lord Hari, Lord Siva, Devi, Lord Rama, Lord Krishna and thinks that Lord Hari is Siva, Rama, Devi or Krishna this is Samarasa Bhakti. He has equal vision. This is also advanced stage of devotion. He

PRACTICE OF BHAKTI YOGA

makes no difference between Rama and Krishna, between Siva and Hari, between Krishna and Devi. He knows and feels that Radha, Sita and Durga are all inseparable Saktis of Lord Krishna, Rama and Siva respectively.

Narada also classifies Bhakti into two kinds, primary and secondary. Secondary devotion is of three kinds according to Sattva, Rajas and Tamas in the devotee. Or it is of three kinds according as the devotees are the distressed (Aartha), the seeker after knowledge (Jijnasu) and the selfish (Artharthi).

Just as you see wood alone in chairs, tables, doors, windows, bed-steads, clay alone in earthen jars, pots and jugs, so also see Lord Krishna alone in all these names and forms. This is Ananya Bhakti. Para Bhakti, Ananya Bhakti, Avyabhicharini Bhakti are one and the same.

7. Five Classes of Worship

Rishis of yore have prescribed five classes of worship to the predominating Tattva in a man or woman. They are worship of Sri Ganesha, Lord Siva, Lord Hari, Sakti and Surya. If Prithivi (earth) Tattva is predominant, one should worship Sri Ganesha. If Apas (water) is predominant, he should worship Hari. If Agni (fire) is predominant, he should worship Surya; if Vayu (air) is predominant he should worship Sakti and if Akasa (ether) is predominant he should worship Lord Siva.

8. Five Kinds of Worship

There is another classification according to the capacity of the individual. Some worship elementals and lower spirits. These worshippers are Tamasic people. Some worship Pitris or forefathers and Rishis and Devas. Some worship Avataras as Lord Krishna and Rama. Some Worship Saguna Brahman. Advanced students worship Nirakara, Nirguna, Avyakta, Satchidananda Brahman of the Upanishads. These are the five kinds of worship.

9. Five Kinds of Bhava

The five kinds of Bhava are: Shanta Bhava, Dasya Bhava, Sakhya Bhava, Vatsalya Bhava and Madhurya Bhava. Dasya Bhava is for the beginners. Madhurya Bhava is most difficult. It is a mode of Vedantic Sadhana. It is merging in the Beloved. In Vatsalya Bhava, Shanta, Dasya and Sakhya Bhavas are hidden. In Sakhya Bhava, Shanta and Dasya Bhavas are hidden. In Dasya Bhava, Shanta Bhava is hidden.

10. Five Thorns in the Bhakti Marga

The five thorns that are found in the path of Bhakti are Abhimana of caste, learning, position, beauty and youth. These thorns should be removed completely if one wants to have God-consciousness.

11. Five Internal Enemies

The five internal enemies that stand in the way of developing Bhakti are lust, anger, greed, infatuated love and hatred. These should be destroyed by Brahmacharya, Kshama, disinterestedness, Vichara, pure love and service.

12. Five External Enemies

The five external enemies of Bhakti are cinema, bad company, obscene songs, Rajasic food and novels that deal with sex and passion. These five items should be shunned ruthlessly if you want to grow in devotion.

13. Four Grades of Bhakti

The four grades of Bhakti are tender emotion, warm affection, glowing love and burning passion; or admiration for God, attraction, attachment and supreme love.

14. Four Classes of Love

The four classes of love are Sneha for inferiors like children, Prem for equals like wife or friends, Sraddha in superiors such as teachers or parents and Bhakti for God.

15. Four Kinds of Mukti

The Bhakta remains in the Loka where Lord Vishnu resides like an inhabitant of a state. This is Salokya Mukti. In Samipya Mukti, the Bhakta remains in close proximity with the Lord like the attendant of a king. In Sarupya Mukti, he gets the same form like that of the Lord like the brother of a king. In Sayujya Mukti, he becomes one with the Lord like salt and water. This is the highest rung in the ladder of Bhakti Yoga.

16. Eight Signs of Bhakti

Asrupata (tears), Pulaka (horripilation), Kampana (twisting of muscles), crying, laughing, sweating, Moorcha (fainting) and Svarabhanga (inability to speak) — these are the signs noticed when a Bhakta develops Bhakti to a higher degree.

17. Requisites for God-realisation

The important requisites for quick realisation of God are:

(1) Bhakti should be of a Nishkamya type. (2) It should be Avyabhicharini. (3) It should be continuous like the flow of oil from one vessel to another (Tailadharavat). (4) The aspirant should strictly observe right conduct (Sadachara). (5) He should have extreme earnestness and sincerity of purpose for Darshan of God, burning Vairagya and Vichara. He should have the same feeling like that of a man who wants the doctor for removal of a foreign body in the eye, like the child in a river who shrieks for coming outside, like the fish out of water which flutters about for re-entry into the water, like the man who runs for the fire-brigade when his house is on fire, like the young wife who pines for meeting her husband who is expected to arrive from a foreign land after a long separation of twelve years. Then alone he will have Darshan of God.

18. Characteristics of a Bhakta

A devotee has equal vision for all. He has no enmity for anybody. He has exemplary character. He has no attachment for anybody, place or thing. He has not got the idea of "mine-ness". He has a balanced state of mind in pain and pleasure, heat and cold, praise and censure. He regards money as pieces of stone. He has neither anger nor lust. He regards all ladies as his own sisters or mother. The name of Hari is always on his lips. He has always inner life or Antarmukha Vritti. He is full of Shanti and Joy.

"These blessed Bhaktas sometimes weep in loving memory of God, sometimes they laugh, sometimes rejoice, sometimes they talk mysterious things that are transcendental, sometimes they dance in divine ecstasy that is simply indescribable, sometimes they sing melodiously His praises and Glory, sometimes they imitate the actions of Lord and sometimes they sit quiet and enjoy the highest bliss of the Self." (*Srimad Bhagavata.*)

PRACTICE OF BHAKTI YOGA

Chapter II

NAME, FAITH AND LOVE

1. Glory of Rama Nam

What is that thing which is superior to Rama even? It is RAM NAM. How? Sri Hanuman told Sri Rama: "O My Lord, there is something superior to Thee." Sri Rama was quite astonished. He asked Hanuman: "What is that thing, O Hanuman, which is superior to Me?" Hanuman replied: "Hey Prabho, Thou hadst crossed the river with the help of a boat. But I crossed the ocean with the help of (and the power and strength of) Thy Name only. Name is indeed superior to Thee."

Mahatma Gandhi says: "You must learn to take the name of Rama with full devotion and faith. When you study the Ramayana, you will learn from Tulasidas the divine power of that blessed Name.

"You might ask me why I tell you to use the word RAMA and not one of the many other names of the Creator. True, His Names are as many as and more than the leaves on the yonder tree and I might for instance ask you to use the word God. But what meaning, what associations would it have for you here? In order to enable you to feel anything when repeating the word God, I should have to teach you some English. I should have to explain to you the foreign people's thoughts and associations.

"But in telling you to repeat the name of RAMA, I am giving you a name worshipped since the beginning of time by the people of this land, a name familiar to the very animals and birds, the very stones of Hindustan through so many thousands of years. You all know the story of Ahalya? No, I see you don't. But you will soon learn it when you study the Ramayana. You will learn how a stone by the roadside sprang to life at the touch of Rama's foot as he passed by. You must learn to repeat the blessed Name of Rama with sweetness and such devotion that the birds and beasts will pause for a moment to listen to you; the very trees will bend their leaves towards you, stirred by the divine melody of that Name. And when you are able to do this, I tell you, I will come all the way on foot from Bombay as on a pilgrimage to hear you. In His sweet Name lies a power which can cure all our ills."

Kamal got a severe scolding from his father Kabir for prescribing RAMA NAM for a rich merchant to be repeated twice for curing leprosy. Kamal asked the merchant to repeat RAMA NAM twice and yet he was not cured of this dire disease. Kabir was very much annoyed and told Kamal: "You have brought disgrace on my family by asking the merchant to repeat Rama Nam twice. Repetition of Rama Nam only once is quite sufficient. Now beat the merchant severely with a stick on his head. Ask him to stand in the Ganga and repeat RAMA NAM once from the very bottom of his heart." Kamal followed the instructions of his father and gave a good thrashing on the head of the merchant who began to bleed profusely. He then repeated Rama Nam once only with Bhava from the very core of his being and was completely cured of his disease.

Kabir sent Kamal to Tulasi Das. Tulasi Das wrote Rama Nam on a Tulasi leaf and sprinkled the juice over five hundred lepers. All were cured. Kamal was quite astonished. Then Kabir sent Kamal to Surdas. Surdas asked Kamal to bring the corpse that was floating in the river. Surdas repeated 'Ra' only once (not the full name Rama) in one ear of the corpse and it was brought back to life. Kamal's heart was filled with awe and wonder. Such is the power of God's Name. My dear friends, my educated college youths, my dear barristers, professors, doctors and judges, don't be puffed up with false, worthless college

PRACTICE OF BHAKTI YOGA

learning. Repeat the Name of the Lord with Bhava and Prem from the very bottom of your hearts with all your beings and realise the supreme bliss, knowledge, peace and immortality right now, this very second.

Kabir says: "If any one utters RAMA NAM even in dream, I would like to make a pair of shoes out of my skin for his daily use."

Who can describe the glory of God's Name? Who can really comprehend the greatness and splendour of the holy Names of the Lord? Even Lord Siva's consort, Parvati failed to describe in adequate terms the very true significance and grandeur of God's Name. When one sings His Name or hears It sung, he is unconsciously raised to sublime spiritual heights. He loses his body-consciousness. He is immersed in joy and drinks deep the divine nectar of immortality. He gets divine intoxication. Repetition of God's Name enables the devotee to feel the Divine Presence, the Divine Glory and the Divine consciousness within himself and also everywhere. How sweet is Hari's Name! How powerful is God's Name! What an amount of joy and peace and strength it brings to one who repeats His Name! Blessed indeed are those who repeat God's Name for they will be freed from the wheel of birth and death and attain Parama Ananda and immortality.

2. Faith Can Work Miracles

Faith in God is the first step to God-realisation. Not an iota of progress is ever possible in the path of spirituality without faith. The faith must be a living faith. It must be unwavering faith. Lack of faith is a stumbling block in the path of realisation. Faith develops into Bhakti or devotion to God. Faith is the gateway to the Kingdom of God. It is the threshold to the Knowledge of God. Faith gives strength and removes anxieties and uneasiness of mind. Faith is therefore a powerful mental tonic.

Faith is an important qualification for an aspirant in the path of spirituality. Students of all Yogas, whether of Karma, Bhakti, Raja and Jnana, should possess this fundamental virtue. No faith, no devotion. No faith, no Jnana. The Sanskrit equivalent of faith is "Sraddha" or "Visvas." The student should have faith in the existence of God, in the teachings of his Guru, in the Vedas and his own self. The whole world runs on faith only. The Raja has faith in his Diwan. The husband has faith in his wife. The shop-keeper has faith in his customers. The patient has faith in his doctor. The client has faith in his lawyer. The engineer has faith in his head-clerk.

Faith is one of the important items in the Shad-Sampat or sixfold virtues of the four means of salvation or Sadhana Chatushtaya in the path of Jnana. Even Patanjali Maharshi, the exponent of Raja Yoga philosophy lays much stress on faith. He says: *"Sraddha veerya smriti samadhi prajna-purvaka itaresham* — to others (this Samadhi) comes through faith, energy, memory, concentration and discrimination of the real." (I-20.) He has placed Sraddha (faith) in the very beginning of this Sutra. He has given prominence to this. If a man has faith, then energy, memory etc., come by themselves. He will collect all his energies and remember the ultimate Tattva and will exert to realise the basic Reality. Let me repeat the words of the Gita here. "He who is full of faith obtaineth wisdom, and he also who hath mastery over his senses; and having obtained wisdom he goeth swiftly to the Supreme Peace. But the ignorant, faithless, doubting self goeth to destruction; nor this world, nor that beyond, nor happiness is there for the doubting self." (IV, 39-40)

"Some by meditation behold the Self in the self by the Self; others by the Sankhya Yoga and others by the Yoga of action. Others also ignorant of this having heard of it form

others, worship; and these also cross beyond death, adher[...]
to what they had heard." (VIII, 24-25)

Dhruva had faith in the words of his mother. So he
retired into the forest, did severe Tapas and came face to
face with Lord Hari. The milk-maid had faith in the words
of the Pandit who said: "Thousands have easily crossed the
ocean by a single Name of God. Could you not cross this
tiny stream?" and crossed the river by reciting His Name,
whereas the faithless Pandit who preached about the power
of the Name to the milk-maid was on the point of drowning
when he himself tried to cross the river on the strength of
the Name after seeing the marvellous spectacle of the girl's
crossing the river by repeating RAMA NAM. Prahalada had
unswerving faith on Narayana. And so he had His Grace.
Fire was transmuted into ice by the Name of Hari. Mira had
absolute faith on her Giridhar Gopal. And so poison was
changed into nectar.

"Life is faith and illumination. Without faith it is lame,
without illumination it is blind. We need today the creative
force of faith, the faith that discerns without logic, the faith
that electrifies, the faith that removes all barriers and
obstacles from its path and is anxious to fill us with divine
enthusiasm and to give expression to the divine in man. Be
strong in faith and be complete in the light faith enkindles
in the heart... If the power of intellect can discern the ideals
of life, the power of faith retains them and makes them
active in us. The delight of life is in the constant striving for
actualising the ideal, and unless we can claim the touch of
divine faith in us, we do not see the joy of a new creation, a
new realisation, a new life, a new dream."

Bad company, lust, greed, infatuated love for wife, son
and property, and unwholesome food are the enemies of
faith. They spoil the intellect, cloud the understanding and
destroy memory. They produce wrong Samskaras or

impressions in the mind and render the intellect gross and impure.

Study of Bhagavata, Ramayana, Gita, Upanishads, Yoga Vasishtha; the elevating company of Sadhus and Mahatmas; service of saints; stay at Prayag, Rishikesh, Ayodhya, Vrindavana, Gangotri, Badrinarayan; prayer; Japa or recitation of Mantra; Kirtan or singing His Name; meditation; remembrance of saints and sages who have realised God and study of their teachings; fasting; pilgrimage; personal contact of a Guru can sow the seed of faith in a man and increase it also till it becomes quite firm and unshakable.

Look at the perfect faith of the boy Nama Dev! His father asked him to place a dish of food before Vittobha (Lord Krishna at Pandharpur). Nama Dev placed the plate before the Murthy and asked the Deity to eat it. He wept bitterly when the Murthy kept quiet. After sometime Lord Krishna came out of the Murthy in the form of a boy and ate the food. The boy brought back the plate empty. The father asked: "Nama Dev, where is the food?" The boy replied: "My Vittobha has eaten it." Such is the power of real faith.

The rare achievements of Visvamitra Rishi in his Tapas and Yoga, the success of Napoleon in the field of battle, the attainments of Mahatma Gandhi in his Karma Yoga and practice of Yama, the awe-inspiring majesty and the soul-stirring magnanimity and the grandeur and nobility of great personages like Tulasidas, Ramdas, Sri Dattatreya, Sri Sankara, Vamadev and Jada Bharata are all due to the work of that simple secret called FAITH.

Faith can work miracles. Faith can work wonders. Faith can move mountains. Faith can reach a realm where reason dare not enter. There is nothing impossible under the sun for the man of faith to accomplish. Have therefore absolute and unshakable faith in God, in the power of RAMA NAM, in the Vedas and the scriptures and in the teachings of your

Guru and, last but not the least, in your own self. This is the master-key for success in life and God-realisation or attainment of Divine Consciousness.

3. Yoga of Universal Love

There is no virtue higher than Love, there is no treasure higher than Love, there is no knowledge higher than Love, there is no Dharma higher than Love, there is no religion higher than Love because Love is Truth, Love is God. This world has come out of Love, this world exists in Love and this world ultimately dissolves in Love. God is an embodiment of Love. In every inch of His creation you can verily understand His Love.

The delicious fruit-juice that quenches your thirst, the palatable vegetable and food that appease your hunger, the silken robes that you wear, the sun, the moon and the stars that illumine this world, the rivers, the mountains and the oceans that bespeak of divine glory, divine beauty and divine splendour, the various kinds of flowers that blossom out in your gardens, the music that lulls you to an agreeable slumber, the scents that give you pleasure, nay, each and everything that gives you happiness and joy has come out of the power of God. When you are tired at night, He envelops this world with darkness to lull you to rest and takes you to His sweet bosom of Love to refresh and soothe your tired nerves. At night He sheds light in the dark to show you the path by taking the forms of stars. God is indeed an ocean of Love! Have you understood the mystery of His creation? Have you realised His magnanimous nature and wonderful love towards His creatures? He serves you in the form of attendants and nurses. He treats you in the form of doctors. He has taken the forms of herbs and medicinal plants to serve your needs. He is the spoon. He is the medicine. He is the patient. He is the doctor. He is the disease. He is the microbe. This great mystery will be unravelled to you when your mind is absorbed in Him through intense and Param Prem.

To love man is to love God alone. Man is the true image of God. He is His Amsa. In the Gita you will find: "A portion of mine own Self transformed in the world of life into an immortal spirit, draweth around itself the senses of which the mind is the sixth, veiled in matter" (XV, 7). "Knowledge of sacrifice (Adhi Yajna) tells of Me as wearing the body, O best of living beings" (VIII, 4). Love is the fulfilling of the law. The aim of charity, social service, altruism, humanitarianism, socialism, bolshevism and so many other 'isms' is to develop this universal love, to expand one's heart *ad infinitum*. Theosophy speaks of universal brotherhood and tries to unite all through the common thread of cosmic love. Love is a great leveller. There is no power on earth greater than Love. You can conquer this world even if you have a ray of this divine commodity which is absolutely free from even a tinge of selfishness. Pure love is a rare gift of God. It is the fruit of one's untiring service of humanity and incalculable virtuous actions in several incarnations. It is a rare commodity indeed.

He who possesses even a ray of this is a veritable god on earth. He is a mighty potentate. St. Paul says: "Though I speak with the tongues of men and of angels and if I have no love, I am become as sounding brass or a tinkling cymbal. And though I have the gift of prophecy and understand all mysteries and all knowledge, though I have all faith so that I could remove mountains and have not love, I am nothing. And though I bestow all my goods to feed the poor and though I give my body to be burned and have not love it profiteth me nothing."

True religion does not consist of ritualistic observances, baths and pilgrimages but in loving all. Cosmic love is all-embracing and all-inclusive. In pure love no one is shut out from its warm embrace. It is wide enough to include the humblest of us, from the tiny ant to the mighty elephant, from the condemned prisoner to the mighty emperor, from the worst scoundrel to the reputed saint on the surface of this earth. It is hatred that separates man from man, nation from nation and country from country. It is pride and egoism that divide a man from another man. Hatred, pride, egoism are mental creations. They are the products of ignorance only. They cannot stand before pure love. Just as darkness is dispelled by the penetrating rays of the burning sun, so also jealousy, hatred and egoism are dispelled by the rays of divine Prem.

It is easy to talk of universal love. But when you come to the practical field, you obviously show signs of failure. If anybody talks ill of you and uses harsh words, at once you are thrown out of balance. You get irritated and show an angry face and pay him in the same coin. Where is universal love? You do not like to part with your possessions when you see people in distress. A man who is struggling to develop cosmic love and realise Him through love, cannot keep anything for himself more than he actually needs for keeping the life going. He will sacrifice even this little to serve a needy one and undergo privation and suffering willingly with much pleasure. He will rejoice that God has given him a rare opportunity to serve Him. People talk of universal love but are very niggardly in action. They show only lip-sympathy and lip-love. This is absolute hypocrisy. Those who have developed pure, cosmic love are very, very rare in this world. But those who talk of universal love are plenty. He who tries to develop universal love should try to possess various Sattvic virtues such as Kshama, patience, perseverance, tolerance, generosity, straightforwardness, mercy, truthfulness, Ahimsa, Brahmacharya, Nirabhimanata, etc. He should serve humanity untiringly with a disinterested, selfless spirit for many years. He has to kill his little self ruthlessly. He must bear calmly insults and injuries. Then only there is the prospect of cultivating cosmic love. Otherwise it is all vain and flowery talk and idle-gossiping only. It is sugar in paper or tiger in the carpet.

Pure divine love consciously felt and spontaneously directed towards all beings including animals and birds is indeed the direct result of one's vision or realisation of the Supreme Being. Let me repeat here the words of Bhagavan Sri Krishna: "He who seeth Me everywhere and seeth everything in Me, of him I never lose hold and he shall never lose hold of Me" (Gita: VI-30). "The self-harmonised by Yoga, seeth the Self abiding in all beings, all beings in the Self; everywhere he seeth the same" (VI-29).

How can that Yogi of pure love who has this grand vision of cosmic consciousness hate another, abuse another and show contempt and anger towards another? He is dear to God. That is the reason why Lord Krishna says: "He who beareth no ill-will to any being, friendly and compassionate, without attachment and egoism, balanced in pleasure and pain, and forgiving, he, My devotee, is dear to Me" (XII-13).

The saints, seers and prophets of the world have spoken of love as the end and aim or goal of life. The Rasa Lila of Sri Krishna is full of Prem and divine mysteries. The stripping of clothes of Gopis means the destruction of egoism. Lord Krishna has preached love through His Flute. Lord Buddha was an ocean of love. He gave up his body to appease the hunger of a cub of a tiger. Raja Sibi gave from his own thigh an equivalent weight of the pigeon's flesh to satisfy the appetite of the hawk. What a noble soul! Lord Rama lived a life of love and showed love in every inch of his activity. My dear children of Love, draw inspiration from their teachings. Tread the path of Love, commune with God and reach the eternal abode of Love. This is your highest duty. You have taken this body to achieve Love which alone is the goal of life.

Dear brothers, if you wish to attain perfection, if you wish to enjoy infinite peace and bliss, if you wish to become immortal, develop pure Divine Love; cultivate universal love by serving and loving all, for Love alone will bring you liberation; Love alone can carry you to the other shore of bliss and immortality, the shore which is beyond all grief, pain and sorrow.

Live in Love. Breathe in Love. Sing in Love. Eat in Love. Drink in Love. Walk in Love. Talk in Love. Pray in Love. Meditate in Love. Think in Love. Move in Love. Write in Love. Die in Love. Purify your thought, speech and action in the fire of Love. Bathe and plunge deep in the sacred waters of Love. Taste the honey of Love and become an embodiment of Love (Prema Vigraha or Prema Murthy).

May the divine flame of Love grow brighter in you all! May we all feel universal brotherhood and cultivate universal love! May we all recognise God in all beings and see God in all faces! May we share what we possess with others! May we speak at all times sweet and loving words! May we serve humanity untiringly with sweet love! May the cultivation of universal love be the goal of life! May we not forget the Flute-Bearer of Vrindavana, the embodiment of Prem, the Joy and Solace of life! May we sing His Name like Radha and repeat His Mantra 'Om Namo Bhagavate Vaasudevaya' at all times! May His blessing be upon us all!

4. Krishna's Flute

There stands my Bansiwala with Flute in His hands underneath the Kadamba tree on the banks of the Yamuna in Vrindavana, my sweet, beloved Krishna, Lover of Radha, the Joy and Solace of my life, my Immortal Friend. On a moon-lit night He played melodiously on His Flute. All the Gopis thronged in front of Him in a breathless state. Some were boiling the milk. Some were nursing their children. Some were serving their husbands. All left their works half done and rushed impetuously with dishevelled hair in a disorderly state to Krishna to hear His sweet Flute. Krishna was their all-in-all. Without Krishna they could not live even for a second.

The ways of Krishna are always crooked. He stands crooked. He holds the Flute in a crooked manner. Vrindavana where he lives is full of crooked gullies. The Yamuna is crooked. His behaviour is crooked. He is full of crooked politics. His philosophy is crooked. Yet He is the most sublime, the most charming personality, an embodiment of Prem, a perfect Yogi. He is Poorna-Avatara with sixteen rays. It is very, very difficult to understand Him.

Amongst all saints, prophets and teachers, Sri Krishna and Sri Sankara are the ideal ones. They were perfect masters. They were Karma Yogis, Bhaktas, Raja Yogis and Jnana Yogis. They preached Karma, Upasana Yoga and Jnana. Lord Krishna drove the chariot in the battle-field and danced with the Gopis in the shady retreats of Vrindavana and taught Yoga and Jnana to Uddhava and Arjuna. The four Yogas are blended in His Gita or the Immortal Song. Sri Sankara fought with the Buddhists, did Parakaya-Pravesa in the body of the Raja of Benares, sang hymns to Hari and Dakshinamurthy, established Mutts in four centres of India, founded the Advaita philosophy, defeated Mandana Misra and did Dik-Vijaya. The world has not yet produced such a brilliant genius as Sankara. This is perfection. This is integral development of head, heart and hand.

No man is a perfect male and no woman is a perfect female. There is always a mixture of masculine and feminine qualities in both. There are some males in whom the feminine elements are predominant in their character. Examples are many in the world. Even so no man is absolutely rational or absolutely emotional. There is a mixture of both. One may be more rational and in him the faculty of reason may be more developed and the other may be more emotional and in him the heart may be more developed. Some foolish, dry Vedantins who pose themselves as "Advaita Vadins" dislike Sankirtan and speak ill of Sankirtan and Nritya. Swami Rama Tirtha, a fine example of a Vedantin, danced in Brahmapuri forests when he was in divine ecstatic mood with *gunguru* tied to his feet. He had a harmonious combination of head and heart. Lord Gouranga was a genius. He was a master of Nyaya. He also did Nritya and Sankirtan. He developed his head and heart. Nritya is an exact science. Nritya is Adhyatmic and celestial. The founders of this science are Lord Krishna and Lord Siva. You will have to exhibit the six Bhavas in your Natanam (dance). These are Utpatti (creation), Vinasa (destruction), Gati (movement), Agati (stability), Vidya (knowledge) and Avidya (ignorance). Mark how Lord Krishna stands with Flute in His hands showing these six Bhavas. O dry, one-sided Vedantins! Give up cavilling. Learn to be wise. Give up dry, idle talking. Develop head, heart and hand and attain perfection. There is no iota of hope for your salvation till you develop your heart. Dear friends, bear this in mind always!

Krishna's Flute is the symbol of the freedom or Pranava. He has preached Prem through His Flute. He has created this world out of the Dhvani OMKARA that proceeds from His Flute. He stands on the right big toe. This signifies the Upanishadic utterance: *"Ekam evadvitiyam Brahma* — one without a second." He shows three curves while standing. This represents the three Gunas by which he has created this world. He gazes at Radha and puts the Prakriti in motion. He is the *primum mobile*. The lotus on which He stands, stands for the universe.

In the esoteric sense heart is the Vrindavana. Mind is Radha. Gopis are the nerves and the Indriyas. Anahata sounds that proceed from the heart are the melodious songs that come out of Krishna's Flute. Sahasrara Chakra is the Param Dhama. Lord Krishna is Para Brahman. The five Koshas are the five fortresses. Pranas are the gate-keepers. The Shad-Chakras are the gates. Immortality is the Yamuna. Crown of the head is Kadamba tree. Mind melts in Brahman. Radha is united with Krishna. This is Rasa Lila.

Radha asked Krishna: "O My dear! Why do you love the flute more than me? What virtuous actions has it done so that it can remain in close contact with your lips? Kindly explain to me, my Lord, the secret of this. I am eager to hear." Sri Krishna said: "This flute is very dear to Me. It has got some wonderful virtues. It has emptied off its egoism before I began to play. It has made its inner hollow quite void and I can bring out any kind of tune, Raga or Ragini, to my pleasure and sweet will. If you also behave towards Me in exactly the same manner as this flute, if you remove your egoism completely and make perfect self-surrender, then I shall also love you in the same manner as I love this flute."

This body also is the flute of Lord Krishna in the macrocosm. If you can destroy your egoism and make total self-surrender, unreserved Atma-Nivedana to the Lord, He will play on this body-flute nicely and bring out melodious tunes. Your will will become merged in His Will. He will work unhampered through your instruments, body, mind and Indriyas. You can rest very peacefully then without cares, worries and anxieties. You can watch the play of the universe as a Sakshi. Then your Sadhana will go on by leaps and bounds, because the divine will or divine grace itself will work through you. You need not do any Sadhana at all. But make the self-surrender from the core of your heart with all your being (Sarva Bhavana). Learn the lesson from the flute and follow its ways. If you have done complete Saranagati at the Lotus Feet of Lord Krishna you have already reached the realm of peace, the Kingdom of Immortality, the dominion of eternal bliss and everlasting sunshine. You have found out a joy that never fades, a life that never decays nor dies. You have reached the other shore of fearlessness, which is beyond darkness, doubt, grief, sorrow, pain and delusion.

O my dear children of immortality! Lord Krishna is still roaming about in the gullies of the Vrindavana. You can find Him in the Seva Kunja in the Kunja gullies if you really want Him. He is the Brij Raj, unprecedented monarch of the three worlds. He is waiting with outstretched hands to embrace you with His warm love in His sweet bosom as He did with Mira, Surdas and others in days of yore. Purify your mind, destroy your evil Vasanas and egoism. Hear once more the flute of the Bansiwala, Banke-Bihari of Vrindavana, His Immortal Song of Gita and allow Him to play on this body-flute of yours. Lose not this rare opportunity. It is very difficult to get this human body.

Call Him fervently with single-minded devotion and purity and sing this song of welcome. He will appear before you.

Hey Krishna Aja Bansi Bajaja,
Hey Krishna Aja Gita Sunaja,
Hey Krishna Aja Makkhan Misri Khaja,
Hey Krishna Aja Lila Dikhaja.

O Lord Krishna come to me and play Thy Flute,
O Lord Krishna come to me and teach me Gita,
O Lord Krishna come to me and eat butter and sugar-candy,
O Lord Krishna come to me and show me Thy Lila.

May we hear once more the Flute of Radha Krishna, the Muraliwala of Vrindavana. May we hear once more the Gita directly from His own mouth as Arjuna had heard in days of yore. May we play with Him in close intimacy and dance in divine ecstasy like the Gopis and the cowherds and merge ourselves in Him. May we eat Makkhan-Misri with Him in Gokul. May we allow Lord Krishna to utilise our bodies also as His flute!

May we sing His Name (Om Namo Bhagavate Vaasudevaya) whole-heartedly like Radha and obtain His Grace, which can take us to His Abode of everlasting peace and infinite bliss! May His blessings be upon us all!

5. Radha — The World Mother

My humble salutations and adorations to Sri Radha, the World Mother, the inseparable devoted partner of the Flute-Bearer of Vrindavana, who took her birth in the sacred village Barsana near Mathura and who was an incarnation of the Goddess Lakshmi. Just as heat is inseparable from fire, just as coolness is inseparable from ice, just as shadow is inseparable from man, so is Radha inseparable from Lord Krishna. Worship of Radha is really worship of Krishna and worship of Lord Krishna really includes worship of Radha. Radha was an embodiment of Prem (Love) and devotion (Bhakti). She had no other thoughts save of Krishna. She had no other image in her mind than that of Krishna. She took her birth to teach the world the true relationship of the lover and beloved, the secret of Madhurya Bhava or Madhurya Rasa, which is only essence of Vedanta.

The gist of the Rasa Lila is essence of devotion (Para Bhakti) or oneness, the merging of the lover and the beloved. The secret of Rasa Lila is that men or women while remaining in the world and doing all sorts of activities can develop Krishna-Prem and can realise Godhead at their very threshold. It teaches: "Give the mind to God, just as Radha did, and the hands to work. Sing. Dance in Divine ecstasy. But forget Him not."

Even the Sufis have admiration and devotion for Radha and Krishna. Their philosophy is founded on Radha's Prem to Lord Krishna. They try to develop the same Bhava which Radha had towards Lord Krishna.

Every nerve, every atom, every cell, every tissue, every

pore in the skin of the body of Radha vibrated the Name of Krishna. She could never forget Him even for one millionth part of a second. She never slept at night. She was singing Lord Krishna's Name throughout the night. She was a Gudakeshi, one who conquered sleep like Arjuna and Lakshmana. A little Dhvani from the flute of Krishna at dead of night would intoxicate her with Krishna-Prem and would bring her out into the dense forest to hear His sweet, heart-rending music of the soul, the melody of Omkara. No power on earth could stop her. She taught to the world the gist of self-surrender, the very core of the highest Bhakti or Atma-Nivedana Bhakti, the highest rung in the ladder of devotion which begins from the first step of Dasya Bhava or the relation of master and servant and culminates in complete merging by total and perfect Saranagati. The name Radha stands for Atma-Nivedana or offering of heart, soul, mind, and the whole being (Sarva Bhava) at the Lotus-Feet of the Lord, just as the name Hanuman stands for the spirit of perfect and supreme service to the Lord.

Radha is Durga. Radha is Parvati. Radha is Rajesvari. Radha is the sweet, untiring nurse of the whole world. She is the world Mother. The whole world rests in Her sweet bosom. She is the creatrix and generatrix of the whole universe. The whole Lila is kept up by Her. She sways the world through Her three Gunas, Sattva, Rajas and Tamas.

She is the doctor. She is the medicine. She is the patient. She is the cup. All these are Her manifestations. She is dynamic Brahman. She is Sakti or power. Without Her not an atom can move. She is the light in the Sun, sapidity in water, Sakti in electricity and will-force, fragrance in flower, beauty in flowers and Himalayan landscape, splendour in the stars, chivalry in warriors, devotion in Bhaktas, revolution in electrons. She is Avidya, Maya, Vidya. She is the Vedas. Whatever you see, hear, feel, taste and smell is Radha. There is no other thing in this world save Radha.

She guides the Sadhakas. She nourishes the babies. She is the untiring gardener of the universe. Her glory is indescribable. Her splendour is ineffable! Her beauty, love and intelligence are inscrutable! Even the thousand-tongued Adisesha will fail to describe Her greatness. Devotees of Radha have written volumes on the philosophy of Radha-Tattva. Lack of space does not allow me to give a full description here.

Without Her grace no spiritual progress is possible. Without Her Anugraha (Grace) no cultivation of devotion, no Darshan of Lord Krishna is possible. Control of mind can hardly be attained without Her blessing. It is She who introduces the thirsty, sincere aspirants to Lord Krishna. She Herself takes care of the Sadhana of Her devotee, if he obtains Her grace. She Herself leads the devotee by holding him in Her hands. How merciful She is! How kind She is! Indescribable!

You can meet Her even now in the Seva Kunja of Vrindavana if you have sincere devotion. Even now she roams about with Lord Krishna in the gullies and Kadamba forests of Vrindavana, and on the banks of the Yamuna. Lo! Now She is there with Her Lord in the Mahavana! If you have the eyes of devotion, the real inner eye of intuition, you can see Her and Her Lord also. She has got the Surma or collyrium to open your blind eyes. She dwells in the chambers of your heart. Run to Her with all Bhava and devotion, right now, this very second. Don't delay even for a second. Delay is practical death. She is waiting on the banks of the Yamuna, to embrace you with outstretched hands. Find Her out. Thirst for Her Darshan. Make yourself fit to approach Her Lotus Feet. Melt in Her Prem. Purify your heart by singing Her Name. Weep sincerely for Her Darshan in solitude. Pray now: "O Mother Radha! When will that blessed day come to me to sit at Your Lotus Feet? I am Thine. All is Thine. Thy Will be done, my Mother!

Beloved of Lord Krishna! Bless Me!" Shed sincere tears of Joy and Prem for Her. Let us sing Her Name now with Bhava, faith and Prem:

Jaya Radhe Jaya Radhe Radhe
Jaya Radhe Jaya Sri Radhe,
Jaya Krishna Jaya Krishna Krishna
Jaya Krishna Jaya Sri Krishna.

May Radha, the World Mother, the sweet untiring World Nurse help us in developing Bhakti or Prem! May She guide us in our daily activities of life. May She introduce us to Her Beloved Lord Krishna, the holder of Govardhan! May She explain to us the full secret of Rasa Lila! May She train us to become qualified students to partake in the Divine Rasa Lila of Seva Kunja at Vrindavana that is going on daily even now and to drink the Krishna-Prema-Rasa or Nectar of Immortality! May the blessings of Sri Radha Krishna be upon us all!

Chapter III

BHAKTI AND JNANA

1. Philosophy of Pratima

Pratima is a substitute or symbol. For a beginner Pratima is an absolute necessity. By worshipping an idol Isvara is pleased. The Pratima is made up of five elements. Five elements constitute the body of the Lord. The idol remains an idol; but the worship goes to the Lord. Just as a man is pleased by shaking hands with his friends by touching a small portion of his body, so also God is pleased when a small portion of His Virat (cosmic) body is worshipped. Just as the child develops the maternal Bhava (mother-feeling) by playing with its imaginary toy-child made up of rags, and suckling it in an imaginary manner, so also the devotee develops the feeling of devotion by worshipping the Pratima and by concentrating upon it. Pictures, drawing, etc., are only a form of Pratima.

A reputed baron of New York came to me one evening for an interview. During the course of conversation the baron said: "Swamiji, I have no faith in image-worship. It is all foolishness." The private secretary of the baron who was also with him had a photo of the baron in his pocket-diary. I took the photo and asked the private secretary to spit on it. The secretary was struck aghast. He hesitated and looked at the baron. I again commanded him: "Go on, spit at the picture. Quick." The secretary said: "Swamiji, the baron is my master. I serve him. How can I spit at the picture? This is his image. I cannot do this ignoble act. I respect him in this picture." I said to him: "This is only a paper. This is not the real baron. It cannot talk, move or eat." Then the secretary said: "Anyhow, I see my baron in this picture. This mean act would affect my feelings as well as wound the feelings of my master. I cannot spit." I said to the baron: "Look here, my friend! Your secretary loves and respects your photo. He associates your presence with the picture although it is just a bit of paper. Is this not image-worship? Even so, the devotee associates the attributes of God with the image and feels His presence or immanence there. He finds it easy to concentrate his mind on the image. The mind wants a concrete prop to lean upon in the beginning stage of practice. Do you see the point now, my dear baron?" The baron replied: "Revered Swamiji! You are quite right. My eyes are opened now. I am quite convinced. Pray, pardon me."

2. Jnani Is the Greatest Bhakta

Bhagavan Sri Sankaracharya defines Bhakti as devotion unto Atman. You cannot entirely separate Bhakti from Jnana. When Bhakti matures, it becomes transmuted into Jnana. A real Jnani is a devotee of Lord Hari, Lord Krishna, Lord Rama, Lord Siva, Durga, Sarasvati, Lakshmi, Lord Jesus and Buddha. He is a Samarasa Bhakta. Some ignorant people think that a Jnani is dry man and has no devotion. This is a sad mistake. A Jnani has a very, very large heart. Go through the hymns of Sri Sankaracharya and try to gauge the depth of his devotion. Go through the writings of Sri Appaya Dikshitar and measure the magnanimous depths of his unbounded devotion.

Swami Rama Tirtha was a Jnani. Was he not a Bhakta of Lord Krishna? If a Vedantin excludes Bhakti, remember, he has not really grasped and understood Vedanta. The same Nirguna Brahman manifests with a little Maya in a corner as Saguna Brahman for the pious worship of His devotees. Isvara is His Tatastha Lakshana only.

Lord Krishna takes a Jnani as a first-class Bhakta. "Of these, the wise, constantly harmonised, worshipping the One, is the best; I am supremely dear to the wise, and he is dear to Me. Noble are all these but I hold the wise as verily Myself; he self-united, is fixed on Me, the highest path." (Gita: VII-17, 18.)

Bhakti is not divorced from Jnana. On the contrary Jnana intensifies Bhakti. He who has knowledge of Vedanta is well established in his devotion. He is steady and firm. Some ignorant people say that if a Bhakta studies Vedanta, he will lose his devotion. This is wrong. Study of Vedanta is an auxiliary to · increase and develop one's devotion. The devotion of a man proficient in Vedantic literature is well-grounded. Bhakti and Jnana are like the two wings of a bird to help one to fly unto Brahman, to the summit of Mukti.

Hear this story with rapt attention. Sukadev was a perfect Jnani. He was an Avadhoota. How is it then that he studied the Bhagavata and held Katha for seven days for Raja Parikshit? This is a wonder of wonders! A perfect Jnani was absorbed in his Brahmanishtha but he came down from his heights and preached devotion. Did he lose his Atma-Jnana? What is the truth here? Sri Veda Vyasa wrote the eighteen Puranas for the benefit of the world. He wrote the Mahabharata which deals more with Pravritti. Yet he was not satisfied in his heart of hearts. He was quite uneasy and restless. Narada met Vyasa and enquired: "What is the matter with you, O Vyasa? You are in a sunken, depressed mood." Vyasa spoke out his heart. Then Narada said: "You will have to write a book which treats of Krishna-Prem and the Lilas of Lord Krishna. Then only you will have peace of mind." Then Vyasa wrote the Bhagavata, a book that overbrims with Bhakti Rasa and Kirtan of Hari. Rishis studied Bhagavata and held Kathas in a lonely forest in the vicinity of Sukadev's hermitage. Sukadev was very much attracted towards the Katha of the Rishis. He directly proceeded to his father and studied the Bhagavata under him. Then only he taught Bhagavata to Raja Parikshit.

Look at the devotion of Sukadev! From this incident it is quite clear that devotion and Jnana are inseparable and a Jnani is greatest Bhakta and those Vedantins who speak ill of devotion are deluded, ignorant persons.

3. Doctrine of Avatarahood

God takes a human form for elevating human beings. There is descent of God for the ascent of man. This is known as Avatara or incarnation of God. In the Gita (IV-6, 7, 8) you will find: "Though unborn, the imperishable Self, and also the Lord of all beings, brooding over nature, which is Mine own, yet I am born through My own power. Whenever there is decay of righteousness, then I Myself come forth. For the protection of the good, for the destruction of evil-doers, for the sake of firmly establishing righteousness, I am born from age to age."

There are various kinds of Avataras: (1) Poorna-avatara, (2) Amsa-avatara and (3) Avesha-avatara. Lord Krishna was a Poorna-avatara, as you already know, with sixteen rays. Lord Rama was an Avatara of fourteen rays. Sri Sankaracharya was an Amsa-avatara. Avataras generally proceed from Brahma, Vishnu and Siva. They cannot come out of Isvara Himself. Just as a tailor who makes coats for others can make a coat for himself also, God who has created the bodies for others, can create a body for Himself as well. There is no difficulty. He is omnipotent and omniscient. As He has control over Maya, He is fully conscious of His divine nature though He assumes a form. Still He is infinite and unconditioned.

Lord Krishna told Arjuna that this was the ancient and imperishable Yoga which he taught to Vivasvan the Sun-God; Vivasvan taught it to Manu; Manu taught it to Ikshvaku and so it was handed down through *Parampara* from royal sage to royal sage till it is decayed in the world by great efflux of time and was now renewed for Arjuna as he was His devotee and friend.

Some ignorant persons object: "How can the unborn God assume a human form? How can the Ruler be limited in a perishable, human body? How can the Lord who stands as the Witness only put on a finite body?" These are all vain, worthless, illogical discussions. The doctrine of Avatarahood is perfectly rational, perfectly logical and perfectly tenable. God is the Antaryamin, the Inner Self of all beings. He is not an absolute landlord of this world. He is not extra-cosmic or super-cosmic deity. He pervades and permeates all atoms and the whole universe. He is the Lord of the breath, mind and all organs. In him we live, move and have our very being.

A simple Jivanmukta is like a star that glitters at night. He throws a little light only. Somehow or other he has crossed to the other shore through some Tapas and Sadhana. He cannot elevate a large number of people. Just as the waters of the small spring in the yonder fields can quench the thirst of a few pilgrims only, so also this Kevala Jnani can bring peace for a few persons only. Whereas an Avatara is a mighty person. He is like the big Manasarovar lake. He removes the veil of ignorance of thousands of men and women and takes them to the land of eternal rest, bliss and sunshine.

There are some premonitory signs that indicate the advent of an Avatara. The ground is well prepared for his descent. People take interest in Sankirtana and some pious people disseminate Sankirtana Bhakti far and wide. Some great souls are born beforehand and these train people in selfless service and right conduct.

The Lord incarnated as Nara and Narayana. The object of the incarnation was to teach by precept and example the performance of duty without desire for reward. Nara and Narayana were doing severe penance at Badrikashram. The

PRACTICE OF BHAKTI YOGA

Lord appeared as a swan to teach Atma-Yoga to Brahma. Dattatreya, the Kumaras, four sons of Brahma are all partial incarnations of Vishnu. Lord Vishnu has taken ten Avataras up till now. Dakshinamoorthy was an Avatara of Lord Siva.

The philosophy of Jesus Christ, the Yogi of Nazareth, is the best of its kind for the European world as is the philosophy of Buddha for Thailand, China, Japan and Sri Lanka. So is the philosophy of Mohammed for Arabia. All are the sons of God made in His image to give to the different parts of the great wide world a message of peace and of the secret of life.

Very few people like Bhishma recognised Lord Krishna as the Avatara. That is the reason why Lord Krishna says: "The foolish disregard Me, when clad in human semblance, ignorant of My Supreme nature, the great Lord of beings." (Gita: IX-11.) "Those devoid of reason think of Me, the unmanifest, as having manifestation, knowing not My supreme nature, imperishable, most excellent." (Gita: VII-24.)

Pseudo-Avataras are abundant these days. They have cropped up like mushrooms. Their disciples pompously advertise these Avataras as Bhagavans, torch-bearers, Perfect Masters, Thakurs, Adepts etc., for collecting money and building Ashrams for their own comfortable living. They get their downfall also soon. All that glitters is not gold. People have lost their faith now in these charlatans. Truth alone can get victory. How long can falsehood stand? The pseudo-Avataras dress themselves as Lord Krishna with crown and peacock-feathers on their heads and appear before credulous disciples and say: "I am Lord Krishna. Drink my Charanamrita. I shall give you Mukti." Any saint who wants to rise up should not allow his disciples to advertise. Otherwise he will lose his respect soon. These pseudo-Avataras who live in the midst of utter darkness but profess themselves to be wise and learned, go round and round, deluded in many crooked ways, as blind people led by the blind.

There is grand possibility of the descent of God in human form as an Avatara. This has occurred several times in the past and will continue to occur in future as well. In the divine scheme of things Avataras are indispensably required for the uplift of humanity. In this Kali-Yuga, Kali-Avatara is expected. May that Avatara bring Supreme Joy and Peace to the world. Glory, Glory unto Avataras!

4. Mutual Dependence of Bhakti and Jnana

We are often confronted with the puzzling question: "Are Jnana and Bhakti conflicting with each other?" My answer is emphatically "No." There is in fact, an inter-relationship between these two, the one supplementing the other. Bhakti is not at all antagonistic to Jnana. There is undoubtedly a mutual dependence between the two. Both lead to the same destination.

Bhakti Yoga and Jnana Yoga are not incompatibles like acid and alkali. One can combine Ananya Bhakti (one-pointed devotion) with Jnana Yoga. The fruit of Bhakti Yoga is Jnana. Highest Love (Para Bhakti) and Jnana are one. Perfect knowledge is love. Perfect love is knowledge. Sri Sankara, the Advaita Kevala Jnani, was a great Bhakta of Lord Hari, Hara and Devi. Jnanadev of Alandi, another great Yogi-Jnani, was a Bhakta of Lord Krishna. Sri Ramakrishna Paramahamsa worshipped Kaali and obtained Jnana through Swami Totapuri, his Advaita Guru. Gouranga Maha Prabhu (Lord Chaitanya) of Bengal was a fine Advaita-Vedantic scholar and yet he danced in the streets singing Hari's Names. It behoves therefore that Bhakti and Jnana can be combined with much advantage.

Action, emotion and intelligence are the three horses that are linked to this body-chariot. They should work in perfect harmony or unison. Then only the chariot will run smoothly.

There must be integral development. You must have the head of Sankara, the heart of Buddha and the hand of Janaka. Vedanta without devotion is quite dry. Jnana without Bhakti is not perfect. How can one, who has realised his oneness with Atman remain without serving the world which is Atman only? Devotion is not divorced from Jnana but Jnana is rather exceedingly helpful to its perfect attainment.

5. Akbar's Four Questions

Akbar asked Birbal the following four questions: (1) Where does God live? (2) What is His duty? (3) What does He eat? (4) Why does He take human form although He can do everything by mere willing?

Birbal replied: (1) God is all-pervading. He gives His Darshan to the holy devotees in their hearts. You can see Him in your heart. (2) He pulls down those who are in a high level and elevates those who are fallen. His duty is to cause constant change. (3) He eats the Ahamkar of the Jivas.

Birbal then asked Akbar to give him some time for thinking out and giving a suitable reply for his fourth question. In the meantime Birbal went to the nurse who was nursing the child of Akbar, and told her: "Look here, you will have to help me today in this matter. I will have to give a proper answer to Akbar on a certain philosophical question. When Akbar comes and sits by the side of the tank to play with the child, hide the child in a certain place and bring this toy-child. Take the toy-child near the tank. Pretend to tumble down and throw the child into the tank. Then you will see the fun. Do the whole thing dexterously. I know you can do it well." He gave her ten rupees as present. She was highly delighted. She at once agreed to do so.

Akbar returned from his evening walk as usual and sat on

a bench by the side of the tank. He then asked the nurse to bring the child. The nurse slowly went by the side of the tank, pretended to tumble down and threw the toy-child into the tank. Akbar at once hastened to jump down into the tank to rescue the child. Birbal intervened and said: "Here is your child. Do not be hasty." Akbar was very much annoyed at the impertinent behaviour of Birbal and ordered him to be punished. Birbal said: "I have now given a practical answer to your fourth question. Why are you angry towards me? Even though there are so many servants to rescue your child, out of affection for the child you yourself wanted to jump into the water. Even so, although God can accomplish everything by mere willing or Sankalpa, yet He comes out Himself out of love for His devotees to give them His Darshan. You see the point?" Akbar was very much pleased. He gave Birbal rich presents of shawl and a diamond ring.

6. Bhakti and Jnana Compared

(1) Jnana Yoga is like crossing a river by swimming. Bhakti Yoga is like crossing a river by a boat. (2) The Jnani gets knowledge by self-reliance and assertion. The Bhakta gets Darshan of God by self-surrender. (3) The Jnani asserts and expands. The Bhakta dedicates and consecrates himself to the Lord and contracts himself. Suppose there is one rupee in the body of a small circle. This rupee contracts and merges itself into the circumference. This is Bhakti. Imagine there is a two-anna piece in the centre of a circle. This coin so expands that it occupies the whole body of the circle and the circumference also. This is Jnana. (4) A Bhakta wants to eat sugar-candy. A Jnani wants to become sugar-candy itself. (5) A Bhakta is like a kitten that cries for help. A Jnani is like a baby-monkey that clings itself boldly to the mother. (6) A Bhakta gets Krama Mukti. A Jnani gets Sadyo-Mukti. (7) A Jnana Yogi exhibits Siddhis through will or

Sat-Sankalpa. A Bhakta gets all the divine Aisvaryas through self-surrender and the consequent descent of Divine Grace.

In the Gita (IV-39) Lord Krishna clearly points out that Bhakti and Jnana are not incompatibles like oil and water. He says: *"Sraddhavan labhate jnanam* — The man who is full of faith obtaineth wisdom."

"Tesham satatayuktanam bhajatam preetipurvakam; Dadami buddhiyogam tam yena mamupayanti te — To these ever harmonious, worshipping in love, I give the Yoga of discrimination by which they come unto Me." (X-10.)

"Bhaktya maamabhijanati yavanyaschasmi tattvatah; Tato mam tattvato jnatva visate tadanantaram — By devotion he knoweth Me in essence, who and what I am; having thus known Me in essence, he forthwith entereth into the Supreme." (XVIII-55.)

To deny Jnana altogether, to say that there is nothing beyond Goloka as some sectarian Bhaktas do, is the height of one's folly. To deny Bhakti and Isvara as some dry Vedantins do is also foolishness. A happy combination of head and heart is perfection.

CHAPTER IV

BHAKTI SADHANA

1. Practice of Japa-Yoga

Japa is an important limb of Yoga. In the Gita you will find: *"Yajnanam Japa-Yajnosmi* — Among Yajnas I am Japa Yajna."* In this Kali Yuga practice of Japa alone can give eternal Peace, Bliss and Immortality. Japa ultimately results in Samadhi or communion with God. Japa must become habitual and must be attended with Sattvic Bhava, Purity, Prem and Sraddha. There is no Yoga greater than Japa-Yoga. It can bestow upon you all Ishta-Siddhis (whatever you want), Bhakti and Mukti.

A Mantra is Divinity. It is Divine Power or Daivi-Sakti manifesting in a sound body. The Sastra says that those who think that an image is a mere stone, that Mantras are merely letters, and that a Guru is a mere man and not a manifestation and representative of the Lord or Supreme Teacher, Illustrator and Director, go to hell. The aspirant should endeavour to realise his unity with the Mantra or the Divinity and to the extent he does so, the Mantra-Sakti supplements his worship-power (Sadhana-Sakti).

Japa is the repetition or recital of a Mantra or the Name of the Lord. Dhyana is the meditation on the form of the Lord with His attributes. This is the difference between Japa and Dhyana. There is Japa with meditation (Japa-Sahita) and without meditation (Japa-Rahita). As you advance, the Japa will drop by itself and meditation alone will remain. It is no doubt an advanced stage. You can practise concentration separately. You can do whatever you like best.

Om is both Saguna and Nirguna Brahman. You can repeat 'Om Ram' for worship of the Saguna Brahman. Om is everything. Om is the name or symbol of God, Isvara or Brahman. Om is your real name. Om covers all the three-fold experiences of man. Om stands for all the phenomenal worlds. From Om this sense-universe has been projected. The world exists in Om and dissolves in Om. Om is derived by adding the letters A + U + M. 'A' represents the physical plane, 'U' represents the mental and the astral plane, the world of spirits, all heavens, and 'M' represents all the deep sleep state as well as in your wakeful state all that is unknown and beyond the reach of the intellect. Om therefore represents all. Om is the basis of your life, thought and intelligence. Om is the centre of all worlds that denote objects. Hence the whole world has come out from Om, rests in Om, and dissolves in Om. As soon as you sit for meditation, chant Om loudly 3 or 6 or 12 times. This will drive away all worldly thoughts from the mind and remove tossing of mind (Vikshepa). Then take to mental repetition of Om.

In the act of breathing, the greatest Mantra SOHAM is repeated automatically by the Jiva 21,600 times within 24 hours. This is called Ajapa Mantra. That is to say, it is a Mantra that is repeated without Japa or willed effort of the Jiva. Breath goes out with HAM and comes in with SO. Soham is Om only. Delete S and H, the consonants. The balance is OM. Soham is the Mantra of a Vedantic student. It means: "I am He" or "He am I." This signifies the identity of Jiva and Brahman. Repetition of this Mantra "HAMSAH SOHAM — SOHAM HAMSAH adds force to the Japa as is the case in "GOD IS LOVE — LOVE IS GOD." In the same way the Mahavakya is repeated *"Aham Brahma Asmi — Brahmaivaham Asmi."*

A Mantra in the Hindu religion has a Rishi who gave it; a metre which governs the inflection of the voice; and a Devata as its informing power. The Beeja (seed) is a significant word or series of words which give it a special power. Sometimes this word is a sound which harmonises with the key-note of the individual using it and varies with the individual. Sometimes this word expresses the essence of the flower springing from this seed. This essence of the Gita is in the words quoted. The Sakti is the energy of the form of the Mantra i.e., the vibration-forms set up by its sounds. These in the Gita carry the man to the Lord. The pillar (Kilakam) is that which supports and makes the Mantra strong. This is the ceasing from sorrow by the freeing from imperfections.

Then follow certain special directions intended to set up relations between the centres in the man's body and the corresponding centres in the body of the Lord (the universe). The thumbs, the earth-symbol, are connected with the physical plane and are utilised in control of its subtle forces. The index fingers, the water-symbol, are connected with the astral plain and are similarly used with astral forces. The middle fingers, the fire-symbol, the apex of the pyramid of the hand, are also similarly used with mental forces. The ring fingers, the air-symbol, are used with Buddhic forces. The little fingers, the most powerful in the subtle worlds, are the Akasa-symbol and are similarly used with Atmic-forces. The other organs of the body are the other poles of the magnet of the body: thumbs and heart; index fingers and head; middle fingers and the point of juncture of the occipital and parietal sutures; the ring fingers and the Sukshma Sarira; the little fingers and the creative organ. These are the positive and negative poles of the magnet we call the body; either may be positive, either negative according to the object aimed at, but they work together.

There is a special, mysterious force or wonderful magnetic power at Sandhi or junction time (sunrise and sunset). The mind will be elevated quickly. It will be filled with Sattva. Concentration will come by itself without any effort at this time. Japa should be done at Sandhis. It is always better to start Japa and meditation at 4 in the morning as soon as you get up from the bed. At this time the mind is quite calm and refreshed. This is the time to catch the meditative wave. Meditation is more important. Then you can take to Asanas and Pranayama and wind up the full course by another short sitting in Japa and meditation. As there is always some drowsiness when you get up and start the practice, it is desirable to do some Asanas and a little Pranayama for five minutes just to drive off this drowsiness and to make yourself fit for Japa and meditation.

The mind gets one-pointedness after the practice of Pranayama. Therefore you will have to take to Japa and meditation after Pranayama is over. Pranayama, though it concerns with the breath, gives good exercise to the various internal organs and the whole body. It is the best of physical exercises known.

Fixing one's eyes between the two eye-brows (Bhrumadhya-Drishti) is an important exercise for the aspirant. Sit on your favourite Asana in your meditation room and practise this gaze gently for half a minute and gradually increase it to half an hour. There should not be any violence in this practice. This Yogic Kriya removes tossing of mind and what is most astonishing, develops concentration. Lord Krishna prescribes this practice. *"Sparsan kritva bahir bahyam-chakshuh-chaivantare bhruvoh* — Shutting out (all) external contacts and fixing the gaze between the eye-brows." (Gita: V-27.) This is known as the "frontal gaze." Sit on your favourite Asana as said before and gently fix your gaze at the tip of the nose from half a minute to half an hour. Do not strain your eyes. This is also prescribed by Lord Krishna in the Gita. You can select either the "nasal gaze" on the "frontal gaze" according to your taste, temperament and capacity.

Some students like to concentrate with open eyes, while some others with closed eyes, while yet some others with half-opened eyes. If you meditate with closed eyes, dust or foreign matter will not injure your eyes. Some students whom lights and jerks trouble, prefer concentration with open eyes. In some who meditate with closed eyes, sleep overpowers within a short time. Use your commonsense and adopt that which suits you best. Overcome other obstacles by suitable, intelligent methods. Remember the story of "Bruce and the Spider." Be patient and persevering. You will have to struggle hard and win the spiritual battle, become a spiritual hero and wear spiritual laurels round your neck.

Loud Japa shuts out all worldly sounds. There is no break. These are the two advantages in loud Japa. In Manasic Japa it is difficult to find when the break comes in the mind in the case of majority of people. Whenever sleep tries to overpower you when you do Japa at night, take the Japa-Maala in your hands and roll the beads. This will put a check to sleep. Repeat the Mantra loudly. Give up Manasic Japa. Now the Maala will remind you when the stoppage takes place. When sleep is hard to overcome, stand up and do the Japa.

Silent repetition of God's Name such as HARI OM or SRI RAM is a potent tonic for all diseases. It should never be stopped even for a day under any circumstances. It is like food. It is a spiritual food for the hungry soul. Lord Jesus says: "Man shall not live by bread alone, but by every word that proceedeth out of the mouth of God." You can drink and live on the nectar that flows during Japa and meditation. Even simple mechanical repetition of a Mantra has got very great effect. It purifies the mind. It serves as a gatekeeper. It intimates to you that some other worldly thoughts have entered now. At once you can try to drive these thoughts and make Smarana of the Mantra. Even during the mechanical repetition, a portion of the mind is there.

If you utter the word "excreta" or "urine" when your friend is taking his meal, he may at once vomit his food. If you think of "Garam Pakoda" your tongue will get salivation. There is a Sakti in every word. When such is the case with ordinary words, what about the Names of the Lord? Repetition or thinking of His Name produces tremendous influence on the mind. It transforms the mental substance — Chitta — overhauls the vicious, old Samskaras in the mind, transmutes the Asuric diabolical nature and brings the devotee face to face with God. There is no doubt of this. O sceptic and scientific atheists! Wake up, wake up. Open your eyes. Chant His Name always. Sing and do Kirtan.

A Maala contains 108 beads. You must increase the number of Japa (recitation of the Name of the Lord) from 200 to 500 Maalas. Just as you are very keen in taking your food twice daily, tea in the morning and cocoa in the evening, you must evince extreme keenness in doing Japa also 4 times: morning, noon, evening and night. Death may come at any moment, without a second's notice. Prepare yourself to meet it with a smile uttering SRI RAM, SRI RAM and merging in RAM — in Eternal Bliss, in Infinite Glory, Ananda and Self-knowledge. Even on tour you must do Japa and reading of the Gita. Do you not eat and drink on your tour? Don't become ungrateful to the Inner Ruler (Antaryamin), who gives your daily bread and looks after you in every way. You can do Japa even in latrines. But do it mentally. Ladies can do Japa mentally even during the monthly periods. There are no restrictions in Japa for those who do it with Nishkamya Bhava, for the attainment of Moksha. Restrictions come only when people repeat any Mantra with Sakama Bhava to get fruits such as wealth, Svarga, son etc. You can wear Maala around your neck while answering the calls of nature also.

If you are a very busy man and if you lead a travelling life always, you need not have a special room and a special time for meditation. Do SOHAM Japa and Dhyana along with the breath. This is very easy. Or associate Rama Mantra along with the breath. Then every moment of breath will become a prayer and a meditation. Remember "SOHAM." Feel His presence everywhere. This will suffice.

Sri Rama's Ishta Devata was Lord Siva. So a Bhakta of Rama should repeat "Om Namah Sivaya", the Mantra of Lord Siva, for six months in the beginning. He can have Rama's Darshan quickly. If you become sleepy during Japa, stand up for half an hour and do Japa. Sleep will pass off. Dash some cold water on the face. At night live on half a seer of milk and some fruits. Heavy diet makes you drowsy.

In 14 hours you can do 2000 Maalas of HARI OM Japa. In 7 hours you can do Japa of one lakh of SRI RAM Mantra. In half an hour you can do 10,000 SRI RAM Japa. If you do Japa of a Mantra 13 crores of times you will have Darshan of your Ishta Devata in physical form. If you are sincere and earnest you can do this in four years' time.

Nama (name) and Rupa (the object signified by the name) are inseparable. Thought and word are inseparable. Whenever you think of the name of your son, his figure will stand before your mental eye and vice versa. Even so when you do Japa of Rama Rama or Krishna Krishna, the picture of Rama or Krishna will come before your mind. Therefore Japa and Dhyana go together inseparably.

The rosary (Maala) is a whip to goad you towards God. Just as the ideas of courts, cases, documents and clients are associated when you see or think of a lawyer, so also the ideas of Sanctity, Purity, Divinity, Glory, Splendour, Wisdom, Power, Love, Omnipotence etc., are associated when you see or think of a Maala. Therefore wear this always round your neck and do Japa. Don't feel shy to wear this, O educated persons! It will always remind you of God

THE TABLE FOR JAPA

No.	Mantras	Speed per minute			No. of Japa that can be done in one hour				Time required for completion of one Purascharana, devoting 6 hours daily			
		Low	Med.	High	Low	Med.	High		Months	Days	Hours	Mins.
1.	OM	140	250	400	8400	15000	24000	Low	0	0	11	54
								Med.	0	0	6	40
								High	0	0	4	10
2.	Hari Om or Sri Rama	120	200	300	7200	12000	18000	Low	0	1	3	47
								Med.	0	0	16	40
								High	0	0	11	7
3.	Om Namah Sivaya	80	120	150	4800	7200	9000	Low	0	17	2	10
								Med.	0	11	3	30
								High	0	9	1	35
4.	Om Namo Narayanaya	60	80	120	3600	4800	7200	Low	1	7	0	15
								Med.	0	27	4	45
								High	0	18	3	15
5.	Om Namo Bhagavate Vaasudevaya	40	60	90	2400	3600	5400	Low	2	23	2	0
								Med.	1	25	3	30
								High	1	7	0	15
6.	Gayatri Mantra	6	8	10	360	480	600	Low	36	16	0	45
								Med.	29	18	5	30
								High	19	15	3	35
7.	Maha-Mantra or Hare Rama Mantra	8	10	15	480	600	900	Low	36	16	0	45
								Med.	29	8	5	30
								High	19	17	3	35

and God-realisation. It is even more valuable than your necklace bedecked with nine precious gems, because it fills your mind with divine thoughts and acts as an instrument to take you to the goal.

Some can do Manasic Japa more quickly than others. The mind becomes dull after some hours. It cannot turn out the work of Japa efficiently. The speed becomes lessened. Those who calculate the Maalas of Japa according to the watch should take recourse to rolling the beads if there be any such dullness. If there be any pain in twirling the beads, you can use the bag for holding the fingers. This gives rest to the hand.

It is always better to take to medium speed. It is not the speed but the Bhava and concentration that bring about the maximum benefits in Japa. There must be Akshara Suddhi in repetition. Every word must be pronounced very, very clearly. There must be no mutilation of any word. This is important. Some people finish one lakh of Japa daily within seven hours in a hurried manner just as a hired carpenter or contractor does the work in order to get the wages. Don't have any contract work with God. There cannot be any real devotion in having any contract with God. There is one advantage in doing Japa with electric speed. If the mind is dull, if the mind is wandering wildly in sensual objects you can keep up very high speed for 15 or 20 minutes. This will stimulate the dull mind and bring it back quickly to the focusing point.

Those who take recourse to Purascharana and keeping up of daily diary should be very exact and accurate in keeping the record. There must be mathematical accuracy. They should watch the mind very carefully and if it becomes dull during Japa they should do more Japa till dullness vanishes. It is better to take into consideration the number of Japa that is done when the mind is in full spirit and to omit that which is done when the mind is lethargic. This is erring on the safe side.

May God give us inner strength and courage to control the Indriyas and the mind and to practise Japa Yoga quite uninterruptedly! May we have unshakable faith in the miraculous power and marvellous benefits of Japa Yoga! May we all recognise and realise the glory of God's Name! May we all spread the glory of the Lord's Name throughout the length and breadth of the land! Victory to Hari and His Name! Glory to Hari and His Name! May the blessings of Sri Siva-Hari-Rama-Krishna be upon us all!

2. God Gives Darshan

There is a village known as Dagheta near Mathura. One Swami Krishnananda was doing Kirtan one night with his party. It was the 10th October, 1934. A certain Bhakta who was much interested in Kirtan locked her little girl in the house and attended the Kirtan. There was none else in the house save the child. When the mother returned, she saw her child playing and laughing. She asked the child: "With whom are you playing, my child?" The child replied: "I am playing with this old man. Do you not see him?" The child repeated these words thrice. The mother was not able to see the old man. The old man was none else but Lord Krishna. He disappeared. Where there is Bhakti and faith, the Lord is always there. Where there is Kama (passion) there is no Rama.

In front of Sankar Kutir, Meerut, where Sannyasins stay, there is a bungalow belonging to Sri Sankar Dayal, an advocate. He has a daughter. She is very devout. She worships Lord Krishna daily. This is all due to her previous virtuous Samskaras. She used to cull flowers in the garden daily. One day when she was doing this work early in the morning, a boy came to her with peacock feathers on the head and said: "Child, repeat this Mantra." He gave a certain Mantra for Japa and disappeared. Who else the boy can be but Lord Krishna? This incident took place on 5th October, 1934. Even in this Kali-Yuga, if you have even a minute trace of faith and devotion, the Lord is ever ready to give His Darshan.

In Farukkabad I met a boy aged about 19 on 14th November, 1934. He was a Bhakta of Lord Siva. He was repeating Om Namassivaya for some months past. But he did not have Darshan of the Lord. He felt aggrieved on account of this and one day he wanted to give up his life by some means or other. Finally when he set about to do a most violent act which it is not necessary for our purpose to mention here, the Lord of Mount Kailas appeared in the midst of a blazing blue light before the boy. The boy heard a voice: "Child what boon do you want?" The boy answered: "I want Your Darshan again for a second time." But Lord Siva did not again appear before him for the second time. Sri Bhagawant Prasad, the Deputy Collector, brought the boy to me to at Sarasvati Bhavan.

3. The Secret of Ramayana

The secret of Ramayana is the attainment of Jivanmukti through control of mind. Killing the ten-headed monster, Ravana of Lanka, is the annihilation of the ten evil Vrittis of mind, viz., Raga (love), Dvesha (hatred), Kama (lust), Krodha (anger), Lobha (miserliness), Moha (infatuation, delusion), Mada (pride), Ahamkara (egoism), Matsarya (Jealousy) and Dambha (ostentation or vanity). Sita represents mind. Rama represents Brahman. Sita unites with her husband Rama. Mind merges in Brahman by concentration and incessant meditation on Rama. This is the esoteric teaching of the Ramayana. Constant repetition of the two-lettered Mantra RAMA (RA + MA) with Suddha Bhavana and perfect concentration leads to the control of mind and Samadhi. The thinker and the thought, the meditator and the meditated, the worshiper and the worshipped, the Upasaka and the Upasya become blended into one. Mind is filled with Rama. It becomes *tadakara, tadrupa, tanmaya* (oneness, sameness) and *talleenata* (as a man thinketh). As you think, so you become. The mind becomes identical with Rama. Jiva's will will become merged with the Cosmic Will or the Will of Rama. Jivatma now vanishes.

The two-lettered Rama Mantra is the best of all the Mantras. Why? Because it is a combination of Panchakshra and Ashtakshara. RA is taken from OM NAMO NARAYANAYA and MA from OM NAMAH SIVAYA. It is therefore very powerful. The shorter the Mantra, the greater the concentration. So repetition of Rama Mantra brings about greater amount of concentration.

By worship and meditation or Japa of Rama Mantra, the mind is actually shaped into the form Rama. The object of worship is made pure through the purity of the object viz., Ishtadevata, Rama. By continual practice (Abhyasa) the mind becomes full of the object (Rama) to the exclusion of everything else, steady in purity and does not stray into impurity. So long as mind exists it must have an object to lean upon and the object of Sadhana is to present to the mind with a pure object.

The sound repeatedly and harmoniously uttered in Japa of a Mantra must create or project into perception the corresponding thing (Devata). The Mantra gathers *creative momentum* by repetition through the force of Samskaras.

A Mantra is a mass of radiant Tejas or energy. It transforms the mental substance by producing a particular thought-movement. The rhythmical vibrations produced by its utterance regulate the unsteady vibrations of the five sheaths (Pancha Kosas). It checks the natural tendencies of the mind to run after objects. It helps the Sadhana-Sakti and reinforces it when it becomes imperfect and meets with obstacles. Sadhana-Sakti is strengthened by Mantra-Sakti.

Mantra awakens super-human powers (Siddhis) when the sleeping consciousness in a Mantra (the Mantra Chaitanya) is awakened.

The famous Tulasi Das had Darshan of Rama by repeating this Rama Mantra. Samartha Rama Das performed his Tapas in Takli village on the banks of the Godavari and chanted Rama Mantra thirteen crores of times and eventually had Darshan of Rama. Ramadas of Bhadrachalam had Darshan of Rama by constantly repeating this Rama Taraka Mantra on the holy banks of the Godavari. Such is the power of Rama Mantra. It purifies the Chitta, gives Ashta Siddhis and eventually leads to Mukti. Have intense faith and Ananya, Avyabhicharini Bhakti towards Sri Rama. Do Antarika (from the bottom of the heart) prayer. Chant this Name constantly with Suddha Bhava. Sing Rama Nam daily for a couple of hours with closed eyes in a solitary room. Serve Bhaktas. You will doubtless be freed from this wheel of births and deaths. You will certainly have Darshan of Rama and through Para Bhakti or Abheda Bhakti will merge yourself in Rama. You will attain the Satchidananda state. There is no doubt of this.

4. Japa of Mahamantra

Hare Rama Hare Rama, Rama Rama Hare Hare;
Hare Krishna Hare Krishna, Krishna Krishna Hare Hare.

At the end of Dvapara-Yuga, Narada went to Brahma and addressed him thus: "O Lord, how shall I, roaming over the earth, be able to cross Kali?" To which Brahma thus replied: "Well asked. Hearken to that which all Srutis (the Vedas) keep secret and hidden, through which one may cross the Samsara (mundane existence) of Kali. He shakes off (the evil effects of) Kali through the mere uttering of the Name of the Lord Narayana, who is the Primeval Purusha." Again Narada asked Brahma: "What is

PRACTICE OF BHAKTI YOGA

the Name?" To which Hiranyagarbha (Brahma) replied thus: (the words are) "1. Hare, 2. Rama, 3. Hare, 4. Rama, 5. Rama, 6. Rama, 7. Hare, 8. Hare, 9. Hare, 10. Krishna, 11. Hare, 12. Krishna, 13. Krishna, 14. Krishna, 15. Hare, 16. Hare. These sixteen Names (words) are destructive of the evil effects of Kali. No better means than this is to be seen in all the Vedas. These (sixteen Names) destroy the Avarana (or the veil which produces the sense of individuality) of Jiva surrounded by the sixteen Kalas (rays). Then like the sphere of the sun which shines fully after the clouds (screening it) disperse, Parabrahman alone shines."

Narada asked: "O Lord! what are the rules to be observed with reference to it?" To which Brahma replied that there are no rules for it. Whosoever in a pure or an impure state, utters these always, attains the same world of, or proximity with, or the same form of, or absorption into Brahman.

Whosoever utters three and a half crores[1] (or thirty-five million) times this Mantra composed of sixteen Names (of words) crosses the sin of the murder of a Brahmin. He becomes purified from the sin of the theft of gold. He becomes purified from the sin of cohabitation with women of low caste. He is purified from the sins of wrong done to Pitris, Devas and men. Having given up all Dharmas, he becomes freed at once from all sins. He is at once released from all bondage. That he is at once released from all bondage is the Upanishad.

---

1 This number can be reached by uttering the Mantra completely within one year if uttered at the rate of a lakh per day; and within ten years if uttered at the rate of 10,000 per day. —*Kalisantarana Upanishad*

5. Meditation on Gayatri

ॐ भूर्भुवः स्वः तत्सवितुर्वरेण्यं ।
भर्गो देवस्य धीमहि धियो यो नः प्रचोदयात् ॥

"Om bhur bhuvah svah tat savitur varenyam;
Bhargo devasya dheemahi dhiyo yo nah prachodayat."

Shabda-Artha

Om	Para Brahman
Bhur	Bhuloka (Physical Plane)
Bhuvah	Antariksha
Svah	Svarga Loka
Tat	Paramatma
Savitur	Isvara (Surya)
Varenyam	Fit to be worshipped
Bhargo	Remover of sins and ignorance
Devasya	Glory (Jnana Svaroopa)
Dheemahi	We meditate
Dhiyo	Buddhi (Intellect)
Yo	Which
Nah	Our
Prachodayat	Enlighten

Bhava-Artha

"Let us meditate on Isvara and His Glory who has created the Universe, who is fit to be worshipped, who is the remover of all sins and ignorance. May he enlighten our intellect."

The aspirant prays to Mother Gayatri, "O Beloved Mother! At the present moment I have taken my body as the self owing to Avidya or ignorance, through my impure intellect. Give me a pure intellect which will enable me to know my real nature. Give me light and knowledge."

This is the Brahma-Gayatri Mantra. Gayatri is the 'Blessed Mother' of Vedas. There is no milk superior to cow's milk. Even so there is no Mantra superior to Gayatri.

As Omkara or Pranava is for Sannyasins, so is Gayatri for Brahmacharis and householders. The fruits that are attained by meditation on Omkara can be attained by meditation on Gayatri. The same goal that is reached by a Paramahamsa Sannyasin can be reached by a Brahmachari or a householder by meditating on Gayatri.

Get up at 4 a.m. in Brahmamuhurta and start Japa and meditation on Gayatri (Panchmukhi or five-faced Devi seated in lotus flower), sitting on Padmasana, Siddhasana or Virasana, facing North or East. Burn incense in the room. In summer you can take a bath. In winter you can simply wash your face, hands and feet and do *achamana* only. Continue the Japa for two hours or more. Have another sitting at night between 7 and 8 p.m. Constantly feel that you are receiving light, purity and wisdom from Gayatri. This is important. Keep the image of the Gayatri at the Trikuti, the space between the eye-brows by closing the eyes and concentrate there, or keep the image in the lotus of the heart and concentrate there. You will have Darshan of Gayatri.

It is better if you do Japa of Gayatri 3000 to 4000 times daily. Your heart will be purified rapidly. If you are not able to do this number, you can do 1008 times daily. If you find it difficult to do this number also, do at least 108 times daily, 36 times at sunrise, 36 times at noon, 36 times at sunset. There is special, mysterious spiritual force or wonderful magnetic power at *Sandhi* or junction of the time, sunrise and sunset. The mind will be elevated quickly. It will be filled with Sattva. Concentration will come by itself without any effort at this time. If you find it difficult to get up at Brahmamuhurta, get up before sunrise. That man who fails to do Gayatri at the *Sandhis* fails in the discharge of his daily duties. He becomes a *Bhrashta* or fallen man. He loses vigour, vitality and *Brahma-tejas.*

In the Gayatri Mantra there are 9 names, viz., 1. Om,

2. Bhur, 3. Bhuvah, 4. Svah, 5. Tat, 6. Savitur, 7. Varenyam, 8. Bhargo and 9. Devasya. Through these nine names the Lord is praised. *Dheemahi* is worship of the Lord. *Dhiyo Yo Nah Prachodayat* is prayer. Herein there are five halts or stops viz., 'Om' is the first stop; 'Bhur Bhuvah Svah' the second; 'Tat Savitur Varenyam' the third; 'Bhargo Devasya Dheemahi' the fourth; and 'Dhiyo Yo Nah Prachodayat' the fifth. While chanting or doing Japa of the Mantra, we should stop a little at every stop or halt.

Savita is the presiding deity of the Gayatri Mantra, Fire (Agni) is the mouth, Visvamitra is the Rishi and Gayatri is the metre. It is recited in the investiture of sacred thread, practice of Pranayama and Japa. What Gayatri is, the same is Sandhya, and what Sandhya is, the same is Gayatri. Sandhya and Gayatri are identical. He who meditates on Gayatri, meditates on Lord Vishnu.

A man can repeat Gayatri mentally in all states while lying, sitting, walking etc. There is no sin of commission and omission of any sort in its repetition. One should thus perform Sandhya three times with this Gayatri Mantra every day, in the morning, noon and evening. It is the Gayatri Mantra alone that can be commonly prescribed for all the Hindus. The Lord commands in the Vedas "Let one Mantra be common to all" "*Samano Mantrah*." Hence the Gayatri should be the one Mantra for all the Hindus. "The secret lore of the Upanishads is the essence of four Vedas, while Gayatri with the three *Vyahritis* is the essence of the Upanishads." He is the real Brahmin who knows and understands thus, the Gayatri. Without its knowledge he is a Sudra, though well versed in the four Vedas.

Three kinds of Japa

Sandilya says in Sandilya Upanishad, "The Vaikhari Japa (loud pronunciation) gives the reward as stated in the Vedas; while the Upamsu Japa (whispering or humming which cannot be heard by any one) gives a reward a

PRACTICE OF BHAKTI YOGA

thousand times more than the Vaikhari; the Manasic Japa gives a reward a crore of times more than the Vaikhari."

Glory of Gayatri

(Manu Smriti, Chapter II)

76. Brahma milked out, as it were, from the three Vedas, the letter A, the letter U, and the letter M; these form by their coalition the three trilateral monosyllable, together with three mysterious words, Bhur, Bhuvah, Svah, or earth, sky, heaven.

77. From the three Vedas also, the Lord of creatures incomprehensibly exalted, successfully milked out the three measures of that ineffable text, beginning with the word Tat, and entitled Savitri or Gayatri.

79. And a twice-born man, who shall 1000 times repeat those three (Om, the Vyahritis and the Gayatri) apart from the multitude (EKANTA) shall be released in a month even from a great offence, as a snake from his slough.

81. The three great immutable words, preceded by the triliteral syllable and followed by the Gayatri which consists of three measures, must be considered as the mouth or principal part of the Veda.

82. Whoever shall repeat day by day, for three years, without negligence, that sacred text, shall hereafter approach the Divine Essence, move as freely as air and assume an ethereal form.

83. The three triliteral monosyllable is an emblem of the Supreme, the suppressions of breath with a mind fixed on God are the highest devotion; but nothing is more exalted than the Gayatri; a declaration of truth is more excellent than silence.

84. All rites ordained in the Veda, oblations to fire, and solemn sacrifices pass away; but that which passes not away, is declared to be the syllable OM, thence called Akshara; since the Japa should be finished before noon daily and

should not be done in the afternoon. All the words should be repeated slowly without mutilation and Akshara Suddhi (clarity in pronunciation). You must not be hasty in the performance of the Japa. You must have always the meaning of Gayatri before the mind's eye. You must perform a Havan in the end to propitiate the Goddess. As a substitute for the Havan you can perform 6 lakhs of Japa. You can make as many Purascharanas as you like.

85. Fruits of three kinds of Japa—The act of repeating Gayatri loudly (Vaikhari Japa), is 10 times better than the appointed sacrifice; a 100 times better when it is heard by no man (Upamasu Japa), done in a whispering tone; and a 1,000 times better when it is purely mental (Manasic Japa).

87. The four domestic sacraments which are accompanied with the appointed sacrifice, are not equal, though all be united, to a sixteenth part of the sacrifice performed by a repetition of the Gayatri.

By the sole repetition of the Gayatri a priest indubitably attains beatitude, let him perform or not perform, any other religious act.

Benefits of Gayatri Japa

Gayatri is the mother of the Vedas and the destroyer of sins. There is nothing more purifying on the earth as well as in the heaven than the Gayatri. The Japa of Gayatri brings the same fruit as the recitation of all the four Vedas together with the Angas. This single Mantra, if repeated three times a day, brings good (Kalyan or Moksha). It is the Mantra of the Vedas. It destroys sins. It bestows splendid health, beauty, strength, vigour, vitality and magnetic aura in the face (Brahmic effulgence).

Gayatri destroys the three kinds of Taapa or pain. Gayatri bestows the four kinds of Purushartha viz., Dharma (righteousness), Artha (wealth), Kama (desired objects) and Moksha (liberation or freedom). It destroys the three Granthis or knots of ignorance, Avidya, Kama and Karma.

Gayatri purifies the mind. Gayatri bestows Ashta Siddhis. Gayatri makes a man powerful and highly intelligent. Gayatri eventually gives liberation or emancipation from the wheel of births and deaths.

The mind is purified by constant worship. It is filled with good and pure thoughts. Repetition of worship strengthens the good Samskaras. "As a man thinks, that he becomes." This is the psychological law. The mind of a man who trains himself in thinking good, holy thoughts, develops a tendency to think of good thoughts. His character is moulded and transformed by continued good thoughts. When the mind thinks of the image of Gayatri during worship, the mental substance actually assumes the form of the image. The impression of the object is left in the mind. This is called *Samskara*. When the act is repeated very often, the Samskaras gain strength by repetition, and a tendency or habit is formed in the mind. He who entertains thoughts of Divinity becomes transformed actually into the Divinity himself by constant thinking and meditation. His Bhava or disposition is purified and divinised. The meditator and the meditated, the worshipper and the worshipped, the thinker and the thought become one and the same. This is *Samadhi*. This is the fruit of worship or Upasana.

Gayatri Purascharana

The Brahma-Gayatri-Mantra has twenty-four Aksharas. So, one Gayatri Purascharana constitutes the repetition or Japa of 24 lakhs of times of Gayatri Mantra. There are various rules for Purascharana. If you repeat 3,000 times daily, you should keep up the number daily all throughout till you finish the full 24 lakhs. Cleanse the mirror of Manas of its Mala and prepare the ground for the sowing of the spiritual seed. His grace is very, very important.

The Maharashtrians are very fond of Gayatri Purascharana. There are in Poona and other places persons who have performed Purascharana several times. Sri Pandit

Madan Mohan Malaviyaji was a votary of Gayatri Purascharana. The success in his life and the establishment of a grand Hindu University at Benares, is all attributable to his Gayatri Japa and the benign Grace of the Blessed Mother Gayatri.

Swami Vidyaranya, the reputed author of the celebrated Panchadasi, performed Gayatri Purascharana. Mother gave him Darshan and granted Vidyaranya a boon. Swami Vidyaranya asked: "O Mother! There is a great famine in the Deccan. Let there be a shower of gold to relieve the immense distress of the people." Accordingly there was a shower of gold. Such is the power or Sakti of Gayatri Mantra.

Yoga-Bhrashtas and pure-minded persons only can have Darshan of Gayatri by doing one Purascharana only. As the minds of vast majority of persons in this Iron Age are filled with various sorts of impurities, one has to do more than one Purascharana according to the degree of impurity of the mind. The more the impurities, the greater the number of Purascharana. The famous Madhusudana Swami did seventeen Purascharanas of Krishna Mantra. He did not get Darshan of Lord Krishna on account of the sins committed in killing 17 Brahmins in his previous births. But he had Darshan of the Lord when he was on the half way of the eighteenth Purascharana. The same rule applies to Gayatri-Purascharana also.

Hints on Gayatri-Japa

1. In days of yore, Hindu ladies also used to wear sacred thread (Yajnopavita) and repeat Gayatri. Manu was not in favour of this.

2. After the Purascharana is over, perform Havan and feed Brahmins, Sadhus and poor people to propitiate the Goddess.

3. Those who wish to do Purascharana may live on milk

and·fruits. This makes the mind Sattvic. One will derive great spiritual benefits.

4. There are no restrictions of any kind when you repeat a Mantra with Nishkama Bhava for attaining Moksha. Restrictions or Vidhis come in only when you want to get some fruits, when you do the Japa with Sakama Bhava.

5. When a Purascharana of Gayatri is done on the banks of the Ganga underneath an Asvattha tree or the Panchavriksha, Mantra-Siddhi comes in rapidly.

6. If you repeat Gayatri 4,000 times daily, you can finish the Purascharana in one year, seven months and twenty-five days. If you do the Japa slowly it will take 10 hours to finish 4,000 daily. The same number should be repeated daily.

7. You must observe strict Brahmacharya when you do Purascharana. Then you can have Darshan of Gayatri easily. Those who are unable to practise strict celibacy should be very moderate in copulation. This is second best thing.

8. The practice of Akhanda Mauna (unbroken silence) during Purascharana is highly beneficial. Those who are not able to practise this can observe full Mauna for a week in a month or on Sundays.

9. Those who practise Purascharana should not get up from the Asana till they finish the fixed number. They should not change the pose also.

10. Counting can be done through Maala, fingers or watch. Count the exact number that you can do in one hour. Suppose you can do in one hour 400 Gayatri Mantras, then Japa for 10 hours means 10x400 =4,000. There is more concentration in counting through watch.

11. There are three varieties of Gayatri pictures for meditation in morning, noon and evening. Many meditate on the five-faced Gayatri only throughout the day.

Gleanings

"Verily all this creation is Gayatri. Speech is Gayatri; by

speech is all this creation preserved. That Gayatri is verily this earth. The Gayatri is verily composed of four feet, and possesseth six characteristics. The creations constitute the glories of Gayatri. That Brahman i.e. the being indicated in the Gayatri, is verily a space which surroundeth mankind." (Chhandogya Upanishad: III-xii.)

"Verily man is Yajna (sacrifice). The first twenty-four years of his life constitute the morning ritual (Pratah savana). The Gayatri includes 24 letters and it is the Gayatri through which the morning ritual is performed." (Chhandogya Upanishad: III-xvi.)

Conclusion

In conclusion I will have to say that the repetition of Gayatri Japa brings the Darshan of Gayatri and eventually leads to the realisation of the Advaitic Brahman or unity of consciousness, or oneness (Tanmayata, Talleenata, Tadrupata, Tadakarata) and the aspirant who asked for light from Gayatri, in the beginning, sings now in exuberant joy, "I am the Light of lights, that gives light to Buddhi."

May Gayatri, the Blessed Mother of Vedas, bestow on us right understanding, pure intellect, right conduct and right thinking! May She guide us in all our actions! May She deliver us from the Samsaric wheel of births and deaths! Glory! Glory unto Gayatri, the creatress, the generatrix of this Universe!

6. How to Do Dhyana?

Fix your mind at the Lotus Feet of Lord Hari. Then rotate the mind on His silk-cloth (Pitambara), Srivatsa, Kaustubha gem on His chest, bracelets on His arm, ear-rings, crown on the head; then conch, disc, mace and lotus, on His hands and then come to His feet. Repeat the process again and again. Think of His attributes also. In this way you can do Dhyana on Krishna, Rama or Siva.

Uddhava asked: "In what form and with what rites should

the devotee think of You? Please inform me of the same fully." Sri Krishna said: "Seated comfortably in a seat neither high nor low, keeping the hands near the body unmoved, control the eye from wandering outwards. (Fix it on the tip of the nose to prevent distraction). Control the breath by taking it through one nostril and letting it out through the other and vice versa. Control the senses. Pronounce the letter OM continuously and with deep devotion both while inhaling and exhaling.

"The above practice daily at the three periods (morning, noon and dusk) will enable the Jiva to get perfect control of breath within a month. Imagine in the heart the lotus flower with its petals as seat, and fancy the sun, moon and fire to be the three lights, at their proper places. Concentrate your mind and imagine My present form as seated in the flower, with calm, dignified, smiling face, the cheeks resplendent with the lustre of the gold ear-rings; of beautiful neck, of sky colour, wearing a white cloth of spotless purity, with the ornament Srivatsa and the Goddess Lakshmi on the chest. With the weapons and other usual appendages, Chakra, mace, conch and lotus flower in My four hands, My feet shining with diamonds; with the splendour of the various ornaments on My body, crown, Kaustubha (diamond) on the chest, waist-ring, and the amulet at the shoulder, overflowing with grace towards My devotees.

"Run your fancy over the whole form till you complete all the details and then fix your mind on the same without thinking of anything else. By thus looking at the form and fixing the mind from wandering elsewhere, the face will gradually wear an ecstatic look. When thus the mind oblivious of everything else (forgetting even the triple differences, conscious at the starting point viz., the person concentrating the mind, the form on which the mind is concentrated and the act of concentration) gets fixed in concentration of My form (Dhyeyam), the Jiva becomes completely merged in Me (in the Tureeya or conscious Anandic ecstatic state), just as a ball of fire gets merged in a big bonfire. By constant practice of this Samadhi or ecstasy the Jiva very soon gets rid of all delusion caused by diversity and attains bliss."

7. Manasic Pooja

Manasic Pooja is preferable to actual Pooja of the Murthy with flowers, sandal-paste etc. But beginners should start with physical Pooja. When they advance in devotion they can take recourse to mental worship. Sri Sankara's mental Pooja in the form *"Atma Tvam, Girija Matih* etc.," is a beautiful way of worshipping God mentally. Get this Sloka by heart and before starting worship repeat this Sloka with Bhava. Mental Pooja consists in offering mentally flowers, Arghya, Achamaneeya, sandal-paste, cloth, ornament, Naivedya, etc., to God. Lord Siva was more pleased with the mental worship of Bhima than the actual offering of Bael leaves by Arjuna.

8. Anushthana

When you get holidays, plunge yourself in doing Anushthana either at home or some holy place preferably at Rishikesh or Prayag on the banks of the Ganga or the Yamuna. Do some lakhs or crores of Japa vigorously living on milk and fruits and observing Mauna. You will realise wonderful results, tremendous purity of heart and actual Darshan of God. If you can do it for six months, it is all the better. Intense Sadhana in solitude is very, very necessary if you want to reap a good spiritual harvest.

9. How to Develop Bhakti

Service of Bhagavatas, Sadhus and Sannyasins; repetition of God's Name; Satsanga; Hari Kirtan; study of Ramayana or Gita; stay in Vrindavana, Pandharpur, Chitrakuta, Ayodhya, or any other place of pilgrimage — these are the six means of cultivating Bhakti. The following nine modes of worship (Navavidha Bhakti) also will develop Bhakti: Sravana (hearing the Lilas of God); Kirtana (singing His praise); Smarana (remembering His Name); Padasevana (worshipping His Lotus Feet); Archana (offerings); Vandana (prostration); Dasya (service); Sakhya (friendship); and Atma-nivedana (complete self-surrender).

10. Secret of Surrender

Sakrudeva prapannaya tavasmeeti cha yachate;
Abhayam sarvabhutebhyo dadamyetad vratam mama.

"I remove all fears of all beings even if they come to Me only once and seek My refuge; calling themselves as Mine – This is My vow." – Sri Ramachandra's vow.

Throughout the Gita there is a ringing note that surrender and devotion are absolutely necessary for the attainment of God-consciousness. In reality, the nine modes of devotion (Navavidha Bhakti) are reducible to one, viz., Atmanivedan. The following Gita Slokas will impress on your mind the importance of devotion and self-surrender:

Tameva saranam gachha sarvabhavena bharata;
Tatprasadat param santim sthanam prapsyasi sasvatam.

"Flee unto Him for shelter with all thy being, O Bharata; by His Grace thou shalt obtain supreme peace, the everlasting dwelling-place." (XVIII-62.)

Manmana bhava madbhakto madyajee mam namaskuru;
Mamevaisyasi satyam te pratijane priyosi me.

"Merge thy mind in Me, be My devotee, sacrifice to Me, prostrate thyself before Me, thou shalt come even to Me." (XVIII-65.)

Sarvadharman parityajya mamekam saranam vraja;
Aham tva sarvapapebhyo mokshayishyami ma suchah.

"Abandoning all duties come unto Me alone for shelter; sorrow not, I liberate thee from all sins." (XVIII-66.)

Slokas 65 and 66 of Chapter XVIII are the most important Slokas of the Gita. The gist of the teaching of Lord Krishna is here. If anyone can live in the true spirit of these Slokas, he will realise the goal of life soon. There is no doubt of this.

The self-surrender must be total, ungrudging and unreserved. You must not keep certain desires for gratification. Mira says: "I have given my whole heart, mind, intellect, soul, my all to my Griridhar Gopal." This is perfect self-surrender.

A real devotee will not ask the Lord even for Mukti. So long as the subtle desire for liberation lingers in one's heart he cannot claim himself to be a true devotee of the Lord. Though the desire for emancipation is of Sattvic nature, yet the devotee has become a slave of Mukti. He is still selfish and so is unfit to call himself a sincere lover of God. He has not yet made total, unreserved self-surrender. To ask for Mukti is a variety of hypocrisy. Can a true devotee dare ask anything from God, when he fully knows that He is an ocean of love and compassion?

A real devotee never complains anything against God. A raw Bhakta speaks ill of God when he is in distress. He says, "I have done 25 lakhs of Japa. I am studying Bhagavata daily. Yet God is not pleased with me. He has not removed my sufferings. God is blind. He has not heard my prayers. What sort of God is Lord Krishna? I have no faith in Him."

A real Bhakta rejoices in suffering, pain and destitution. He welcomes grief and sorrow always, so that he may not forget God even for a second. He has the firm belief that God does everything for his good only. Kunti Devi prayed to Krishna: "O Lord! Give me pain always. Then only I will remember Thee always."

In Puri a saint who completely dedicated himself to Lord Hari was seriously ailing from chronic dysentery. He became quite helpless. Lord Jagannath was serving him for months in the form of a servant. The law of Prarabdha is inexorable. Nobody can escape from the operation of this infallible law. The Lord did not want the Bhakta to take another birth for the exhaustion of his Prarabdha. So His devotee had to suffer from protracted ailment. This was his Karmic purgation. But He Himself served him, as the devotee surrendered himself completely. Look at the unbounded mercy of the Lord! He becomes a slave of His devotees when they entirely depend upon Him.

Self-surrender does not mean retirement into the forests. It does not mean giving up of all activities. Tamas or inertia is mistaken for self-surrender. This is a sad mistake. What is wanted is internal surrender. The ego and desire must be annihilated. This will constitute real surrender. The Rajasic mind stands obstinate to effect complete self-surrender. Obstinacy is a great obstacle in surrender. The lower nature again and again raises up to assert itself. There is resurrection of desires. Desires get suppressed for some time. Again they manifest with redoubled force. Man is dragged hither and thither by these desires. Believe in the divine possibilities. Completely dedicate yourself to the Lord. Have full trust in Him. Rest in peace. All cares, worries, anxieties, tribulations and egoistic efforts will terminate now.

Look at Prahlada's surrender and faith in God! He completely resigned himself to Lord Hari. No other thought save thoughts of God occupied his mind. He had His full Grace and benediction even though he was ill-treated by his father in a variety of ways. He was hurled down from the top of a cliff. He was trampled by the elephant. He was poisoned. He was thrown into the sea with the legs tied by iron chains. Cobras were thrown over him. His nose was filled with poisonous gases. He was thrown over fire. Boiled oil was poured over his head. Yet his faith in Narayana was not shaken a bit. The Name of Narayana was always on his lips. Such must be the faith of every devotee.

The lower nature must be thoroughly overhauled. All old, wrong habits must be completely destroyed. Then the surrender becomes complete. Do not make plans and speculations. "Sufficient for the day is the evil thereof." Keep the mind and the intellect passive. Allow the Divine Will and Grace to work through your mind and Indriyas. Become silent. Feel His Grace and Love and enjoy the Divine Ecstasy. Be at ease.

Pray to God fervently, "O Lord! Make my will strong to resist all temptations, to control my Indriyas and lower nature, to change my old evil habits and to make my surrender complete and real. Enthrone Thyself in my heart. Do not leave this place even for a second. Use my body, mind and organs as instruments. Make me fit to dwell in Thee for ever."

Give up all ideas of duty and responsibility. Allow the Divine Will to work unhampered now. This is the secret of surrender. You will feel yourself a changed being. This exalted state is ineffable. A great transformation will come upon you. You will be enveloped by a halo of divine effulgence. You will be drowned in indescribable bliss, peace and joy. Your old little self is dead now. You are now a changed spiritual being. Your individual will is merged in the Cosmic Will. You are now illumined by the Divine Light. All ignorance has melted now. Enjoy the immortal, divine life wherein there is neither despair nor fear, neither hunger nor thirst, neither doubt nor delusion. Shine in Divine Splendour and Glory, O my beloved Visvanath! Radiate peace and joy all around.

11. Background of Thought

The background of thought of a Marwadi is about his money. His mind is always on the safe. He plans, speculates and schemes as how to increase his money in the bank from one lakh to two lakhs. The background of thought of a young man is about his wife. The background of thought of a doctor is about his patients, dispensary and drugs. The background of thought of a lawyer is about his clients, courts and rulings of the High court. The background of thought of an old grand-mother is about her grand-children. The vast majority of people indulge in thoughts of jealousy and hatred and these thoughts form their background.

But the background of thought of a Bhakta is about his Ishta-Devata. A devotee of Lord Krishna always thinks of Krishna with flute in hand. He has a concrete background. A Vedantin or a student of Jnana Yoga has an abstract background. He meditates on abstract ideas. A Sattvic background keeps the mind always pure and takes the devotee to the goal. The mental image of Lord Krishna destroys all other worldly thoughts. A sacred background of thought either concrete or abstract is a valuable spiritual asset for a man. A habit to think of the image is formed by constant thinking of one's Ishta Devata. Even in the office when you leave the pen on the table, the mind through the force of habit will at once move to the background of thought and think of the picture of Lord Krishna. Even in dream you will have vision of Lord Krishna only. The greater the Sadhana, the stronger the background of thought of the mental image. Even when you work in the office, just close your eyes for a couple of minutes every hour and think of the picture of Lord Krishna and repeat His Mantra: *Om Namo Bhagavate Vaasudevaya*. This is an excellent practice. This is solid Sadhana. You will have an unruffled state of mind always. You can turn out more work with great concentration.

In the beginning you may not be able to bring the full image before the mind's eye. When you think of the face of Lord Krishna, the feet and hands will disappear. When you think of His feet, His face will slip away. Through constant Sadhana, you can visualise a well-defined, clear-cut, full image.

A ray of the mind goes forth to the object, which in turn shapes and moulds the mental substance into the form of the object. When a man thinks of an image of Lord Krishna or Lord Rama constantly with a single-minded or one-pointed concentration like unbroken flow of oil (*Avicchinna Tailadharavat*), his mental substance takes the form of the image. The image leaves a definite impression on the mind. This is called Samskara. If this impression is repeated very often, a tendency or habit is formed in the mind. That is the reason why the aspirant is asked to repeat the Mantra several lakhs of times. A man can shape his mind for good or bad. It depends upon the nature of food he gives to the mind. Every thought produces a definite change in the substance of the brain also.

One has to create a Sattvic background of thought through continued struggle. The mind will run back to its old ruts and manufacture images of worldly objects. The Sadhaka will have to bring back again and again the mind to the Sattvic background of thought that he has developed. The struggle will be keen in the beginning. Later on the mind will quietly rest in the spiritual background of thought.

12. How to See God

The personal aspect of that Being is termed 'Isvara', 'Allah', 'Hari', 'Jehovah', 'Father in Heaven', 'Buddha', 'Siva', etc.

The impersonal aspect is called "Brahman" by Vedantins, "Unknowable" by Herbert Spencer, "Will" by Schopenhauer, "Absolute", "Noumenon" by some, and "Substance" by Spinoza.

Religion is faith for knowing God and worshipping Him. It is not a matter for discussion at a club-table. It is the realisation of the true Self. It is the fulfilment of the deepest craving in mind.

Therefore hold religion as the highest prize of your life. Live every moment of your life for its realisation. Life without religion is real death.

"Remove selfishness. Calm the passions. Remove egoism. Purify the heart. Analyse your thoughts. Scrutinise your motives. Cleanse the dross or impurity. Realise God." This has been the essence of the preachings of all prophets, seers and sages of all times. Read the teachings of Buddha, Jesus, Mohammed, Confucius, Shinto, Chaitanya, Sankara or any other prophet. This is the essence of Sadhana. This is the way to God. God-realisation is your chief duty.

Just as a charioteer restrains the restive horses through the reins, so also you will have to curb the restless "Indriyas" (the horses) through the reins of Viveka and Vairagya (discrimination and dispassion). Then alone you will have a safe journey to Atman or God, the sweet, eternal abode of peace and bliss.

Be righteous always; never deviate from the path of righteousness. You are born to practise righteousness and lead a virtuous life. Truth is established in righteousness. Stand upright. Be bold. Be fearless. Practise Truth. Proclaim it everywhere.

A man who speaks truth, who is merciful and liberal, who has Kshama and Santi, who is free from fear, wrath and greed, who is innocent and loving is really God or Brahman. He is the real Brahmin. Those who are destitute of the above virtues are Sudras only.

How can you obtain His Grace, if you have no humility and if you do not make ungrudging, unreserved, unconditioned self-surrender to the Lord? The Lord knows what is good for you better than you do. To resign yourself absolutely to His Will is even higher form of worship than visiting temples and shaking the bell, and doing all sorts of ritualistic ceremonies. The Lord does not want your external show. He wants your heart. Say once more: "Thy Will be done. I am Thine. All is Thine" from the bottom of your heart, Antarika. Be sincere. Weep for Him out of Prem (pure love). Cry in solitude out of devotion. Let the cloth be drenched in profuse tears.

Close your eyes. Destroy the Vasana (of body, world and book-lore). Withdraw the mind. Merge in Him. Drink the nectar of immortality now.

A real devotee of Lord Krishna sees Krishna and Krishna alone in the whole world. He has a new Yogic eye, a new spiritual vision.

It is simple foolishness to think that you are separate from the rest of the world. You are one with all. In injuring Visvaranjan you injure yourself. In loving Chandrasekhar you love yourself. Separation is death. Unity is eternal life.

O friends! It is not very difficult to have Darshan of God. It is not very difficult also to please Him. He is everywhere, within all. He is seated in your hearts. Think of Him always (Sakara, Saguna). Pray fervently: "O Lord! Have mercy upon me. Open my inner eye – the Divyachakshus. Let me have Thy Grand vision – Visvaroopadarshan. Bhaktas sing about Thee as "Patitapavana" (purifier of the fallen ones), "Bhaktavatsala" (lover of the devotees), "Deenadayalu" (merciful towards the helpless). Just as the bird protects the young ones under its wings so also protect me under Thy wings, O Ocean of Mercy!"

13. Glory of Lord Siva

Om. I bow with folded hands to Lord Siva, Who is the Lord of the universe (Jagat-Pati), world's teacher (Jagad-Guru), Who is the destroyer of Tripuras (3 cities, egoism, lust and anger), Who is the Lord of Uma (Uma Sankar), Gauri (Gauri Sankar), Ganga (Ganga Sankar), who is full of light (Jyotirmaya), knowledge and bliss

(Chidananda Maya), Who is the Lord of Yogins (Yogeesvara), Who is the storehouse of knowledge and Who is known by the various names as Mahadeva, Sankara, Hara, Sambhu, Sadasiva, Rudra, Soolapani, Bhairava, Uma-Mahesvara, Neelakantha, Trilochana or Tryambaka (the three-eyed), Visvanatha, Chandrasekhara, Ardhanareesvara, Mahesvara, Neelalohita, Parama Siva, Digambara, Dakshinamurti, etc.

How merciful He is! How loving and kind He is! He even wears the skulls of His devotees as a garland around His neck. He is an embodiment of renunciation, mercy, love and wisdom. It is a mistake to say that He is the destroyer. Lord Siva in reality is the regenerator. Whenever one's physical body becomes unfit for further evolution in this birth either by disease, old age or other causes, He at once removes this rotten physical sheath and gives a new, healthy, vigorous body for further quick evolution. He wants to take all His children to His Lotus Feet quickly. He desires to give them His glorious "Siva-Pada". It is easier to please Siva than Hari. A little Prem and devotion, a little chanting of His Panchakshra is quite sufficient to infuse delight in Siva. He gives boons to His devotees quite readily. How large is His heart! He gave Pasupatastra to Arjuna without any difficulty for his little penance. He gave a precious boon to Bhasmasura. In Kalahasti near Tirupati He gave Darshan for Kannappa Nayanar, the devoted hunter who plucked his two eyes to replace the weeping eyes in the Murti. In Chidambaram even the untouchable saint Nandanar had Darshan of Lord Siva. He ran with tremendous speed to make the boy Markandeya immortal when he was in the clutches of the God of Death – Yama. Ravana of Lanka pleased Siva with his Sama chantings. He initiated the four virgin youths Sanaka, Sanandana, Sanatana and Sanatkumara into the mysteries of Jnana in the form of Guru Dakshinamoorthy. In Madurai in Tamil Nadu,

Sundaresvara (Lord Siva) assumed the form of a boy and carried earth on his head for a devoted lady for the sake of *Puttu* (a kind of sweetmeat) as wages when an anicut was erected in the Vaigai river. Look at the unbounded mercy for His devotees! When Brahma and Lord Vishnu went to find out the head and feet of Lord Siva, He assumed an infinite, expansive blaze of light (Jyotirmaya). They were baffled in their attempts. How magnanimous and self-effulgent He is! He lived in the house of Pattinattu Swami in Southern India for several years as his adopted son and disappeared after giving him the small note: "Even the broken needles will not follow you after your death." The reading of this note was the starting point for attainment of Jnana for Pattinattu Swami. Why not you all attempt this very second with sincerity to realise God (Lord Siva)?

Hatha Yogins awaken the Kundalini Sakti that is lying dormant in the Muladhara Chakra by Asana, Pranayama, Kumbhaka, Mudra and Bandha, take it above through different Chakras (centres of spiritual energy) Svadhishthna, Manipura, Anahata, Visuddha and Ajna and join it with Lord Siva at the Sahasrara, the thousand-petalled lotus at the crown of the head. They drink the nectar of Immortality (Siva-Jnana-Amritam). This is termed Amrita-srava. When the Sakti is united with Siva, full illumination comes for the Yogi.

Lord Siva represents the destructive aspect of Brahman. That portion of Brahman that is enveloped by Tamo-Guna-Pradhana-Maya is Lord Siva who is the all-pervading Isvara and who also dwells in Mount Kailas. He is the Bhandar or store-house for wisdom. Siva minus Parvati or Kaali or Durga is pure Nirguna Brahman. With Maya (Parvati) He becomes the Saguna Brahman for the purpose of pious devotion of His devotees. Devotees of Rama must worship Lord Siva also. Rama Himself worshipped Lord Siva at the famous Ramesvaram. Lord Siva is the Lord of ascetics and Lord of Yogins robed in space (Digambara).

His Trisul (trident) that is held in His right hand represents the three Gunas — Sattva, Rajas and Tamas. That is the emblem of sovereignty. He wields the world through these three Gunas. The Damaru in His left hand represents the Sabda Brahman. It represents OM from which all languages are formed. It is He who formed the Sanskrit language out of the Damaru sound.

The wearing of the crescent moon on His head indicates that He has controlled the mind perfectly. The flow of the Ganga represents the nectar of immortality. Elephant represents symbolically the Vritti, pride. Wearing the skin of the elephant denotes that He has controlled pride. Tiger represents lust. His sitting on the tiger's skin indicates that he has conquered lust. His holding a deer in one hand indicates that He has removed the Chanchalata (tossing) of the mind. Deer jumps from one place to another swiftly. The mind also jumps from one object to another. His wearing of serpents on the neck denotes wisdom and eternity. Serpents live for a large number of years. He is Trilochana, the three-eyed One, in the centre of whose forehead is the third eye, the eye of wisdom. Nandi, the bull that sits in front of Sivalingam represents Pranava (Omkara). The Lingam represents Advaita. It points out "I am one without a second. *Ekam eva Advaiteeyam*" just as a man raises his right hand above his head pointing out his right index finger only.

Kailas hills in Tibet are a huge range with a central, beautiful, naturally carved and decorated shining peak, eternally clad with silvery snow 22,980 feet above sea-level. Some take the height to be 22,028 feet. This particular peak is in the form of a natural, huge Siva Linga (Virat Form). This is worshipped as the form of Lord Siva from a distance.

There is neither a temple nor a Poojari nor a daily Pooja there. I had the fortune to have Darshan of Kailas through the grace of Lord Siva on July 22, 1931. I even climbed with panting breath to the foot of Kailas peak where the Indus takes its origin. It is a very picturesque, soul-stirring scenery. You will have to ascend from Didipha Gupha, the first halting stage in Parikrama of Kailas. The Indus gushes out as a small streamlet through blocks of ice from behind the back portion of Kailas peak. Though in the pictures of Lord Siva it is shown that the Ganga flows from His head, it is really the Indus that takes its origin from the head of Siva (Kailas) in the physical plane. Parikrama of Kailas covers 30 miles. It takes three days. On the way comes the famous and sacred Gauri Kund which is eternally covered with snow. You will have to break the snow when you take a bath.

Jyotirlingas

The following are the twelve Jyotirlingas of Lord Siva:

1. Somanath in Gujarat.

2. Mallikarjuna in Srisaila Parvat in Andhra Pradesh.

3. Mahakala in Ujjain in Madhya Pradesh.

4. Omkaresvar on the banks of Narmada in Amalesvarm.

5. Baijnath near Gaya (Paralya).

6. Naganath in Southern India.

7. Kedarnath in Himalayas, Uttar Pradesh.

8. Tryambak, near the source of the Godavari in the Nasik District, Maharashtra.

9. Ramesvaram, in Ramnad district, Tamil Nadu.

10. Bhima Sankar, near Poona.

11. Visvanath in Benares.

12. Grishnesvar (Gokarna) in Karwar district, Karnataka.

Even if people remember these 12 places both morning and evening, the sins of seven births will be destroyed.

PRACTICE OF BHAKTI YOGA

In Southern India, there are five famous Siva Lingas which represent the five elements.

1. In Shiyali, Tanjore district, there is Prithvi Lingam.

2. In Tiruvana Koil, Trichinopoly district, there is Appu Lingam. The Lingam is always in water. Tiruvana Koil is otherwise known as Jambukesvaram.

3. In Kalahasti, Andhra Pradesh, there is a Vayu Lingam.

4. In Tiruvannamalai, via Villupuram Junction, North Arcot District, there is the Tejolingam (Arunachalesvar).

5. In Chidambaram, there is the Akasa Lingam.

During my recent travels, I used to hold Sankirtan in Monghyr (All-India Kirtan Sammelan 1932), Sitapur, Lakhimpur, Ayodhya, Lucknow, Kakinada, Calcutta and other places. People were very much attracted towards my three charming Siva Namavalis. I shall mention them here.

Panchakshara Namavali

1. Sivaya Nama Om Sivaya Namah;
   Sivaya Nama Om Namah Sivaya.

2. Siva Sambho Sadasiva,
   Sambho Sadasiva,
   Sambho Sadasiva Bhum Bhum Bhum.

3. Hara Hara Siva Siva Sambho,
   Hara Hara Siva Siva,
   Hara Hara Sambho,
   Siva Siva Sambho.

Rudra is the destructive aspect of Siva. There are eleven Rudras in the cosmic hierarchy. Esoterically the Pranas and the mind represent the eleven Rudras. Sri Hanuman is a manifestation or aspect of Siva only.

These are the 25 Lilas (sportive plays) or manifestations of Lord Siva.

1. Wearing of moon on the head. 2. Living with Uma Devi. 3. Riding on Nandi. 4. Tandava dancing with Kaali.

5. Marriage with Parvati. 6. Begging. 7. Burning of Manmatha or the God of Love. 8. Victory over Yama the God of death. 9. Burning of Tripuras. 10. Killing of Jalandarasura. 11. Killing of Gajasura. 12. Incarnation of Virabhadra. 13. Harihara. 14. Ardhanareesvara. 15. Transforming into Kirata. 16. Assuming the form of Kankala. 17. Blessing Chandusvara. 18. Drinking poison. 19. Giving of Chakra. 20. Destroying of obstacles. 21. Having sons of Uma with Him. 22. Becoming Ekapada Rudra. 23. Being in easy pose (Sukhasana). 24. Assuming the form of Dakshinamoorthy. 25. Assuming Linga form.

In Me the universe had its origin,
In Me alone the whole subsists;
In Me it is lost—this Siva
The Timeless, It is I Myself!
Sivoham! Sivoham!! Sivoham!!!

14. Lord Krishna and His Teachings

Om Sri Krishna Rukminee-Kanta Gopeejanamanohara,
Samsarasagare magnam mamuddhara jagadguro.

Lord Krishna was born in Mathura which is situated on the banks of the beautiful river Yamuna, in U.P. He showed superhuman physical strength and very mysterious powers on various occasions even as a boy. He killed many wild beasts and birds and is especially famous for killing the demoniac snake called Kaaliya which used to live in the waters of the Yamuna. His Flute was the signal for a general onrush towards the beautiful grooves where everything was love and pleasure. He organised several kinds of plays, games and picnics in the gardens and shady retreats of Vrindavana for the amusement of the maids and boys of Gokula. He gradually gave up all his boyish pranks and soon turned out to be a most astute statesman when he reached the age of adolescence. He became a powerful and able ruler and had much to do in the field of politics.

At the holy hermitage of Rishi Sandeepani, he and his brother Balaram learnt philosophy and theology, science and politics, and several other arts such as archery etc. He settled up all internal dissensions that were rending the country from one corner to another. He chastised Kamsa and Jarasandha for their tyranny and restored peace and order in place of bloodshed and misery.

Lord Krishna was a statesman of a very superior order. He was a reformer, a Yogi and a Jnani to boot. He was a master of Vajroli Mudra. Hence He is termed as a Bala-Brahmachari though he lived in the midst of Gopis. His love towards the Gopis was one of Divine type. It was not physical love. How can you expect carnality in a boy of eleven years? He always identified Himself with Nirguna, Anatma Brahman and used his mind and body as His instruments in Vyavahara. He was a Sakshi of Prakriti's activities.

Lord Krishna is popularly known as "Bansiwala". When Lord Krishna played on the Flute it conveyed a different, divine message altogether to the Gopis (the incarnations of the classical Devatas). It was not a mere musical sound.

Kling is the Beeja Akshara of Lord Krishna. It is a powerful Mantra. It produces a powerful vibration in the mental stuff and transforms the Rajasic nature of the mind. It produces certain kind of powerful spiritual idea in the mind which greatly helps purification of mind, concentration and contemplation. It induces Vairagya and Antarmukha Vritti and attenuates the force of Vasanas and Samskaras. It completely checks the thought-force. It produces rhythmical vibrations of the five sheaths.

The following is the "Mahamantra" of Lord Krishna. It is found in the Gopala Tapani Upanishad. Those who repeat this Mantra 18 lakhs of times with concentration, Suddha Bhava and intense Sraddha will doubtless have direct Darshan of Lord Krishna. It is 18 Akshara Mantra.

"Om Kling Krishnaya Govindaya
Gopijana Vallabhaya Svaha."

The following is the Nyasa for the Mantra:

(a) "Om Kling Krishnaya Divyatmane Hridayaya Namah".

(b) "Govindaya Bhumyatmane Sirase Svaha".

(c) "Gopijana Surya-atmane Sikhaya Vashat".

(d) "Vallabhaya Chandra-atmane Kavachaya Hum".

(e) "Svaha Agnyatmane Astraya fut."

"Om Namo Bhagavate Vaasudevaya" is a 12 Akshara Mantra of Lord Krishna. Dhruva repeated this Mantra and obtained His Darshan. Repeat it 12 lakhs of times. Even ladies can repeat this Mantra.

You need not go to Vrindavana, to have the Darshan of Lord Krishna. Your own heart is the real Vrindavana. You will have to search Him in your Hridaya-Vrindavana. Rukmini and Radha are the two Saktis (Kriya Sakti and Jnana Sakti) of Lord Krishna. Arjuna is Jiva. Kurukshetra is the battlefield within. The real battle is the one with the mind, Indriyas, Vishaya Samaskaras, Vishaya Vrittis, and Svabhava. Draupadi is the mind. Pandavas are the Indriyas. Blind Dhritarashtra is the original Avidya. Gopis are the nerves or Nadis. Enjoyment with Gopis is enjoyment of Atmic Bliss by controlling the various nerves. This is the esoteric exposition.

Just as Lord Dattatreya is still moving about with his astral body in the reputed Girnar hills and gives Darshan even now to His sincere Bhaktas, just as Sri Jnana Dev is still moving about with his astral body in Alandi near Poona, and gives Darshan even now to his sincere devotees, so also Lord Krishna is still moving about in Vrindavana and gives Darshan to His sincere Bhaktas even now.

The Bhagavad Gita contains the teachings of Lord Krishna. It is a wonderful book for constant study. Aspirants should study this book with great care daily. The first six chapters deal with Karma Yoga and represent the "Tat" Pada of "Tat Tvam Asi" Mahavakya. The next six chapters deal with Bhakti Yoga and represent the "Tvam" Pada. The last six chapters deal with Jnana Yoga and represent the "Asi" Pada.

Lord Krishna summarised His teachings in the following words in the 12th Chapter (8-11) of the Gita: "Fix thy mind in Me only, thy intellect in Me, (then) thou shalt no doubt abide in Me alone hereafter (Yoga of Meditation). If thou art unable to fix thy mind steadily on Me, then by the Yoga of constant practice (Abhyasa Yoga — Yoga Practices) do thou seek to reach Me, O Dhananjaya. If thou art unable to practice even this Abhyasa Yoga, be thou intent on doing actions for My sake; even by doing actions for My sake, thou shalt attain perfection (Assiduity of Love). If thou art unable to do even this, then, resorting to union with Me, renounce the fruits of all actions, with the self controlled, (doing one's duties without desires)."

Act but act only with devotion to God without desire for fruits. Is this impossible? Sri Krishna said: "No". I shall explain His words by quoting an example. The soldiers in an army fight: they kill men and are killed but they act without any desire, without any mind: they are under the orders of their general. They know not what they do, they move, they march, they run, they fire, but they know not for what object. They are like dolls in the hands of their general. They do what they are commanded to do. Their lives, their objects, their desires are all in their general's hand. To obey their general's command is their duty, and in performing it they give their own lives or take the lives of others — the others sometimes being their dearest or the nearest relatives. They know that whatever they do under orders from their general must be good, good for them and good for the country and the cause for which they fight. Their minds, with their conscience and all, are placed in the hands of their general. From this illustration it is evident that it is not impossible to act without desires and without a mind. It is possible only when man fully depends upon another. If I know that I am not responsible for my acts, if I know that I have a General under whose orders I act and who will be responsible for all my acts, if I know I am not to think for myself, I have got one who will think for me to do that which would be good to me—surely I can go on acting without troubling myself in any way; surely in such a case I can act without any desires whatsoever and without any mind and anything else I possess.

Sri Krishna asked man to consider himself as a doll in the hands of God: He asked man to think himself as a soldier, God as his great General, his worldly acts as duties under orders. He asked him to act on the faith and belief that whatever he does is the work of God. He said:

Sarvadharman parityajya mamekam saranam vraja;
Aham tva sarvapapebhyo mokshayishyami ma suchah.

"Abandoning all duties, take refuge in Me (God) alone: I will liberate thee from all sins; grieve not." (Gita: XVIII-66.)

I shall conclude my article with the last Sloka of the 18th chapter of the Gita:

Yatra Yogesvarah Krishno yatra partho dhanurdharah;
Tatra sreer vijayo bhutir dhruva neetir matirmama.

"Wherever is Krishna, the Lord of Yoga; wherever is Arjuna, the wielder of the bow; there are prosperity, victory, happiness and firm policy; such is my conviction."

15. Sankirtan Movement

Kirtan is singing God's Name with feeling (Bhava), love (Prem) and faith (Sraddha). In Sankirtan people join together and sing God's Name collectively in a common place. There is accompaniment of musical instruments such as harmonium, violin, cymbals, Mridanga or Kole etc.

Christians sing hymns in the churches with piano. This is only Sankirtan. There are nine modes of Bhakti (Nava-Vidha-Bhakti). Kirtan is one of the nine modes. One can realise God through Kirtan alone. This is the easiest method for attainment of God-consciousness. Sri Tuka Ram, Sri Ram Prasad, Lord Gauranga had attained Godhood through Kirtan and Kirtan alone.

The Sankirtan movement which had its revival during the time of Lord Gouranga began gradually to decline owing to several causes as time passed on. But thanks to the great change in the atmosphere of the present day, there is a striking revival of this movement in U.P., Bengal, Maharashtra, Tamil Nadu and Punjab. The party of the late reputed Sri Roopkalaji of Ayodhya is holding[2] all-India Sankirtan in the various places in U.P. and Bihar. Sri Krishna Premi also known as Mr. Nixon, M.A. of Uttara Vrindavan, Almora, is a great Bhakta and a fine Sankirtanist. He evinces very keen interest in the movement. He sings and dances in divine ecstasy forgetting himself in Krishna Prem. He delivers lectures in Hindi and has now become a Sanskrit scholar. When an Englishman takes so much interest in Sankirtan, our Hindu brothers are lethargic and spend their time in sleeping only. What a shame!

Sri Hari Babaji is also a well-known Bhakta staying in Bhand in U.P. He is a devotee of Lord Krishna and belongs to the Sampradaya of Lord Gouranga. He has disseminated Sankirtan in Aligarh, Delhi and other places. He has done remarkable service to the villagers all round Bhand by constructing an anicut up to a distance of six miles on the bank of the Ganga and saved several villages from being swept away during the recent floods. He collected six lakhs of rupees for this noble work. He is known as Bhandwala. He holds Akhanda Kirtan for several months. He held

2 This book was written in 1937

BHAKTI SADHANA

several Kirtan Utsavas in Delhi, Bulandsahar, Aligarh and other places.

The reputed Sri Odiya Babaji always accompanies him wherever big religious functions are held. Rasa Lila and Kathas are also held. He is now holding Akhanda Sankirtan for one year at Bhand. He hails from Punjab. He got Vairagya when he was a medical student and immediately left his studies and renounced the world. He never wastes a single minute. He always plunges himself in Katha and Kirtan.

Sri Swami Ekarasanandaji is another veteran Swami who stays sometimes at Kanpur. He has got Ashram at Kanpur and Farukkabad. He has established the Daivi Sampat Mandal there. He is a noble, pious soul full of humility and love. Though he is aged 75 now, he could deliver lectures standing three or four hours at a stretch. He is a Bhakta-Jnani. He is very fond of Sankirtan. He helps the Sankirtan movement a good deal. His lectures impress people very much. His disciples Sri Bhajananandaji, Sri Naradanandaji and Sri Sukadevanandaji are disseminating his ideals and views in religion.

Pandit Bindhuji Sharma, a nice Katha-Vachak, Sangeeta Bhushan, Kavya Kaustubh Vani Visarad and poet of Vrindavana is another important figure in the field. He has disseminated Sankirtan in Gwalior, Jhansi, Sagar, Jammu and other places. He is a learned man and is greatly skilled in music. Sri Swami Ramananda Saraswati, another Sankirtan Acharya is spreading Sankirtan in Layalpur, Sitapur, Lakhimpur and other places.

Sri Hanuman Prasad Poddar, the Editor of "Kalyan" is now holding Akhanda Kirtan in Gorakhpur for one year. Sri Jayadayal Goyandka is another Bhakta who has stirred the whole Marwari community in the path of devotion. He holds Sankirtan on Ekadasi and Poornima. Sri Hanuman Prasad Poddarji and Sri Jayadayalji are the corner-stones for the edifice of Sankirtan in Gorakhpur. Through the medium of the Gita Press they are nicely spreading the message of Sankirtan Bhakti. In this connection it is but right to mention that two important journals issued from Meerut viz., "Svadharma" and "Sankirtan" are the leading organs of the movement.

Professor Ganga Saran Sheelji, M.A., of Chandosi Intermediate College is working very hard in disseminating Sankirtan Bhakti. He is very energetic and can be rightly said to be an enthusiastic worker in the field. He has stirred Meerut, Rawalpindi and other places. Sri Prabhu Dutt Brahmachariji held Akhanda Kirtan in Jhusi near Allahabad for one full year. He is also another important man in the movement.

There are twelve Sankirtan Sabhas in Lahore (now in Pakistan). Various other Sankirtan Mandals also have been started in U.P. and Punjab. Pt. Durga Prasad, a retired Advocate and Managing Editor of the "Sankirtan", Meerut, is labouring in this direction. Pt. Ramdasji may be rightly described as the heart and soul of the Sankirtan Mandal at Lakhimpur-Kheri. Lala Chetu Ramji, the prop of Sankirtan Sabhas in Lahore, Seth Bhagath Ram of Lahore, Dr. Parsram of Jammu, Sri Karamchand Bhagat of Ambala Cantt. are doing very good work in this direction.

In this Kali Yuga Sankirtan alone is the easiest, quickest and surest path for God-realisation. Wherever Sankirtan is held there you will find Munis, Rishis like Sri Narada, Nitya-Siddhas, Sri Hanuman, Lord Krishna and Lord Rama. Workers in the field should not relax their efforts but should keep the divine flame burning steadily. They should see that Sankirtan is held in every Mohalla, in every house of a town or village. They should direct their energies in villages. They can do much work there. The villagers are more devotional than the people in towns. There you will find more purity, more simplicity and faith in the innocent villagers. Fashion, civilization and cunningness have not yet penetrated their hearts. Ladies of Punjab and U.P. are now evincing keen and lively interest. Fashion and passion are slowly giving place to Bhakti and devotion.

It is my great desire to mention the names of some more men, both Sannyasins and householders, in this connection. The keen and active co-operation with which Sannyasins like Sri Swami Krishnanandaji (Sakhi Bhava), Sri Swami Yoganandaji (Lucknow), Swami Atmanandaji, Swami Svaroopanandaji and Swami Mahesvaranandaji work with householders like Sri Balmukandji, Sri Nagarji Bhakkat, Sri Takore Mahendra Pal Singhji, Pandit Radha Ramana, Sri Pitambhar Dayal Saxena and Sri Krishna Svaroop Bhatnagar etc., reminds one of the days of the Upanishads and the glories of the past. All these Sannyasins mentioned above and also the householders are highly educated, cultured and polished people which is the most pleasing feature of the movement. Yes, Sankirtan is no doubt spreading like wild fire and has brought with it the glorious Satya Yuga. Victory to Hari's Name! Glory to Sankirtanists! Glory to one and all who spread Bhakti throughout the length and breadth of the land!

Need for Organisation

An All-India Sankirtan organisation is indispensably requisite. The idea is laudable indeed. But how this will materialise and how this will become practicable and feasible, is the present problem. Large-hearted leaders in the Sankirtan field are wanted. Then there is the possibility of systematic organisation. Then only union can be expected. Bear in mind: where there are different sects with fighting attitude for superiority, where jealousy, Abhimana, Gurudom and petty-mindedness, canker of name and fame prevail, there is not an iota of hope of an all-India organisation. It is an Utopian scheme only. There may be honest differences in opinion amongst the leaders of the

Sankirtan world, but they should be united in their hearts by the thread of Suddha Prem. To avoid rupture and dissension amongst the members of a Sabha, I would also suggest to you the advisability of removing the names of President and Secretary and substituting "Hari Das" for the one and "Krishna Das" for the other, and not to collect any money at all as subscription.

I shall suggest some means to help the growth of Sankirtan and its dissemination. People do Sankirtan with great enthusiasm of two or three years. Afterwards they do not evince real interest. They become slothful and torpid. This is a sad mistake. The zeal should be kept up all throughout life. Just as food and water are not stopped even for a day, so also Sankirtan should not be stopped even for a day. Sankirtan is a spiritual food, a physical and mental tonic as well. You can live on Sankirtan alone.

Of late, you are perfectly aware that there is a great revival in the Sankirtan movement. Various "Mandalis" are formed now in various parts of U.P., Punjab, M.P., Tamil Nadu and Bengal. Many English educated persons, many atheists, agnostics and ladies as well are doing vigorous Kirtan with Kartals and cymbals in their hands. Several Sankirtan Utsava conferences were held in Bulandsahar, Bandha (Badayun), Gwalior, Roorkee, Lahore, Etawah and other places. You will be glad to hear that in Lahore more than eight thousand ladies are doing vigorous Kirtan now. It is hoped, therefore, that the advent of a great Avatar within a short time is expected. The ground is prepared now by the Sankirtan Utsavas for His descent.

If you want to make the Sankirtan movement grow, a powerful organisation of all Sankirtan Sabhas in India is an imperative necessity. A well-conducted organisation is a great *desideratum*. As there are now dissensions and splits in these Sabhas owing to lack of selfless workers, the Mandalis break down soon like mushroom growths. All the present

Sankirtan Sabhas must be well united. There must be a head-office or a central Maha-Sabha with different nuclei or centres throughout India. All the Sabhas must be affiliated to this central Maha-Sabha.

Petty-minded, jealous, selfish people cause many obstacles in the growth of Sankirtan. They create dissensions and party-feelings amongst Sankirtanists. New rival Sabhas with a hostile spirit are started. The Secretary of a Mandal should be a man of pluck and amiable disposition. He should unite all with all-embracing love. Everybody wants to make the Kirtan-Sabha his own personal property.

Where there is the personal element with self-interests, with desire for name and fame, there cannot be any growth in Sankirtan. It becomes a business. It becomes a commercial enterprise. God is far from these men who work with ulterior motives but outwardly profess to be Bhaktas. Can there be any religion in business? The secretary of a Sankirtan Sabha should not work with a view to get name and fame. People ascend the platforms to exhibit their devotion. This is highly despicable!

Sannyasins and other Sankirtan propagandists who are desirous of doing Sankirtan on the platform and of disseminating Sankirtan far and wide should train themselves first before they appear on the stage. They should have a perfectly trained Mandali of their own. Then only they will be able to produce a lasting impression on the public. Lord Gouranga did the same. He had an organised Mandali of his own. He gave them good training in the beginning within the four walls of his compound. There must be perfect harmony and concord, one Svara, one Tala when Sankirtan is done. Then only there will be joy, Ananda and elevation of mind. No propaganda work is possible without a trained Mandali.

"Union is strength". In Kali Yuga Sangha Sakti is a potent factor in the Sankirtan propagandic activities. If all the patrons of Sankirtan, Acharyas and renowned Sannyasins who are interested in the growth and development of Sankirtan join together whole-heartedly and work in perfect concord and unison, tremendous work can be turned out and marvellous, indescribable influence will be produced in the minds of the public. They should sit in one place and conduct Sankirtan-Utsava or conference for two or three months continuously. Then the people will develop the habit of doing Sankirtan daily. Utsavas for four days do not produce a lasting impression on the minds of the public.

Benefits of Sankirtan

Lord Hari says to Rishi Narada:

"I dwell not in Vaikuntha nor in the hearts of the Yogins, but I dwell there where My devotee sings My name, O Narada!"

If one does Sankirtan from the bottom of his heart with full Bhava and Prem, even the trees, birds and animals will be deeply influenced. They will respond. Such is the powerful influence of Sankirtan. Rishis and Siddhas visit the place where Sankirtan is held. You can see brilliant lights all around the Pandal.

Melodious music soothes the nerves. In America doctors cure diseases by music. Shakespeare says: "The man who hath no music in himself nor is not moved by the concord of sweet sounds, is fit for treason, stratagem and spoils. The motions of his spirit are dull as night, his affections dark as Erebus. Let no such man be trusted. Mark the music."

Vedanta and Jnana can only be understood by the microscopic minority. Vast majority are fit for Sankirtan-Bhakti only. Even highly intellectual people will derive immense benefit by doing Sankirtan. Their minds will be elevated for practising Nididhyasana (meditation). The Vikshepa in their minds will also be removed.

There is no Yajna greater than Akhanda Kirtan. It does

not cost you anything. Whenever you get holidays, start Akhanda Kirtan for twenty-four hours. Change the batch of people every two hours. Those who take an active part in it should wear clothes washed by their own hands and take milk and fruits or Phalahar that day. They should observe strictly the vow of celibacy (Brahmacharya) and walk bare-footed to the place where the Yajna is held. The Kirtan can be continued for a week also. The longer, the better.

In Jhusi there had been Akhanda Kirtan for full one year. In Lakhmipur-Kheri, Pandit Rama Dasji had Akhanda Kirtan for three months. You will also have to follow suit. Remember, Akhanda Kirtan produces tremendous purity of mind and other incalculable benefits. Utsavas for three days may not produce a lasting impression. To induce Samadhi and Divine ecstatic mood quickly, there is no other agent more powerful than Akhanda Kirtan. You should have Akhanda Kirtan, Prabhata Kirtan and also daily Kirtans at night in your own house.

We are often confronted with the puzzling question: Are Jnana and Bhakti conflicting with each other? My answer will be in the negative. There is, in fact, an inter-relation between the two, the one supplementing the other. Bhakti is not at all antagonistic to Jnana. There is doubtless a mutual dependence. Both lead to the same destination. Jnana intensifies Bhakti. A Jnani is truly a highest Samarasa Bhakta. He is a Saivite, Vaishnavaite and a Sakta. He has an all-inclusive, all-embracing heart.

How patiently and cautiously the fisherman watches the bait to catch a single fish! How energetically and untiringly a student works for passing his M.Sc. examination! How vigilant is the man who wants to catch the train at 2 a.m.! How smart and careful is the surgeon in the operation-theatre when the patient is on the table! How alert is the lawyer when he argues a case in the court! How vigilant is the captain of a ship when there is a cyclone or an ice-berg! Even so, you will have to work hard in the practice of Sankirtan if you care to realise fully the fruits of Sankirtan Bhakti-Yoga.

Do Prabhata Kirtan in a common place and at home at 4 a.m. Do Prabhata Pheri Kirtan around Mohallas. Do Akhanda Sankirtan. Do Nagar Kirtan. Do daily Kirtan in a common place and at home. Establish Hari Kirtan Mandalis in every Mohalla.

Train your children in Kirtan. Do Utsava every year. Let ladies do vigorous Sankirtan. Ladies are the backbone of religion. Religion is maintained through the devotion of our women alone. If they are inspired, the whole world will be inspired. Disseminate Sankirtan Bhakti far and wide. Bring Vaikuntha on earth in every house.

Do actions for His sake only. Be intent on His service. Work with controlled Indriyas and disciplined mind. Be fully devoted to Him. Sacrifice everything to Him. Service of humanity (Desa-Seva) is only Padaseva of God. Prostrate before Him with Bhava and sincerity. Have Lord Krishna as your be-all and Supreme Goal. Take refuge under His Lotus Feet. Constantly think of Him. He will give you liberation. He will give you freedom and perfection.

Now then, stand up friend! Gird up the loins. Push on in your practice. Be true and sincere. Be not troubled; be not anxious if there is a little delay in your progress and advancement. You will have to thoroughly overhaul old Samskaras and fight with the Indriyas and mind. Have full trust in Isvara. Destroy all doubts and desires in the burning ground of mind by the fire of devotion.

March cautiously and boldly in the field of Sankirtan with Vairagya coat-of arms, with the band of Hari Bol, Hari Bol. Remove the five thorns viz., Abhimana of caste, learning, position, beauty and youth, that lie in the path. That man who is humbler than the blade of grass, who has more endurance than the tree, who cares not for honour and yet honours all is only fit to sing Hari's Name always. Therefore acquire these four qualifications if you want to become real Sankirtanists and desire to get the grace of Hari and His Darshan quickly.

Ask the Lord when you fervently pray, "Tell me honestly, O Hari of compassion. I am sincere now. Will a day come to me in the near future, a day when tears will gush out from my eyes in silence out of sincere devotion unto Thee and drench my clothes as in the case of Lord Gouranga; when I will cry bitterly, 'O Hari! Hey Krishna!' and roll about on earth in Divine ecstasy forgetting my body, relatives and surroundings and all differences and seeing everywhere Hari and Hari alone like the devotee of yore, Prahlada of happy memory? Withdraw me within, O Love! Take me into Thy sweet bosom that I may be lost in Thee for ever." Now sing once more His Name:

Hare Rama Hare Rama, Rama Rama Hare Hare;
Hare Krishna Hare Krishna, Krishna Krishna Hare Hare.

Sing His Name from the bottom of your heart. Merge in Him. Be established in Him. Be with Him. Be like Him. Become a Jivanmukta and Bhagavata in this very birth. Don't lose this golden opportunity. Weep not afterwards. Remember, delay in God-realisation is but death. Blessed is the place where Sankirtan Sammelan is held. Sacred is the land trodden by the feet of Bhagavatas. Twice blessed are those who daily do Sankirtan. Thrice blessed are those who organise Sankirtan Sammelan. Hail! Hail to the Name of the Lord, which bringeth infinite bliss, peace and immortality! May Joy, Bliss, Peace and Kaivalya abide in you for ever!

Sankirtan Dhvanis

(Sing with Bhava and enjoy the spiritual bliss)

(Thars: Sunaja)

1. Bhajo Rama   Hari Rama Hari Rama Hari Ram

Bhajo Krishna Hari Krishna Hari Krishna Hari Shyam
Bhajo Siva   Hari Siva Hari Siva Hari Bhum
Bhajo Guru   Hari Guru Hari Guru Hari Om.

2. (i) Jaya Siva Sankara Jaya Tripurari
        Jaya Gangadhara Jaya Madanari

   (ii) Jaya Muralidhara Jaya Asurari
        Jaya Manamohana Kunjabihari
        Jaya Sarangadhara Jaya Asurari
        Jaya Manamohana Rama Murari

3. Siva Sambasadasiva Sambasadasiva
   Sambasadasiva Sambasiva Hara.

4. Sambho Sankara Gaureesa
   Siva Samba Sankara Gaureesa.

5. Sankara Siva Sankara Siva
   Sankara Siva Sankara Siva Hara

6. Hari Om Ram Ram Hari Om Ram
   Hari Om Ram Sita Hari Om Ram
   Hari Om Hari Om Hari Om Ram
   Siva Om Siva Om Siva Om Shyam
   Hari Om Tat Sat Tat Sat Om
   Hari Om Santi Tat Sat Om.

7. Radha Krishnane, Trilokanathane
   Venugana-lola Neela-Megha-Shyamane
   Pita Raghuvara, Mata Raghuvara
   Bhrata Sakha Prabhu Guru Hita Raghuvara.

8. Natesa Saranam — Saranam Venkatesa

9. Rama Rama Rama Rama Rama Nama Tarakam
   Ramkrishna Vaasudeva Bhaktimuktidayakam.

10. Achyutam Kesavam Rama Narayanam
    Krishna Damodaram Vaasudevam Harim
    Sridharam Madhavam Gopikavallabham
    Janakee-Nayakam Ramachandram Bhaje.

11. Jaya Siyaram Jaya Jaya Siyaram

Jaya Radheshyam Jaya Jaya Radheshyam
Jaya Hanuman Jaya Jaya Hanuman
Audh Bihari Sitaram Kamala Vimala Mithila Dham
(Jaya Siyaram.....)

12. Ramaho Krishnaho Radha Krishna Devaho,
Venugana-Lola Neela Megha Shyama Krishnaho.

16. Vairagya Maala

Poets describe in their fanciful, passionate moods that honey flows from the lips of a young, beautiful lady. Is this really true? What do you actually see? The stinking pus from the sockets of the teeth that are affected with dreadful pyorrhoea, the nasty and abominable sputum from the throat, and foul saliva at night dribbling on the lips — do you call all this as honey and nectar? And yet the passionate, lustful and sex-intoxicated man swallows these filthy excretions when he is under the sway of excitement! Is there anything more revolting than this? Are not these poets culpable, when they have given such a false description, when they have caused great havoc and damage to passionate young men? Well then, let the Great Court decide this vital issue. Or else I will surely take this matter to the Grand Council of Lord Hari.

Marriage is a curse and a life-long imprisonment. It is the greatest bondage. The bachelor who was once free is now tied to the yoke and his hands and feet are chained. This is the experience of all married people invariably, as it were. They weep after marriage.

Wife is a sharp knife to cut the life of the husband. Anasuya and Savitri are very, very rare. If the gold necklace and Benares silk saries are not supplied, the wife frowns at the husband. The husband cannot get his food at the proper time. The wife lies down in bed under false pretext of acute abdominal colic. You can see this spectacle in your own house and daily experience. Indeed I need not tell you much. Therefore be wedded to Santi and have Vairagya the worthy son and Viveka the magnanimous daughter and eat the delicious divine fruit of Atma Jnana which can make you immortal.

This world is full of difficulties and troubles. No one save a Yogi or a Bhakta or a Jnani is free from these worldly miseries and anxieties. Go wherever you may. It is all the same. Kashmir is a lovely place. But pissus (small insects) bite at night. Man does not get sleep. Uttarkasi is a good place for meditation. It has good spiritual vibrations. But peculiar flies bite you there. They cause severe itching, bleeding and inflammation. Deva Prayag in the Himalayas has very good scenery. The Ganga and the Alakananda meet here. But there are horrible scorpions. There is sun-stroke at Benares and pneumonia and dysentery at Badrinath. Develop therefore power of endurance. Lead a life of Tyaga and Vairagya (renunciation and dispassion). Then and then alone you can be happy in the world, no matter which part of it.

Man feels that this world is fraught with pain and misery when he gets severe knocks and blows, when his wife dies, when he loses his job and when he himself suffers from cataract, diabetes and blood-pressure at the same time. When a little fortune comes, when his pockets begin to jingle with a few coins, when a grandson is born, when a little fat accumulates in his body, he begins to smile and laugh and forgets all about the past. The world appears to be full of pleasure. This is the jugglery of Maya. Learn to discriminate, O Prem, and attain wisdom.

Trishna means an intense craving or sense-hankering. Through constant repetition of enjoyment of an object, the longing for the object becomes very keen and acute. This is Trishna. It is all easy to become a big research scholar in the Oxford or Cambridge University and to get a M.A., Ph.D. degree. But it is extremely difficult to eradicate these

Trishnas. That is the reason why Vasishthaji says in the Yoga Vasishtha to Sri Rama: "You can even uproot the Himalayas. You can even drink the waters of the whole Pacific Ocean. You can even swallow balls of fire. But it is difficult to destroy the Trishnas. Cravings cause incessant trouble in many different ways. These cravings are the seeds of this Samsara."

A worldly man is always drowned in sorrow. He is ever struggling to get something, some money, some power, some position and so on. He is always anxious as to whether he will get it or not. Even when he is in possession of the thing he so passionately longed to possess, he is very anxious lest he should lose it. There is pain in earning money. There is more pain in taking care of it. There is still more pain if it gets decreased. And when it is lost all of a sudden, imagine for a moment the magnitude of the climax and the amount of pain it gives a man! Therefore renounce money and rest in peace in the blissful Self.

Lord Buddha says: "On the whole life is sorrow". You will find an echo of this statement in Patanjali's Raja Yoga Philosophy. *"Sarvam Duhkham Vivekinah* – All indeed is pain for a man of discrimination." This is not the philosophy of the pessimists. This is wonderful optimism as it induces deep Vairagya, weans your mind from sensual objects and directs it towards God to realise eternal, infinite bliss.

Mamsa-lubdho yatha matsyo lohasamkum na pasyati;
Sukha-lubdhasthatha dehi yama-bandham na pasyati.

"Just as a fish in its desire to eat flesh does not see the hook that lies beneath, so also a man in his passionate desire to get sensual pleasure does not see the noose of death."

Wife is only a luxury. It is not an absolute necessity. Every householder is weeping after marriage. He says: "My son is ailing from typhoid. My second daughter is to be married. I have debts to clear. My wife is worrying me to purchase a gold necklace. My eldest son-in-law died recently."

If you really want God and God alone, kick this world mercilessly. Enough, enough of tea and coffee, enough of soda and lemonade; enough of father, mother, sons and daughters, brothers, sisters, friends and relations. You have had countless fathers and mothers, wives and children in the past. You came alone, you will go alone, none will follow you save your own actions. Realise God. All miseries will come to an end.

17. Science of Worship

Man does not get full satisfaction from sensual pleasures. He always feels that he is in want of something. He is restless and discontented. Then he longs to come into conscious communion with the Lord of the Universe and to attain immortality and everlasting peace. This ultimate craving of a man finds its satisfaction in worship. The individual soul desires to unite himself with his father, the Supreme Soul. This is done through worship. Love and devotion naturally rise in his heart when he hears the glory and greatness of the Lord. An object of worship is therefore necessary for man to pour forth his love and devotion. Worship helps spiritual evolution and eventually brings the devotee face to face with God. As the Absolute or Infinite cannot be comprehended by the limited and finite mind, the conception of the impersonal God in His lower, limited form came into existence. The Nirguna Brahman assumes forms for the pious worship of the devotees.

Worship is the expression of love and devotion by the devotee to the Lord, of extreme reverence towards Him, of keen longing to be in conscious communion with Him, of eager aspiration to be always at His feet, of intense craving to be united with Him. The devotee feels the pangs of his separation from the Lord, sheds profuse tears, and sings His praise, glory, splendour and greatness. Worship may take the form of prayer, of praise, of meditation or of Kirtan.

Worship differs according to the growth and evolution of the individual. There is nature worship. Parsees worship the element fire. Hindus worship the Ganga, cows, *asvatta* tree, etc. In the Vedas there are hymns to Indra, Varuna, Agni, Vayu. This is nature worship. There is hero-worship. Great heroes like Sivaji, Napoleon are worshipped even now. In hero-worship the individual imbibes the virtues of the person whom he worships. Birthday celebrations of great persons, anniversary celebrations are forms of worship. Then there is relic worship. Hairs and bones of departed souls are also worshipped. Then there is Pitru-worship, or worship of forefathers.

There is worship of Gurus or Rishis or Devatas. As man evolves, he passes from one stage of worship to another. The lower stages drop down by themselves. A man of higher stage should not condemn his brother who is in a lower stage. One should not forget the underlying, indwelling, interpenetrating, one Essence or Intelligence when he does the worship of any kind. The fundamental object in worship is union with the Lord, who pervades or permeates all these names and forms, by developing intense love. Isvara has different aspects or forms such as Brahma, Vishnu, Siva, Rama, Krishna, Ganapathy, Karttikeya, Durga, Lakshmi, Sarasvati, Indra, Agni, but in whatever name and form, it is Isvara who is adored. The Lord in the form is worshipped. The devotion goes to the Lord.

All are worshipping the one basic Reality, Isvara. The differences are only differences in names and forms on account of differences in the worshipers. Worship of Lord Jesus or Lord Mohammed or Sri Guru Nanak or Lord Buddha or Lord Mahavira is really worship of Isvara only. These are all His forms. "However men approach Me, even so do I welcome them, for the paths men take from every side is Mine, O Partha." (Gita: IV-11.)

"Whatsoever form any devotee desires to worship with faith — that (same) faith of his I make firm and unflinching." (Gita: VII-21). Ignorant, petty-minded people fight unnecessarily amongst themselves and disturb the peace of the country. The essentials of all religions are the same. Non-essentials must differ. There is quarrel on these non-essentials only. All religions agree: "One should attain salvation by right living, by speaking truth, by celibacy, by loving all, by developing virtuous qualities, by meditation, by devotion."

The term "Sadhana" comes from the root "Sadh", which means "to exert", "to endeavour to get a particular result or Siddhi." He who does the attempt is called Sadhaka. If he achieves the desired result, Siddhi, he is called Siddha. A fully developed Siddha is one who has attained full knowledge of Brahman. Self-realisation or Darshan of God is not possible without Sadhana. Any spiritual practice is called Sadhana. Sadhana, Abhyasa are synonymous terms. That which is obtained through Sadhana is Sadhya (God or Brahman).

Upasana means worship. It means to sit near God. One who does Upasana is an Upasaka. The object of worship is Upasya. Upasana is a broad term which includes many forms of worship. It includes meditation, Japa, daily Sandhya, prayer, Stotra etc. It is of two kinds, viz., Ahamgraha Upasana or meditation on Nirguna, Nirakara Brahman and Saguna Upasana or meditation on Isvara (with form and attributes). The former is called Avyakta Upasana, and the latter Vyakta Upasana. Upasana is again either gross (Sthula) or subtle (Sukshma) according to the nature of the Adhikari, his degree of competency or advancement in the path. He who worships a Murthy, rings bells and offers sandal-paste, flowers, etc., does gross form of worship.

Whereas he who visualises the image of his Ishtam, meditates on it and offers mental offerings, does subtle form of worship. Manasic Pooja is Sukshma Upasana.

Pooja comes from the Sanskrit root *"Pooj"* which means to worship. Pooja is a simple form of worship. A picture or image is used for worship. Mantras are recited. Water is poured over the image. Flowers are offered. Sandal-paste is applied. Naivedya and Arghya are offered, camphor and incense are burnt. The devotee pours forth his love and devotion to the Isvara who is hidden in the picture or image. One important point is that he who does Pooja must abandon the idea of ownership of the articles of worship etc., and must think that all the articles and wealth belong to Isvara and he is only the caretaker. Then only his worship will bring the desired result. Prostrations, offering, etc., are outer worship. Meditation is inner worship.

Lord Krishna gives a description of worship to Uddhava in the eleventh chapter of Bhagavata: "The Sun, fire, earth or clay, water, a Brahmin, any image of Mine in the concrete, clearly thought out as seated in the heart, may be worshipped in My name sincerely with such articles as could be obtained by him. The worship should be sincere and whole-hearted and the devotee should imagine Me as his preceptor. The devotee should begin My worship for obtaining My Grace and not for any other desire. In ordinary images I should be invoked and released at every time of worship. I can be pictured in the mind. The worship of My image in the heart should be with accessories pictured in the mind.

"The image should be washed or bathed, cleaned and adorned with ornaments and marks. The devotee should not rise in the midst of worship to get some articles. Once seated in worship, he must finish it before he rises for anything. He should be seated on *Darbha* grass or other clean seat. He must put My image facing North or East or must himself sit also facing North or East. He must sit facing Me or sideways. (The devotee must be facing the North while the image faces the East). He should repeat the Mantras for purifying himself. He should clean his body by control of breath. He should sit quiet and meditate on Me for some time.

"He should fancy Me as seated in a lotus with eight petals, overflowing with fragrance and radiant with light. The emblems conch, Chakra, mace, lotus, the ornament of Kaustubha, the necklace and the mark or spot in the heart Srivatsa should be imagined at the proper place and worshipped. Sandal-wood, saffron, camphor, Kumkum and fragrance should be used. Purusha-Sukta and other sacred literature should be repeated. My devotee may adorn Me with cloths, gems, sacred thread, sandal, flowers, saffron and ointments etc. The devotee should give water for washing the feet, Achamana, sandal, words of greeting, invitation and hospitality. He should also show fragrance, light and camphor at My altar. He can sing aloud hymns in My praise. He can sing songs and dance in My altar reciting My various deeds and achievements. He should seek My Grace prostrating himself duly before Me. Putting his head on My feet, he should ask for My Grace to protect him and save him for the wheel of births and deaths.

"He should adorn himself with the flower and sandal used in such worship — The devotee may worship Me in any form in all objects or in himself in the manner that appeals most to his mind and inclinations, as I am immanent in all things. My devotee worshipping Me thus with rituals, Mantras or both, attains not only bliss and Self-realisation but also all things he desires. By building temples and altars etc., devotees attain powers over all the worlds. By worship of Me they attain Brahma-Loka. By all the acts, they attain My powers and immanence."

The devotee invokes the deity into the image by what is

called the welcoming (Avahana) and life-giving (Prana-pratishtha) ceremonies. When the worship is over, he bids the deity farewell. This is called Visarjana. The offerings of water, light, fragrance, sandal, flowers etc., to God are called Upachara.

The mind is purified by constant worship. It is filled with good and pure thoughts. Repetition of worship strengthens the good Samskaras. "As a man thinks, so he becomes." This is the psychological law. The mind of a man who trains himself in thinking good, holy thoughts develops a tendency to think good thoughts. His character is moulded and transformed by continued good thoughts. When the mind thinks of the image of God during worship, the mental substance actually assumes the form of the image. The impression of the object is left in the mind. This is called a Samskara. When the act is repeated very often, the Samskara gains strength by repetition and a tendency or habit is formed in the mind. He who entertains thoughts of divinity becomes transformed actually into the divinity himself by constant thinking and meditation. His Bhava or disposition is purified and divinised. The meditator and the meditated, the worshipper and the worshipped, the thinker and the thought, become one and the same. This is Samadhi. This is the fruit of worship or Upasana.

Man sows an action or thought and reaps a habit of doing or thinking. He sows a habit and reaps a character. He sows a character and reaps a destiny. Habit is second nature or rather first nature itself. Man has made his own destiny by thinking and acting. He can change his destiny. He is the master of his own destiny. There is no doubt of this. By right thinking and Vichara and strong Purushartha he can become master of his destiny. Markandeya changed his destiny through Tapas and worship of Lord Siva. Visvamitra became a Brahmarshi through vigorous Tapas and changed his destiny. You can also do so, if you have a strong will and iron determination. Vasishthaji preached Purushartha to Sri Rama in Yoga Vasishtha. Savitri changed the destiny of her husband Satyavan through her power of 'Pativrata-dharma'. Just as you can change your way of writing in a slanting manner, into a vertical manner, so also you can change your destiny by changing your mode of thinking. Now you are thinking, "I am Mr. So and So," by identifying with the body and other Upadhis or limiting adjuncts. Now start the anti-current. Think, "I am Brahman. I am the immortal Self in all. I am all-pervading, light, intelligence or pure consciousness." Your destiny will be changed. Just as you think, so you will become. This is the Sadhana. This is the Ahamgraha-Upasana. Practise it steadily. Feel and realise.

18. Bhakti Yoga Sadhana

God is the Inner Ruler of your heart and mind. He is the silent witness of your thoughts. You cannot hide anything from Him. Become guileless and straightforward.

A devotee of Hari is always meek and humble. Name of God "Hari" is always on his lips. He sheds profuse tears when he is alone. He is very pious. He is friendly towards all. He has equal vision. He does good always. He never hurts the feelings of others. He has a spotless character. He never covets the property of others. He sees Hari in all beings.

Bhakti can move mountains. Nothing is impossible for it. It was the devotion of Mira that converted a snake into a flower-garland, poison into nectar and an iron bed of needles into a bed of roses. It was the devotion of Prahlada that turned fire into ice.

A devotee should become an embodiment of goodness. He must be ever ready to do good to living beings. That devotee who is intent upon the welfare of all beings obtains the peace of the Eternal. He who rejoices in the welfare of all, gets the Darshan of the Lord. He develops Advaitic consciousness eventually.

Service of Bhagavatas, repetition of God's Name, Satsanga, singing His Name, study of Bhagavata or Ramayana, stay in Vrindavan, Pandharpur, Chitrakuta or Ayodhya—these are the six means of developing Bhakti.

Anger and lust are the two inner enemies that stand in the way of developing Bhakti. From lust follow ten vices that are mentioned in Manusamhita: "Love of hunting, gambling, sleeping by day, slandering, company with bad women, drinking, singing love-songs, dancing, vulgar music, aimlessly wandering about."

Anger begets eight kinds of vices. All evil qualities proceed from anger. If you can eradicate anger all bad qualities will die of themselves. The eight vices are: "Injustice, rashness, persecution, jealousy, taking possession of others' property, killing, harsh words and cruelty."

How are Bhaktas to be known? Lord Krishna has given a description of them. You will find it in Bhagavata. "They do not care for anything. Their hearts are fixed on Me. They are very humble. They have equal vision. They have no attachment towards anybody or anything. They are without 'mine-ness.' They have no egoism. They make no distinction between sorrow and happiness. They do not take anything from others. They can bear heat, cold and pain. They have love for all living beings. They have no enemy. They are serene. They possess exemplary character.

Here is Sadhana for advanced students. This is highly useful for getting quick, solid progress in the spiritual path. Get up at 4 a.m. Start your Japa on any Asana you have mastered. Do not take any food or drink for 14 hours. Do not get up from the Asana. Control passing urine till sunset if you can. Do not change the Asana if you can manage. Finish the Japa at sunset. Take milk and fruits after sunset.

Householders can practise this during holidays. Practise this once in a fortnight or once in a month or once weekly.

Here is another Sadhana for ten days. You can do this during Christmas holidays or Pooja holidays or summer vacation. Shut yourself up in an airy room. Do not talk to anybody. Do not see anybody. Do not hear anything. Get up at 4 a.m. Start Japa of the Mantra of your Ishta Devata or your Guru Mantra and finish it at sunset. Then take some milk and fruits or Kheer (milk and rice boiled with sugar). Take rest for one or two hours; but continue the Japa. Then again start Japa seriously. Retire to bed at 11 in the night. You can combine meditation along with Japa. Make all arrangements for bath, food etc., inside the room. Have two rooms if you can manage, one for bath and one for meditation. Repeat this four times in a year. This practice can be kept up even for 40 days. You will have wonderful results and various experiences. You will enter into Samadhi. You will have Darshan of your Ishtam. I assure you.

Here is the Anushthana for 40 days. You will have to do Japa of Rama Mantra one lakh and twenty-five thousand times for 40 days in the following manner. Do Japa at the rate of 3000 daily for 35 days and 4000 daily during the last five days. Get up at 4 a.m. Write down in a thin paper Rama, Rama 3000 times. Then cut it into small pieces. Each piece will contain one Rama Nama. Then roll it with a small ball of Atta (wheat flour paste). Writing will take two or three hours according to your strength and capacity. Then you will have to cut it one by one. You will have to do the whole process by sitting on one Asana. If you will find it difficult to sit on one Asana you can have change of Asana. But you should not leave your seat. Some use a special ink made up of saffron, mush-kapoor etc., and a special writing pen made up of sharp pointed thin Tulasi stick. You can use ordinary ink and pen if you cannot get the above special ink and special pen. You will have to do Anushthana on the bank of the Ganga, Yamuna, Godavari, Kaveri or Narmada, at Rishikesh, Benares, Haridwar or Prayag. You can do it at home, if you find it difficult to move to these places. Take milk and fruits or Phalahar during these days. Throw the balls in the Ganga or any river for fishes. You will develop wonderful patience. You will get divine grace.

Study the whole Ramayana 108 times with purity and concentration. This can be done in three years if you can devote three hours daily. You can go through the book three times in a month. You will acquire Siddhis. You will have Darshan of Lord Rama.

19. Bhaktas of Chitrakuta

Chitrakuta is a wonderful place for meditation. There is the river Mandakini with clear, sparkling water. Bhaktas of Sri Rama can have Darshan of Lord Rama within six months if they do Japa of Rama Nam in Chitrakuta in right earnest intently living on a diet of milk and fruits. So says Sri Tulasi Dasji in a Chaupai.

Mowni- Baba is a great Titikshu. He is a Vairagi. He lives in a forest two miles from Chitrakuta. He stands in the terribly hot sun in summer from 8 o'clock in the morning to five in the evening. What a wonderful power of endurance the saint has! Remarkable indeed!

Vishnu Das is another advanced saint. He lives in the forest two miles from Chitrakuta. He sleeps in a place which abounds in serpents. He has childlike simplicity. That is a marked feature of a Bhakta.

20. Why Should We Believe in God?

Belief in God is an indispensable requisite for every human being. It is a *sine qua non*. Owing to force of Avidya or ignorance pain appears as pleasure. The world is full of miseries, troubles, difficulties and tribulations. The world is a ball of fire. The Antahkarana charged with Raga, Dvesha, anger and jealousy is a blazing furnace. We have to free ourselves from birth, death, old age, disease and grief. This can only be done by faith in God. There is no other way. Money and power cannot give us real happiness. Even if we exercise suzerainty over the whole world, we cannot be free from care, worry, anxiety, fear, disappointment etc. It is only the faith in God and the consequent God-realisation through meditation that can give us real, eternal happiness and free us from all kinds of fear and worries which torment us at every moment. Faith in God will force us to think of Him constantly and to meditate on Him and will eventually lead us on to God-realisation.

Belief in God and God-realisation will give us Parama Santi (supreme peace). In that peace comes the extinction of all pains. We will be no longer bewildered. We will be released from the bondage of actions. We will become immortal. We will obtain eternal Divine Wisdom. We will reach a place whence there is no return to this world of miseries, our sins being dispelled by Divine Wisdom. Our minds will ever remain balanced. We will never rejoice on obtaining what is pleasant nor feel sorry on obtaining what is unpleasant. We will have an icy cool Antahkarana. We will be ever established in the Divine Consciousness. We will get "Akshaya Sukha," happiness exempt from decay. We will become one with God (Samadhi) and get eternal (Nitya), infinite (Ananta), unbroken (Akhanda) Bliss. When we are established in the Divine Consciousness we will not be shaken even by heavy sorrow. We will get "Ateendriya Sukha", happiness beyond the reach of senses (Supreme Bliss).

God will give us full security if we worship Him with unswerving devotion and undivided attention. He gives us the Yoga of discrimination to enable us to reach Him easily. Out of pure compassion for us He destroys the ignorance-born darkness by the shining lamp of wisdom. He speedily lifts us from the ocean of Samsara if we fix our minds on Him steadily with devotion and faith. We will cross over the three qualities and, liberated from birth, death, old age, and sorrow, drink the nectar of immortality. By devotion and faith we will know Him in essence and will enter into His very Being. Through His Grace we will overcome all obstacles (Parama Pada — Parama Dhama).

21. Where Is the Harm in Not Believing in God's Existence?

If we have no faith in God we will be born again in this world and will undergo considerable miseries. The ignorant, faithless doubting self goes to destruction. He cannot enjoy the least happiness. Neither this world, nor that beyond is there for the doubting self. Those who have no faith in God do not know what is right and what is wrong. They have lost the power of discrimination. They are untruthful, proud and egoistic. They are given to excessive greed, wrath and lust. They hoard up money by unlawful means. They become men of demoniacal nature. They commit various sorts of atrocious crimes. They have no ideals for their lives. They are thrown into demoniacal wombs. They sink into the lowest depths, deluded birth after birth.

Some one hundred and fifty years ago there lived a very famous Yogi-jnani by name Sadasiva Brahmendra Sarasvati in Nerur in the district of Trichinopoly, Tamil Nadu. He is the author of Brahma Sutra Vritti and Atma-Vidya Vilas and various other books. He has done innumerable miracles. Once when he was absorbed in Samadhi on the banks of the Kaveri he was carried away by the flood and thrown somewhere else. He was deeply buried underneath the sand. Labourers went to plough the fields. They hit against the head of the Yogi and some blood oozed out. They dug out and to their great astonishment they found a Yogi seated in Samadhi.

On another occasion as an Avadhoota he entered the *zenana* (ladies' quarters) of a Mahommedan chief naked. The chief was quite enraged at the sage. He cut off one of the arms of the Mahatma. Sadasiva Brahman walked away without uttering a word and without showing any sign of pain. The chief was greatly astonished at this strange condition of the sage. He thought that this man must be a Mahatma, a superhuman being. He repented much and followed the sage to apologise. Sadasiva never knew that his arm was cut off. When the chief narrated to the sage what had happened in the camp, Sadasiva excused the chief and simply touched his maimed arm. Sadasiva Brahman had a fresh arm. It is the life of this sage that made a very deep impression in my mind. I came to a very definite conclusion that there is a sublime divine life independent of objects and the play of mind and the senses. The sage was quite unconscious of the world. He did not feel a bit when his arm was cut off. He ought to have been absorbed in the Divine Consciousness (one with the Divine). Ordinary people yell out even when there is a pin prick in their bodies. When I heard the marvellous incident of Sage Sadasiva from some persons and when I read in the book, it gave me a very strong conviction of the divine existence and a divine eternal life where all sorrows melt, all desires are satisfied and one gets Supreme Bliss, Supreme Peace and Supreme Knowledge.

Chapter V

OBSTACLES IN GOD-REALISATION

1. Introduction

Just as volunteers come in front and obstruct the path of those who want to enter a conference pandal without tickets, so also the old Samskaras of enmity, hatred, lust, jealousy, fear, honour, respect etc., assume definite forms and obstruct the path of aspirants.

An intelligent and comprehensive understanding of the various obstacles that act as stumbling blocks in the path of God-realisation is indispensably requisite for an aspirant. Then alone he will find it easy to conquer them one by one. Just as the sailor sails in and out of a harbour along a dangerous coast, so also a detailed knowledge of these obstacles and the methods to conquer them will act as a guide in steering clear the ocean of spirituality. Hence I have given a very lucid exposition of the various obstacles and the effective methods to conquer them. Aspirants are requested to go through them very carefully often when they encounter difficulties on the path.

Reference

2. Raja-Yoga and Yoga-Kundalini Upanishad

According to Patanjali Maharshi the following are the obstacles in God-realisation:

Vyadhi-styana-samsaya-pramada-alasya-avirati-bhranti
darsana-alabdha bhumikatva-anavasthitatvani
chitta-vikshepaste-antarayah.

Diseases, remission of Sadhana, doubt, carelessness, laziness, worldly-mindedness, illusion, false perception, tossing of mind and inability to remain in the state of

Samadhi on account of Vikshepa are the obstacles in the path of God-Realisation. (I-30.)

You will find in the Yoga-Kundalini-Upanishad:

"Diseases are generated in one's body through the following causes, viz., sleeping in the day time, late vigils overnight, excess of sexual intercourse, moving in crowd, the checking of the urine and faeces, the evil of unwholesome food and laborious mental operations with Prana. If a Yogin is afraid of such diseases (when attacked by them), he says: 'My diseases have arisen from the practice of Yoga'. Then he will discontinue his practice. This is said to be the first obstacle to Yoga. The second (obstacle) is doubt; the third, carelessness; the fourth, laziness; the fifth, sleep; the sixth, not leaving of objects (of sense); the seventh, erroneous perception; the eighth, sensual objects; the ninth, want of faith; and the tenth, the failure to attain the truth of Yoga. A wise man should abandon these ten obstacles after great deliberation."

3. Poor Health

God-realisation is not possible without Sadhana or spiritual practice. Spiritual practice is not possible without good health. A sickly, dilapidated body stands in the way of doing Abhyasa or discipline. The aspirant should try his level best to keep good health always by regular exercise, Asana, Pranayama, moderation in diet, walking, running in open air, regularity in his work, meals, sleep, etc. He should avoid drugging as far as possible. He must take recourse to nature cure such as fresh air, wholesome food, cold bath and dietetic adjustment. He should always keep a cheerful attitude of mind, under all conditions of life. Cheerfulness is a powerful mental tonic. There is intimate connection between body and mind. If one is cheerful, the body is also healthy. That is the reason why doctors now prescribe laughing three times daily in the treatment of diseases.

Some foolish aspirants refuse to take medicine when they are ailing seriously. They say: "It is Prarabdha. We should not go against Prarabdha. Taking medicine is against the Will of God. Body is Mithya. It is Anatma. If I take medicine, it will increase Deha-Adhyasa and body-idea." This is foolish philosophy. Take medicine. Do Purushartha. Leave the results to Prarabdha. This is _wisdom. These foolish people unnecessarily torture the body, allow the disease to strike a deep root and spoil their health. They cannot do any Sadhana. They ruin this instrument by wrong conception of Vedanta. Vedanta says: "Have no attachment for this body. But keep it clean, strong and healthy for constant rigid Sadhana. This body is a boat to cross to the other shore of Immortality. It is a horse to take you to the destination. Feed the horse well—but give up 'mine-ness'." Tell me friend, which is better? To take a purgative, to take some medicine for a couple of days, to tide over difficulties in a few days and to start again Sadhana quickly or to neglect the disease, not to take any medicine, to allow the disease to assume a grave form, to suffer for a month or two by negligence, to make the disease chronic and incurable, and to allow the Sadhana to suffer for a month?

There is a class of people in India called the Rasayanas. They try to make the body strong and healthy by taking Siddha-Kalpas. They claim that this body can be made immortal. They say: "This is an instrument for God-realisation. No realisation of God is possible without a healthy and strong body. Man makes some progress in Yoga and dies before he attains perfection. He takes another birth and then practises Yoga for some years and then again dies. In this way much time is lost in recurring births and deaths. If the body is kept strong and healthy for a long time, a man can have God-realisation in one birth alone." Therefore they prescribe Kalpas made up of neem-essence, nux-vomica, gold, arsenic, sulphur, mercury etc. No disease can enter a body which is rendered adamantine by a course of these tonics. They begin spiritual Sadhana after making the body quite strong and healthy in the beginning.

4. Impure and Immoderate Food

Mind is formed out of the subtlest portion of food. If the food is impure, the mind also becomes impure. This is the dictum of sages and psychologists. Food plays an important part in the evolution of mind. It has direct influence on the mind. Meat, fish, eggs, stale, unwholesome food, onions, garlic etc., should be avoided by spiritual practitioners as they excite passion and anger. The food should be simple, bland, light, wholesome and nutritious. Liquors and narcotics should be strictly abandoned. Chillies, condiments, spiced dishes, pungent articles, hot things, things that are sour, sweetmeats etc., must be rejected.

In the Gita (XVIII-8, 9, 13) you will find: "The foods that augment vitality, energy, vigour, health, joy and cheerfulness, delicious, bland, substantial and agreeable, are dear to the pure. The passionate desire foods that are burning, and which produce pain, grief and sickness. That which is stale and flat, putrid and corrupt, leavings also and unclean, is the food dear to the dark". Aspirants should not overload the stomach. Ninety per cent of diseases take their origin in immoderation in diet. People have developed a strong habit of eating more food than what is actually necessary from their very boyhood. Hindu mothers stuff the stomachs of their children with too much food. This is not the way of caressing and loving children. Overloading brings drowsiness and sleep immediately. If there is no hunger, you must not take any food. The night-meals should be very light for Sadhakas. Half a seer of milk, with one or two plantains is quite sufficient. *Overloading is the chief factor in bringing night-pollutions.* Sannyasins and aspirants should take their Bhiksha from the hands of those householders who earn their livelihood by honest means.

5. Doubt

(Samsaya)

An aspirant begins to doubt whether God exists or not, whether he will succeed in his God-realisation or not, whether he is doing his practices rightly or not. Lack of faith is a dangerous obstacle in the spiritual path. The student slackens his efforts when these doubts crop up. Maya is very powerful. Mysterious is Maya. It misleads people through doubting and forgetfulness. Mind is Maya. Mind deludes people through doubting. Sometimes he gives up his Sadhana altogether. This is a serious mistake. Whenever doubt tries to overpower any student he should at once take recourse to the company of Mahatmas and remain with them for some time under the influence of their currents. He should clear his doubts by conversing with them. Generally an aspirant starts Sadhana with expectation of so many Siddhis within a short time. When he does not get them he gets dejection and stops his practices. This is the trouble in almost all cases. He thinks that Kundalini will be awakened within six months and he will have clairvoyance, clairaudience, thought-reading, flying in the air etc. He entertains so many fantastic and romantic ideas.

There are various kinds of impurities in the mind. It takes a long time for purification of the mind and getting a one-pointed mind. Concentration is a question of practice for several lives. Concentration is the most difficult thing in the world. One should not get dejected after some practice for some months or one or two years. Even if you do a little practice the effect is there. The Samskaras are there. Nothing is lost. That is the immutable law of nature. You will not be able to detect the little improvement that has come out of a little practice, as you have no subtle intellect and as you have many kinds of impurities from beginningless time. You must develop virtues, Vairagya, patience and perseverance to a maximum degree; you must have an unshakable conviction in the existence of God and in the efficacy of spiritual practices. You must have a strong determination: "I will realise God right now in this very birth, nay in this very second. I will realise or die."

6. Tandri-Alasya-Nidra

Tandri is half-sleepy state. Alasya is laziness. Nidra is sleep. The first two are the precursors of sleep. These three are great obstacles in the path of realisation. Sleep is a powerful force of Maya. It is called Laya. It is Nidra Sakti. You will be imagining that you are meditating. The mind will immediately run through the old groves into the Moola-Ajnana for resting, in the twinkling of an eye. You will be doubting: "Did I go to sleep? Or did I meditate now? I think I have a small nap, as I feel heaviness of lids and body now." Sleep is the greatest obstacle as it is very powerful. Even though a Sadhaka is very careful and vigilant, yet it overpowers him somehow or other. This is a very strong habit. It takes time and demands great strength of will to tear this old, old habit.

Arjuna is called Gudakesa or conqueror of sleep. Lord Krishna addresses him: "O Gudakesa". Lakshmana also had conquered sleep. Besides these two persons who had conquered sleep, we have not heard of anyone. There are people who have reduced the sleep to 2 or 3 hours. Even Yogins and Jnanins sleep for two or three hours. Sleep is a psychological phenomenon. Brain needs rest at least for a short time. Otherwise man feels drowsy and tired. He can neither work nor meditate. The sleep of a Jnani is different from the sleep of a worldly man. In a Jnani the powerful Samskaras of Brahmabhyasa are there. It is something akin to Brahma-Nishtha. One should be careful in reducing his sleep. It should be done gradually. Go to bed at 10 p.m. and get up at 3.30 a.m. Reduce half an hour in one month. Then get up at 3 a.m. in the next month and so on.

Sadhakas can gain time for their Sadhana by reducing sleep. The practice of reducing sleep will be very troublesome in the beginning. When the habits are changed, it will be pleasant in the end. When drowsiness tries to manifest, stand up and do the Japa. Dash cold water on the face and head. Take milk and fruits only at night. Avoid overloading the stomach at night. Take the night meals before sunset. Do Pranayama morning and evening before starting meditation. Do Sirshasana and Sarvangasana. Run for five minutes in your compound. Drowsiness and sleep will vanish. Aspirants do meditation in the morning for one hour between 4 and 5 a.m. Then they are overpowered by sleep. They begin to sleep again after 5 a.m. This is a great complaint. Do 10 or 20 rounds of Pranayama at 5 a.m. Do Sirshasana for 2 minutes. Again you will be fresh for meditation. Use your commonsense always. The old habit may recur again and again. Tear it also again and again by suitable practices, strength of will, by prayer etc. The Practice of keeping vigils on Sivaratri and Sri Krishna Janmashtami is highly commendable. The Christians also keep vigils on Christmas and New Year's night.

7. Manorajya

Manorajya is building castles in the air. This is a trick of the mind. Look at this wonder! The aspirant is meditating in an isolated cave in the Himalayas. He plans in the cave: "After finishing my meditation, I must move about in San Francisco and New York and deliver lectures there. I must start a centre of spiritual activity in Columbia. I must do something new to the world. I must do something which no one has done upto this time." This is ambition. This is egoistic imagination. This is a great obstacle. This is a powerful Vighna. This will not allow the mind to rest even for a second. Again and again there will be resurrection of some scheme, speculation or plan or other. The aspirant will be thinking that he is having deep meditation, but if he closely watches his mind through introspection and self-analysis, it will be a pure case of building castles in the air. One Manorajya will subside and another will crop up in the twinkling of an eye. It will be a small Sankalpa or ripple in the mind-lake. But it will gain tremendous force within a few minutes by repeated thinking. The power of imagination is tremendous. Maya havocs through the power of imagination. Imagination fattens the mind. Imagination is like musk or Siddha-Makaradhvaja. It renovates and vivifies a dying mind. The power of imagination will not allow the mind to keep quiet even for a second. Just as swarms of locusts or flies come forth in a continuous stream, so also currents of Manorajya will stream forth incessantly. Vichara, discrimination, prayer, Japa, meditation, Satsanga, fasting, Pranayama, practice of thoughtlessness will obviate this obstacle. Pranayama checks the velocity of the mind and calms the bubbling mind. A young ambitious man is unfit to remain in a solitary cave. He who has done selfless service in the world for some years, and who has practised meditation for several years in the plains in solitary rooms can live in a cave. Such a man only can really enjoy the solitude of Himalayan retreats.

8. Lack of a Preceptor

The spiritual path is thorny, rugged and precipitous. It is enveloped by darkness. The guidance of a Guru who has already trodden the path is imperatively necessary. He will be able to throw light and remove the obstacles on the path. The knowledge of the Self is revealed through *Parampara* and handed down from Guru to the disciple in succession. Matsyendranath taught Brahma-Vidya to Nivrittinath. Nivrittinath gave the knowledge to Jnana Dev and so on. Gaudapada initiated Govindapada into the mysteries of Kaivalya. Govindapada instructed Sankaracharya. Sankaracharya instructed Suresvaracharya and so on.

The spiritual path is quite a different line altogether. It is not like writing a thesis for M.A. examination. The help of a teacher is necessary at every moment. Young aspirants become self-sufficient, arrogant and self-assertive in these days. They do not care to carry out the orders of the Guru. They do not wish to have a Guru. They want independence from the very beginning. They apply in an absurd manner with a perverted intellect the Neti-Neti Doctrine and Bhaga-Tyaga Lakshana in the case of Guru also and say: *"Sarvam Khalvidam Brahma — Na Gurur Na Sishyah — Chidananda-Rupah Sivoham Sivoham."* They think they are in the Turiya Avastha when they do not know even the A.B.C. of spirituality or truth. This is the philosophy of Asuras or devils or satans. They mistake licentiousness or "having their own ways and sweet will" as freedom. This is a serious, lamentable mistake. That is the reason why they do not grow. They lose the faith in the efficacy of Sadhana and in the existence of God. They wander about in a happy-go-lucky manner without any aim from Kashmir to Gangotri and from Gangotri to Ramesvaram, talking some nonsense on the way, something from Panchadasi and posing as Jivanmuktas.

He who lives under the guidance of a Guru for twelve years, who carries out implicitly the orders of the Guru, who serves the Guru sincerely taking him for Brahman, can really improve in the spiritual path. There is no other way for spiritual progress. So long as there is world, there are spiritual teachers and spiritual books. The number of Jivanmuktas may be less in Kali Yuga than in Satya Yuga. If you cannot get an ideal Guru, you can take even a man who has been treading the path of realisation for some years, who is straightforward and honest, who is selfless, who is free from pride, egoism, who has good character, who has knowledge of Sastras as your Guru. Live with him for some time. Study him carefully. If you are satisfied, take him as your preceptor and follow his instructions strictly. After you have accepted him once as your Guru never suspect him and never find fault with him. Do not change the Guru also very often. You will be bewildered. You will get different conflicting ideas. Everybody has got his own Sadhana. You will find no improvement if you change frequently your method of Sadhana. Stick to one Guru and stick to his instructions. Stick to one method. You will evolve quickly. Single-minded devotion to Guru, ideal, one kind of Sadhana and whole-hearted application are indispensably requisite for God-realisation.

Beware of pseudo-Gurus. They are knocking about in abundance in these days. They will exhibit some tricks or feats to attract people. Think that those who are proud, who are roaming about to make disciples and to amass money, who talk of worldly matters, who speak untruth, who boast of themselves, who are talkative, who keep company with worldly people and women, and who are luxurious, are false impostors. Do not be deceived by their sweet talk and lectures.

In this connection it will not be out of place to mention the story of a man who was in search of a Sat-Guru. He found out after all one Sat-Guru. The student asked the Guru: "O Venerable Sir, give me Upadesh." The Guru asked: "What sort of Upadesh do you want?" The disciple asked: "O Beloved Master! Who is superior, disciple or Guru?" The Guru said: "Guru is superior to disciple." The disciple said: "O Revered Guru! Make me a Guru. I like that." Such sort of disciples are plenty in these days.

9. Vishayasakti

This is the greatest of all obstacles. The mind refuses to leave completely the sensual pleasures. Through the force of Vairagya and meditation, the desires get suppressed for some time. All on a sudden the mind thinks of sensual pleasures through the force of habit and memory. There arises mental disturbance. Concentration decreases. The mind moves outwards in sensual objects. In the Gita (II-60, 67) you will find: "The turbulent senses, O Arjuna, do violently carry away the mind of a wise man, even though he be striving (to control them). For the mind, which follows in the wake of the wandering senses, carries away his discrimination, as the wind carries away a boat on the waters." "The objects of senses turn away from the abstinent man leaving the longing (behind); but his longing also turns away on seeing the Supreme." (II-59.)

Some desires lurk in the corners of the mind. Just as old dirt from the corners of the room comes out when you sweep, so also through the pressure of Yogic practices, these old lurking desires come out to the surface of the mind with redoubled force. The Sadhaka should be very careful. He should be ever watching the mind vigilantly. He must nip the desires in the bud by developing his Vairagya, Viveka and increasing his period of Japa and meditation. He must observe Akhanda Mauna and do vigorous meditation and Pranayama. He should live on milk and fruits for 40 days. He should observe fast on Ekadasi days. He should give up mixing with anybody completely. He should never come out of the room. He should plunge himself deep into the Sadhana. Kashaya means hidden Vasanas. This comes under the category of Vishayasakti. Worldly ambition of all sorts can be included under this head. Ambition makes the mind very restless. Man should have the one laudable ambition of getting Self-realisation.

10. Lack of Brahmacharya

No spiritual progress is possible without the practice of celibacy. The semen is a dynamic force. It should be converted into Ojas or spiritual energy by pure thoughts, Japa and meditation. Those who are very eager to have God-realisation should observe unbroken celibacy strictly. Householders break their vows owing to their weakness and hence do not find much advancement in the spiritual path. They place two steps on the spiritual ladder and fall down immediately to the ground by lack of celibacy. This is a sad mistake. They should sleep separately. They should be very serious. They should understand clearly the gravity of the situation. Taking a vow is a very sacred act. It must be kept up at all costs. Man only is the real culprit. He violates rules and laws. Women have got greater self-restraint than men, though Sastras say that they are eight times more passionate than men.

Remember the advantages of Brahmacharya and evils of loss of semen. Wastage of semen brings nervous weakness, exhaustion and brings premature death. Sexual act destroys vigour of mind, body and Indriyas and annihilates memory, understanding and intellect. This body is meant for God-realisation. It must be well utilised for higher, spiritual purpose. It is very difficult to get a human birth. Remember those Brahmachari-saints who had earned undying reputation and glory. You can also achieve greatness if you preserve this vital energy and utilise it for divine contemplation. You are not crawling now. You have learnt to stand up and walk. You are a man. Behave like a real man. Observe the vow of Brahmacharya strictly. Let your wife also understand and realise the importance and glory of Brahmacharya. Get for her religious books for daily study. Ask her to fast on Ekadasi and to do Japa of any Mantra 21,600 times daily. Take refuge in God's Name and Japa. All obstacles will be removed. You can keep up this sacred vow.

St. Paul said: "It is good for a man not to touch a woman." Lord Buddha said: "A wise man should avoid married life as if it were a burning pit or live coal."

Ojas

Ojas is spiritual energy that is stored up in the brain. By sublime thoughts, meditation, Japa, worship and Pranayama the sexual energy can be transmuted into Ojas-Sakti and be stored up in the brain. This energy can be utilised for divine contemplation and spiritual pursuits.

Anger and muscular energy can also be transmuted into Ojas. A man who has great deal of Ojas in his brain can turn out immense mental work. He is very intelligent. He has a magnetic aura in his face and lustrous eyes. He can influence people by speaking a few words. A short speech can produce tremendous impression on the minds of hearers. His speech is thrilling. He has an awe-inspiring personality. Sri Sankara, an Akhanda Brahmacharin, worked wonders through his power of Ojas. He did Digvijaya and held controversies and heated debates in different parts of India with the learned scholars through his power of Ojas. A Yogi always directs his attention in the accumulation of this divine energy by unbroken chastity.

Socrates and His Disciple

(Conversation on Brahmacharya)

One of the disciples of Socrates asked his teacher, "My Venerable Master, kindly instruct me how many times a householder can visit his legal wife?"

Socrates replied: "Only once in his life time."

The disciple replied: "O my Lord! This is absolutely impossible for worldly men. Passion is dreadful and troublesome. This world is full of temptations and distractions. Householders have not got strong will to resist temptations. Their Indriyas are very revolting and powerful. The mind is filled with passion. Thou art a philosopher and a Yogi. You can control. Pray, kindly prescribe an easy path for the men of the world." Then Socrates said: "Well – a householder can have copulation once in a year." The disciple replied, "O my Venerable Sir! This is also a hard job for them. You must prescribe an easy course." Socrates then said, "Well my dear disciple, once in a month. This is suitable. This is quite easy. I think you are satisfied now." The disciple said, "This is also impossible, my revered preceptor! Householders are very fickle-minded. Their minds are full of sexual Samskaras and Vasanas. They cannot remain even for a single day without sexual intercourse. You have no idea of their mentality." Then Socrates said "Well said, my dear child. Do one thing now. Go direct to the burial ground. Dig a grave and purchase a coffin and the winding sheet for the corpse beforehand. Now you can spoil yourself any number of times as you like. This is my final advice to you." This last advise pierced the heart of the disciple. He felt it keenly. He thought over the matter seriously and understood the importance and glory of Brahmacharya. He took to spiritual Sadhana in right earnest. He took a vow of strict, unbroken celibacy for life. He did meditation with sincerity of purpose. He slept on a coarse mat, ate a little Sattvic food, shunned the company of ladies and plunged himself into deep meditation. He became an Oordhvareto-Yogi and had Self-realisation. He became one of the pet disciples of Socrates.

11. Name and Fame
(Kirti and Pratishtha)

One can renounce even wife, son, property, but it is difficult to renounce name and fame. Pratishtha is established name and fame. This is a great obstacle in the path of God-realisation. This brings downfall in the end. This does not allow the aspirant to march forward in the spiritual path. He becomes a slave of respect and honour. As soon as the aspirant gets some purity and ethical progress, ignorant people flock to him and pay homage and salutations. The aspirant gets puffed up with pride. He thinks he is a great Mahatma now. He becomes eventually a slave of his admirers. He cannot notice his slow downfall. The moment he mixes up freely with householders, he loses what little he had gained during eight or ten years. He cannot influence the public now. The admirers also leave him because they do not find any solace or influence in his company.

The people imagine that the Mahatma has got Siddhis and they can get children through his grace, wealth and herbs for removal of diseases. They always approach a Sadhu with various motives. The aspirant through bad association loses his Vairagya and Viveka. Attachment and desires crop up now in his mind. Therefore an aspirant should hide himself always. Nobody should know what sort of Sadhana he is doing. He should never attempt to exhibit any Siddhi. He should be very humble. He should pass for quite an ordinary man. He should not accept any rich present from householders. He will be affected by the bad thoughts of those who offer presents. He should never think that he is superior to anybody. He should not treat others with contempt. He should always treat others with respect. Then only respect will come by itself. He should treat respect, honour, name and fame as dung or poison. He should wear disrespect and dishonour as a golden-necklace. Then only he will reach the goal safely.

Building of Ashrams and making of disciples bring about the downfall of the aspirant. They are also stumbling blocks in the path of God-realisation. The aspirant becomes another sort of householder. He develops institutional egoism. He gets attached to the Ashram and disciples. He gets 'Mamata' 'mine-ness' for the buildings and Chelas. He has the same cares, worries and anxieties for running the Ashram and magazine and feeding his disciples. He develops slave mentality and weak will. Thoughts of the Ashram revolve in his mind when he is in a dying condition. Some Ashrams are nicely conducted by the 'spiritual head' of the institution while he is alive. When he passes away, the disciples who are petty-minded fight amongst themselves. Cases in the courts are going on. The Ashram becomes a fighting centre afterwards. Ashram owners have to flatter the donors and have to appeal for funds very often. How can thoughts of God remain in his mind, when one has his mind fixed in collection of money and developing the Ashram? Those who have started the Ashram may say now: "We are doing good to the people in various ways. We are having religious classes daily. We feed poor people in various ways. We are training religious students."

It is quite true that an Ashram that is run by a selfless dynamic Yogi and a realised Jivanmukta is a dynamic centre of spirituality. It is a spiritual nucleus for the spiritual uplift of thousands of people. Such centres are needed in all parts of the world. Such Ashrams can do immense spiritual good to the country. But such ideal Ashrams with ideal spiritual heads to run the institution are very, very rare nowadays. Money is collected in a variety of ways. Some portion is spent in some useful purposes. The rest goes to the comforts of the founders of the Ashram.

Goshalas are not really meant for the protection of the cows. The inner real motive is for getting pure fresh milk in the early morning for their own use. Milk is not shared equally with the workers of the Ashram. It is the sole monopoly of the President Sahib. Hence trouble comes in the Ashram. The workers feel the wide gulf of separateness which the founder keeps between himself and the inmates. Where is the feeling of unity or oneness even in small trifling matters? Milk should be equally shared between the workers. *"Sarvabhuta hite ratah"* should be put in actual practice. Then there is real joy and supreme peace.

The founders of the Ashram in course of time become unconsciously slaves of worship and Pooja. Maya works in various ways. They are quite eager that people should drink their Charanamrita. How can a man who has the Bhava that he should be worshipped as Avatara, serve the public? Workers are petty-minded. They fight amongst themselves for trifling matters and disturb the peaceful atmosphere of the Ashram. Where is peace in the Ashram then? How can outsiders who visit the Ashram for getting Santi, enjoy peace there?

The founders of the Ashram should live on daily Bhiksha from outside. They should lead an ideal life of absolute self-sacrifice, a life of ideal simplicity, like the late Kali-Kambli-Wala of Rishikesh who carried water-pot on his head for the Ashram and who lived on Bhiksha from outside. Then only they can do real good to the people. Founders of the Ashram should never appeal for funds to the public. It brings great discredit to those who tread the path of God-realisation. It is another way of respectable begging. The habit of begging destroys the subtle, sensitive nature of the intellect and those who appeal for funds frequently do not know what they are exactly doing, just as the lawyers and those who visit the houses of ill-fame have lost the discriminative faculty of finding out truth from untruth, purity from impurity. Intelligent people use intelligent methods for collecting money. Nowadays there are intelligent thieves who knock away the money in tramcars by giving morphine injection. The following one is an intelligent way of modern begging. An intelligent young educated boy boards the trains with a dozen printed cards in his hands and distributes them to the passengers. There it is written, "I am the grandson of the Dewan of Mysore. My father died all on a sudden. My mother is aged 85. One brother is dumb. Another is blind. Kindly help me with some money." This is begging on modern lines. He never stretches a plate or bowl for begging nor talks anything. But he distributes printed cards. He appears with neat open coat, collar, tie, shirt, pants and Ellwood hat. He collects some money, gets back the cards, quietly walks down and then enters another compartment. Begging kills Atma-Bal. It produces wrong impression on the minds of the public. Where is freedom if one begs? People have lost faith in the founders of the Ashram. If anything comes by itself without asking it can be accepted. Then you can do some work independently. Householders who conduct Ashrams can appeal for funds.

It is very difficult to get good workers for the Ashram. Then why do you bother about building Ashrams when you have neither money, nor workers, nor dynamic, spiritual force? Keep quite. Do meditation. Evolve yourself. Mind your own business. Reform yourself first. How can you help others, when you yourself grope in darkness, when you are blind? How can a blind man lead another blind man? Both will fall in the deep abyss and break their legs.

Lastly, I have to point out that though we have not got at present the first class type of Ashrams, yet there are many good Ashrams of the second class type that are run by noble, Sattvic souls, who do great service to the country in a variety of ways, bring out valuable philosophical books and train students in the practice of meditation and Yoga. They render selfless service. Their works are to be greatly congratulated indeed. It is the duty of rich people to render them spontaneously financial help and help of all sorts. May they live long! May God bestow on them inner spiritual strength to disseminate their message of love, service and peace! My silent homage and salutations to these rare, exalted, selfless souls!

12. Evil Company

The effects of evil company are highly disastrous. The aspirant should shun all sorts of evil company. The mind is filled with bad ideas by contact with evil companions. The little faith in God and scriptures also vanishes. A man is known by the company he keeps. Birds of the same feather flock together. These are all proverbs or wise maxims. They are quite true. Just as a nursery is to be well fenced in the beginning for protection against cows etc., so also a neophyte should protect himself very carefully from foreign evil influences. Otherwise he is ruined totally. The company of those who speak lies, who commit adultery, theft, cheating, double-dealing, who are greedy, who indulge in idle talks, back-biting, tale-bearing, who have no faith in God and in the scriptures etc., should be strictly avoided. The company of women and of those who associate with women is dangerous.

Bad surroundings, obscene pictures, obscene songs, novels that deal with love, cinemas, theatres, the sight of pairing of animals, words which give rise to bad ideas in the mind, in short anything that causes evil thoughts in the mind constitute evil company. Aspirants generally complain: "We are doing Sadhana for the last fifteen years. We have not made any solid spiritual progress." The obvious answer is that they have not totally shunned evil company. Newspapers deal with all sorts of worldly topics. Aspirants should entirely give up reading of newspapers. Reading of newspapers kindles worldly Samskaras, causes sensational excitement in the mind, makes the mind outgoing, produces an impression that the world is a solid reality and makes one forget the Truth that lies underneath these names and forms.

13. Tooshnimbhoota and Stabdha Avasthas

Sometimes the mind remains quiet for a short time. You will find neither Raga nor Dvesha in the mind. This silent state of the mind is called Tooshnimbhoota Avastha. The aspirant mistakes this for Samadhi. This is a neutral state of the mind. This is an obstacle on the path of God-realisation. He should overcome this state of the mind by careful introspection and vigorous meditation. A careful Sadhaka, through experience and acute acumen, can find out exactly the nature of the various states of the mind. He should adopt effective methods to control those states. Mere study of books will not help him much. Experience and practice will do him much real good.

Stabdha Avastha is another kind of mental state. It is akin to Tooshnimbhoota Avastha. This is also another obstacle on the path. When you experience some fear, when you hear some wonderful astounding news, the mind gets stunned for some time. This is Stabdha Avastha. Tooshnimbhoota and Stabdha are Jada states. There is no perfect awareness. The mind remains like a log of wood in a state of inertia. It becomes unfit for active meditation. When these states prevail, there is heaviness of body. The mind is dull. There is lack of cheerfulness. The mind also becomes dull for the time being. The student can find out these states by these symptoms. An intelligent Sadhaka who practises meditation daily can easily find out the different states into which the mind passes. A beginner finds meditation dry in the beginning. But an advanced student who has an intelligent and comprehensive understanding of the nature of the mind and its operations and the laws of the mental plane, will find meditation very interesting. The more he meditates, the more he gains control of the mind. He can understand the nature of the Vrittis and the different mental states. He can control them. He will actually feel that he is gaining inner spiritual strength and that he cannot be easily swayed by the mind now.

14. False Tushti and Rasasvada

The Sadhaka gets some experience during the course of his Sadhana. He sees wonderful visions of Rishis, Mahatmas, astral entities of various description, etc. He hears various melodious Anahata sounds (Nada). He smells Divya Gandha. He gets the powers of thought-reading, foretelling etc. The Sadhaka now foolishly imagines that he has reached the highest goal and stops his further Sadhana. This is a serious mistake. He gets false Tushti or contentment. These are all auspicious signs that manifest on account of a little purity and concentration. These are all encouragements which God gives as a sort of incentive for further progress and intense Sadhana. The aspirant gets more strength of conviction by having these experiences.

Rasasvada is another kind of experience. It is bliss that comes from lower Savikalpa Samadhi. The Sadhaka who has experienced this supersensual bliss imagines that he has reached the final destination and gives up his Sadhana. Just as a man digs the earth very deep to find out the most precious hidden treasures and gems, just as a man is not satisfied with the petty things he has found out just beneath the surface of the ground, so also the Sadhaka should continue his Sadhana till he gets the unconditioned Bhuma, or highest goal of life. He should never be satisfied with *alpam* or lower experiences. He should compare his experiences with the highest experiences of sages that are described in the Upanishads and find out whether they exactly tally with them or not. He should exert till he reaches the seventh Jnana Bhumika, till he becomes a Brahma-varishtha. He should struggle till he gets the inner feeling of Apta-Kama, Krita-Kritya, Prapta-Prapya. "I have obtained all desires, I have done everything, I know everything. There is nothing more to be known. There is nothing more to be obtained."

15. So-called Friends

The so-called friends are your real enemies. You cannot find even a single, unselfish friend in this universe. Your real friend in need who attends on you sincerely is God, the indweller of your heart. Worldly friends come to you to get money and other comforts when you are rolling in a Rolls Royce, when you have got plenty of money. When you are in adverse circumstances no one will care to look at you. Even your sons and wife forsake you. The world is full of avarice, hypocrisy, double-dealing, flattery, untruth, cheating and selfishness. Be careful. Friends come to have idle talk with you and to waste your time. They have no idea of the value of time. They want to pull you down and make you also worldly. They will say: "Friend, what are you doing? Earn money as much as possible. Live comfortably now. Eat, drink, be merry. Let us go to talkies. Today there is a good new American Hollywood production running at so and so theatre. There is beautiful American dance. Who knows about the future? Where is God? Where is heaven? There is no rebirth. There is no Mukti. It is all gup and gossip of Pundits. Enjoy now. Why do you fast? There is nothing beyond this world. Give up all Sadhana and meditation. You are wasting your time." You will get such sort of advice from such worldly friends. Cut off all connections ruthlessly. Don't talk to any of your friends, however sincere he seems to be. Hide yourself away. Live alone at all times. Trust in that Immortal Friend only who dwells in your heart. Then alone you are perfectly safe. He will give you whatever you want. Hear His sweet counsel from within with one-pointed mind and follow.

16. Depression

Aspirants get moods of depression occasionally. These moods may be due to indigestion, cloudy condition, influence of lower astral entities, and revival of old Samskaras from within. Treat the cause. Remove the cause. Do not allow depression to overpower you. Immediately take a brisk, long walk. Run in the open air. Sing divine songs. Chant Om loudly for one hour. Walk along the sea-side or river-side. Play on the harmonium if you know the art. Do some Kumbhakas and Sitali Pranayamas. Drink a small cup of orange-juice or hot tea or coffee. Read some of the elevating portions of Avadhoota Gita and Upanishads.

17. Religious Hypocrisy

(Dambha)

There are as many fashions in Sadhus as there are in worldly persons.

Just as hypocrisy prevails in the worldly persons, so also hypocrisy manifests in aspirants, Sadhus and Sannyasins who have not completely purified the lower nature. They pretend to be what they are not in reality. They pose for big Mahatmas and Siddha Purushas when they do not know even the alpha-beta of Yoga or spirituality. They put on serious Sunday faces. This is a dangerous Vritti. They cheat others. They boast and brag too much of themselves. They do mischief wherever they go. They practise hypocrisy to get respect, honour, good food and clothing and to cheat credulous simpletons. There is no greater crime than trading in religion. This is a capital sin. Householders can be excused. There cannot be any excuse for aspirants and Sadhus who are treading the path of spirituality and who have renounced everything for God-realisation. Religious hypocrisy is more dangerous than hypocrisy of worldly persons. A long drastic course of treatment is needed for its eradication. A religious hypocrite is very far from God. He cannot dream of God-realisation. Thick Tilaka, elaborate painting of the forehead, wearing of too many Tulasi and Rudraksha Maalas on neck, arms, forearms, ears are some of the external signs of religious hypocrisy.

18. Moral and Spiritual Pride

As soon as an aspirant gets some spiritual experiences or Siddhis he is puffed up with vanity and pride. He thinks too much of himself. He separates himself from others. He treats others with contempt. He cannot mix with others. If any one has some moral qualifications such as spirit of service or self-sacrifice, or Brahmacharya, he will say: "I am Akhanda-Brahmachari for the last twelve years. Who is pure like myself? I lived on leaves and gram for four years. I have done service in an Ashram for ten years. No one can serve like myself." Just as worldly people are puffed up with the pride of wealth, so also Sadhus and aspirants are puffed up with their moral qualifications. This kind of pride is also a serious obstacle in the path of God-realisation. It must be eradicated thoroughly. As long as a man boasts himself, so long he is the same little Jiva only. He cannot have Divinity.

19. Prejudice, Intolerance and Bigotry

Prejudice is unreasonable dislike for something or some person. Prejudice makes the brain callous. The brain cannot vibrate properly to grasp the things in their light. One cannot endure honest differences of opinion. This is intolerance. Religious intolerance and prejudice are great obstacles in the path of God-realisation. Some orthodox Sanskrit Pundits strongly think that only Sanskrit-knowing people will have God-realisation. They think that English-knowing Sannyasins are barbarians and they cannot have Self-realisation. Look at the thick foolishness of these bigoted Pundits! Incorrigible, petty-minded, narrow-hearted, crooked sectarians! If one has prejudice against Bible or Quoran, he cannot grasp the truths that are inculcated there. His brain becomes hard, stony and callous. A man can realise by studying and following the principles that are laid down in Quoran, Bible or Zend Avesta or the Pali books of Lord Buddha.

Aspirants should try to remove prejudice of all sorts. Then only they can see truth everywhere. Truth is not the sole monopoly of the Sanskrit Pundits of Benares or the Vairagis of Ayodhya. Truth, Rama, Krishna, Jesus are the common property of all. Our Bengalee brothers think that Ramakrishna Paramahamsa and Vivekananda belong to the Bengalees only. There is a general complaint that the Bengalees and Bengalee Sannyasins are clannish and provincial. It is high time now for them to remove this undesirable spirit in them. This is a great taint. They are famous for their intelligence. Those Sannyasins who have gone abroad to the continent and those who are educated in the West are exceptions. They are broad-hearted.

Sectarians and bigoted people confine themselves to a small circumscribed circle or area. They have no large heart. They cannot see the good points in others on account of their jaundiced vision. They think that their principles and doctrines only are good. They treat others with contempt. They think that their Sampradaya only is superior to others and that their Acharya only is a man of God-realisation. They always fight with others. There is no harm in praising one's own Guru and sticking to his principles and teachings. But one should pay equal regard to the teachings of other prophets and other saints. Then only the feeling of universal love and universal brotherhood will manifest. This will eventually lead to the realisation of God or Atman in all beings. Prejudice, intolerance, bigotry, sectarianism should be thoroughly eradicated. Prejudice and intolerance are forms of hatred.

20. Shilly-Shallying

(Vikshepa)

Vikshepa is tossing or oscillation of mind. This is an old habit of mind. All Sadhakas generally complain of this trouble. The mind never stays at a fixed point for a long time. It jumps hither and thither like a monkey. It is always restless. This is due to the force of Rajas. Whenever Sri Jaya Dayal Goyandka came to me for an interview he used to put always two questions: "Swamiji, what is the remedy to control sleep? How to remove Vikshepa? Give me an easy and effective method." My answer was: "Take light diet at night. Do Sirshasana and Pranayama. Sleep can be conquered. Trataka, Upasana and Pranayama will remove Vikshepa." It is better to have a combined method. This will be more effective. Patanjali Maharshi prescribes Pranayama for destroying Rajas which induces Vikshepa and for getting one-pointed mind.

In the Gita (VI-26, 24, 25) Lord Krishna prescribes a Sadhana for removing Vikshepa. "From whatever cause the restless and unsteady mind wanders away, from that let him restrain it and bring it under the control of the Self alone. Abandoning without reserve all desires born of imagination, and completely restraining the whole group of senses by the mind from all sides, little by little let him attain quietude by the intellect held firmly; having made the mind establish itself in the Self, let him not think of anything". Trataka is an effective method in destroying Vikshepa. Practise this for half an hour on a picture of Lord Krishna or on a black point on the wall. First do this for two minutes and gradually increase the period. Close the eyes when tears come. Look steadily at the object without winking. Do not strain the eyes. Look gently. There are students who can do Trataka for 2 or 3 hours. For full description read my book *"Kundalini Yoga"*.

21. Easy, Comfortable Pranayama (Sukha Purvak)
Loma-Viloma (For removing Vikshepa)

Sit in Padmasana or Siddhasana in your meditation room, before the picture of your Ishta Devata (guiding deity). Close the right nostril with the right thumb. Draw in the air very, very slowly through the left nostril. Then close the left nostril also with the little and the ring finger of the right hand. Retain the air as long as you can comfortably do. Then exhale very, very slowly through the right nostril after removing the thumb. Now half the process is over.

Then draw the air through the right nostril. Retain the air as before and exhale it very, very slowly through the left nostril. All these six processes constitute one Pranayama. Do 20 in the morning and 20 in the evening. Gradually increase the number. Have a Bhavana (mental attitude) that all the Daivi Sampat (Divine qualities) such as mercy, love, forgiveness, Santi, joy, etc., are entering into your system along with the inspired air and all Asura Sampat (devilish qualities) such as lust, anger, greed, etc., are being thrown out along with the expired air. Repeat OM or Gayatri during Purak, Kumbhak and Rechak. Hard-working Sadhakas can do 320 Kumbhaks daily in four sittings at the rate of 80 in each sitting (morning, evening, night and midnight). Purak is inhalation, Rechak is exhalation and Kumbhak is retention of air.

This Pranayama removes all diseases; purifies the Nadis; removes Vikshepa, steadies the mind in concentration, improves digestion, increases the digestive fire (Jatharagni) and the appetite, helps in maintaining Brahmacharya and awakens the Kundalini that is sleeping at the Muladhara Chakra. Purification of Nadis will set in rapidly. You will have levitation (raising from the ground).

Do not produce any sound during inhalation and exhalation. Close the eyes during the practice. Take a little rest when one Pranayama is over. Take three long breaths — inhalation and exhalation. This will give you rest.

If you want to have Mantra during the first week, inhale till you count 1 Om; retain the breath till you count 4 Oms and exhale till you count 2 Oms. The ratio is 1:4:2. Use the fingers of your left hand for counting. In the second week increase the ratio to 2:8:4. In the third week you can increase it to 3:12:6 and so on till you get the maximum ratio of 16:64:32. When you increase the ratio, if you find it difficult to retain the breath, have the same practice for two or three weeks more with the same ratio till you gain the capacity and strength to increase the ratio further. Use your commonsense all throughout the practice. There must not be the least suffocation during the practice.

22. Dilly-Dallying

(Aimless Wandering)

Some aspirants have got a habit of wandering aimlessly. They cannot stick to one place even for a week. The wandering habit must be checked. They want to see new places, new faces and want to talk with new people. A rolling stone gathers no moss. A Sadhaka should stick to one place at least for a period of twelve years (one Tapah period). If his health is delicate, he can stay for six months in one place during summer and rainy season and in another place for six months during winter. During winter he can stay either at Rajpur (Dehradun) or Rishikesh. During summer he can go to Badrinath or Uttarkashi. Sadhana suffers if one wanders constantly. Those who want to do rigorous Tapas and Sadhana must stay in one place. Too much walking produces weakness and fatigue.

23. Jilly-Jallying

(Lingual Diarrhoea)

Too much talking is Jilly-Jallying. If a man talks too much, he suffers from diarrhoea of the tongue. Quiet people cannot sit even for a second in the company of these loquacious or garrulous people. They will talk five hundred words per second. There is an electric talking-dynamo in their tongues. They are restless people. If you lock these people for a day in a solitary room, they will die. Much energy is wasted by too much talking. The energy that is spent in talking must be conserved and utilised for divine contemplation. The Vag-Indriya distracts the mind considerably. A talkative man cannot dream of having peace even for a short time. An aspirant should talk only a few words when necessary and that too on spiritual matters only. A talkative man is unfit for the spiritual path. Practise Mauna daily for two hours and especially during meals. On Sundays observe full Mauna for 24 hours. Do a lot of Japa and meditation during Mauna. The Mauna that is observed during meditation cannot be taken as Mauna. Mauna should be observed by householders at such a time when there are great opportunities for talking and when visitors come to meet. Now only the impulses of speech can be checked. Ladies are very talkative. They create troubles in the house by idle talk and gossiping. They should observe Mauna particularly. You should speak measured words only. Too much talking is Rajasic nature. Great peace comes by observance of Mauna. By gradual practice, prolong the period of Mauna to six months and then to two years.

24. Villy-Vallying

(Discussing too much)

Some people in whom the reason has developed have got the habit of entering into unnecessary controversies and discussions. They have got Tarkik Buddhi. They cannot remain quiet even for a second. They will create opportunities for heated debates. Too much discussions end in enmity and hostility. Much energy is wasted in useless discussions. Intellect is a help if it is used in the right direction of Atmic Vichara. Intellect is a hindrance if it is used in unnecessary discussions. Intellect takes the aspirant to the threshold of intuition. Thus far and no further. Reason helps in inferring the existence of God and finding out suitable methods for Self-realisation. Intuition transcends reason but does not contradict reason. Intuition is direct perception of Truth. There is no reasoning here. Reasoning concerns matters of the physical plane. Wherever there is 'why' and 'wherefore', there is reasoning. In transcendental matters which are beyond the reach of reason, reason is of no use.

Intellect helps a lot in reflection and ratiocination. But people in whom reasoning has highly developed become sceptical. Their reason becomes perverted also. They lose faith in Vedas and in the teachings of Mahatmas. They say: "We are rationalists. We cannot believe anything which does not appeal to our reason. We do not believe the Upanishads. We reject anything that does not come within the domain of reason. We have no faith in God and Sat-Gurus". These so-called rationalists are a type of atheists only. It is very difficult to convince them. They have an impure, perverted reason. Thoughts of God cannot enter their brains. They will not do any kind of spiritual Sadhana. They say: "Show us your Brahman of the Upanishads or Isvara of the Bhaktas." Those who are of doubting nature will perish (*samsayatma vinasyati*). Reason is a finite instrument. It cannot explain many mysterious problems of life. Those who are free from the so-called rationalism and scepticism can march in the path of God-realisation.

25. Irregularity of Sadhana

This is also a great obstacle in the path of realisation. Just as a man is regular in taking his food, so also he must be strictly regular in his Sadhana. He must get up punctually at 3.30 or 4 a.m. and start his Japa and meditation. One can get the meditative mood quite easily without effort if he does his Sadhana at fixed hours, both morning and night. In winter one can have four sittings. One should have the same pose, the same room, the same seat, the same Bhava or the same mental attitude, the same hours for meditation. Everybody should have his daily routine or Dinacharya and should strictly adhere to it at all costs. Leniency to the mind will upset the whole programme. One should meditate regularly. He should do the spiritual Sadhana untiringly with indefatigable energy, asinine patience, adamantine will and iron determination. Then only sure success is possible. Meals should be taken at regular hours. One should go to sleep at fixed time. See how the sun is very regular in its rising and daily work!

26. Cessation of Sadhana

The aspirant is very enthusiastic in his Sadhana in the beginning. He is full of zeal. He takes a great deal of interest. He expects to get some results. When he does not get these results, he gets discouraged. He loses his interest in his Abhyasa and slackens his efforts. He gives up his Sadhana completely. He loses his faith in the efficacy of the Sadhana. Sometimes the mind gets disgusted with one particular kind of Sadhana. It wants some new kind of Sadhana. Just as mind wants some variety in food and other things, so also it wants variety in the mode of Sadhana also. It rebels against monotonous practice. The aspirant should know how to coax the mind on such occasions and to extract work from it by a little relaxation of mind. The cessation of Sadhana is a grave mistake. Spiritual practices should never be given up under any circumstances. Evil thoughts will be ever waiting to enter the gates of the mental factory. If the aspirant stops his Sadhana, his mind will be Satan's workshop. Do not expect anything. Be sincere and regular in your daily routine, Tapas and meditation. The Sadhana will take care of itself. You mind your own daily business. The fruit will come by itself. Let me repeat here the words of Lord Krishna: "Thy business is with the action (Tapas, Sadhana and meditation) only, never with its fruit; so let not the fruit of action be thy motive, nor be thou to inaction attached." (Gita: II-47.) Your efforts will be crowned with sanguine success by the Lord. It takes a long time for purification of the mind and getting a one-pointed mind. Be cool and patience. Continue your Sadhana regularly.

27. Fault-finding

This is a detestable old habit of man. It clings to him tenaciously. The mind of the aspirant, who always tries to poke his nose into the affairs of other men, is always outgoing. How can he think of God, when his mind is ever engaged in finding the faults of others? If you spend even a fraction of the time that you waste in finding your own faults you would have become a great saint by this time. Why do you care for the faults of others? Improve yourself first. Reform yourself first. Purify yourself first. Wash the impurities of your own mind. He who applies himself diligently to his spiritual practices cannot find even a single second to look into the affairs of others. If the fault-finding nature dies, there will be no occasion for criticising others. Much time is wasted in back-biting, scandal-mongering etc. Time is most precious. We do not know when will Lord Yama take away our lives. Every second must be utilised in Divine contemplation. Let the world have its own ways. Mind your own affairs. Clean your mental factory. That man who does not interfere with others is the most peaceful man in the world.

28. Fear

This is a very great obstacle in the path of God-realisation. A timid aspirant is absolutely unfit for the spiritual path. He cannot dream of Self-realisation even in one thousand births. One must risk the life, if he wants to attain immortality. The spiritual wealth cannot be gained without self-sacrifice, self-denial or self-abnegation. A fearless dacoit who has no Deha-Adhyasa is fit for God-realisation. Only his current will have to be changed. Fear is not an imaginary non-entity. It assumes solid forms and troubles the aspirant in various ways. If one conquers fear, he is on the road to success. He has almost reached the goal. Tantrik Sadhana makes the student fearless. There is one great advantage in this line. He has to make practices in the burial ground, by sitting over the dead body at mid-night. This kind of Sadhana emboldens the student. Fear assumes various forms. There are fear of death, fear of disease, scorpion-phobia, fear of solitude, fear of company, fear of losing something, fear of public criticism in the form of "What will people say of me?" Some are not afraid of tigers in the forests. They are not afraid of gun shots in the battlefield. But they are awfully afraid of public criticism. Fear of public criticism stands in the way of an aspirant in his spiritual progress. He should stick to his own principles, and own convictions, even though he is persecuted and even though he is at the point of being blown up at the mouth of a machinegun. Then only he will grow and realise. All aspirants suffer from this dire malady, fear. Fear of all sorts should be totally eradicated by Atma-Chintana, Vichara and devotion and cultivation of the opposite quality, courage. Positive overcomes negative. Courage overpowers fear and timidity.

29. Force of Old Samskaras

When the aspirant does intense Sadhana to obliterate the old Samskaras, they try to rebound upon him with a vengeance and with redoubled force. They take forms and come before him as stumbling-blocks. The old Samskaras of hatred, enmity, jealousy, feeling of shame, respect, honour, fear etc., assume grave forms. Samskaras are not imaginary non-entities. They turn into actualities when opportunities crop up. The aspirant should not be discouraged. They will lose their force after some time and die by themselves. Just as the dying wick burns with intensity just before it gets extinguished, so also those old Samskaras show their teeth and force before they are eradicated. The aspirant should not get unnecessarily alarmed. He will have to increase the force or momentum of spiritual Samskaras by doing Japa, Dhyana, Svadhyaya, virtuous actions, Satsanga and cultivation of Sattvic virtues. These new spiritual Samskaras will neutralise the old vicious Samskaras. He should plunge himself into his spiritual practices. This is his Kartavya or duty.

30. Jealousy

This is also a great obstacle. Even Sadhus who have renounced everything, who live with one Kowpeen only in the caves of Gangotri and Uttarkashi in Himalayas are not free from this evil Vritti. Sadhus are more jealous than the householders. Their hearts burn when they see some other Sadhu in a flourishing condition, when they notice that his neighbouring Sadhu is respected and honoured by the public. They try to vilify their neighbour and adopt methods for his destruction or elimination. What a sad sight! What a deplorable spectacle! Horrible to think! Dreadful to imagine! When the hearts burn, how can you expect peace of mind? Even highly educated people are very mean and petty-minded. Jealousy is a worst enemy of Peace and Jnana. It is the strongest weapon of Maya. Aspirants should be always alert. They should not become slaves of name and fame and jealousy. If there is jealousy, he is small little being only. He is far from God. One should rejoice at the welfare of others. One should develop Mudita (complacency) when he sees others in prosperous conditions. He should feel Atma-Bhava in all beings. Jealousy assumes various forms such as Irshya, Asuya, Matsarya etc. All forms of jealousy must be totally eradicated. Just as milk again and again bubbles out during the process of ebullition, so also jealousy bursts out again and again. It must be entirely rooted out.

31. Habit of Self-justification

This is a very dangerous habit for an aspirant. It is an old-standing habit. Self-assertion, self-sufficiency, obstinacy, dissimulation, speaking falsehood are the constant retinues or attendants of self-justification. He who has developed this can never improve himself, as he will never admit his faults. He will always try his level best to justify himself in various ways. He will not hesitate to tell several lies to support his false statements. He will tell one lie to cover another lie and he will speak lies *ad infinitum*. The aspirant should always admit his faults, mistakes, weaknesses etc., then and there. Then only he can improve quickly.

32. Backbiting

This is a dirty, abominable habit of petty-minded people. Almost all are victims of this dire malady. This has become an ingrained habit of narrow-hearted, mischievous people. This is a Tamo-Guna Vritti. The Lila of this world is kept up by this evil habit of man. It is Maya's strong weapon to spread restlessness throughout the world. If you see four men sitting in a group, think that some backbiting is surely going on there. If you behold that four Sadhus are talking, you can at once infer without any shadow of doubt that they are backbiting against some person or other. A Sadhu who is engaged in contemplation will always be alone. The Sadhu will be talking: "The food of that Kshetra is very bad. That Swami is a very bad man." Backbiting is more prevalent amongst the so-called Sadhus than householders. Even educated Sannyasins and householders are not free from this dreadful disease.

The root-cause of backbiting is ignorance or jealousy. The backbiter wants to pull down or destroy the man who is in a prosperous condition by false vilification, slander, calumny, false accusation etc. There is no other work for a backbiter except scandal-mongering. He lives on backbiting. He takes pleasure in backbiting, mischief-making. This is his Svabhava. Backbiters are a menace to society. They are worst criminals. They need capital punishment. Double-dealing, crookedness, diplomacy, chicanery, quibbling, tricks, artifices are the retinues of backbiting. A backbiter can never have a calm, peaceful mind. His mind is always planning or scheming in wrong directions. An aspirant should be absolutely free from this dreadful vice. He should walk alone, live alone, eat alone and meditate alone. If a man who has not removed jealousy, backbiting, hatred, pride, selfishness says: "I am meditating for six hours daily," it is all gassing nonsense. There is no hope of getting a meditative mood even for five minutes unless a man removes all these evil Vrittis and purifies his mind first by selfless service for six years.

33. Anger

It is a gate to hell. It destroys the knowledge of Self. It is born of Rajas. It is all-consuming and all-polluting. It is the greatest enemy of peace. It is a modification of lust. Just as milk is changed into curd, so also lust or desire becomes transmuted into anger. When a man's desire is not gratified, he becomes angry. Then his mind becomes confused. He loses his memory and understanding. He perishes. A man when he is angry will talk anything he likes and do anything he likes. He commits murder. A hot word results in fighting and stabbing. He is under intoxication. He loses his senses for the time being. He does not know what he is exactly doing. He is a prey to anger. He is under the sway of anger. Anger is a form of Sakti or Devi. In Chandipatha you will find, *"Yaa Devee Sarvabhuteshu Krodharupena Samsthita; Namastasyai Namastasyai Namastasyai Namo Namah."* "I bow to that Devi who is seated in all beings in the form of anger."

Resentment, indignation, fury, wrath and irritation are all varieties of anger according to degree or intensity. If a man wants to correct another man and uses slight anger unselfishly as a force to check and improve him, then it is called "religious anger." Suppose a man molests a girl and tries to outrage her, and a by-stander becomes angry towards this criminal, then it is called 'righteous indignation.' This is not bad. Only when the anger is the outcome of greed or selfish motives, it is bad. Sometimes a religious teacher has to express a little anger outwardly to correct his disciples. This is also not bad. One has to do it.

But he should be cool within and hot and impetuous outside. He should not allow the anger to take deep root in his Antahkarana for a long time. It should pass off immediately like a wave in the sea.

If a man becomes irritable for trifling things very often, it is definite sign of mental weakness. One should control irritability by developing patience, Vichara, Kshama, love, mercy and spirit of service. When anger is controlled, it becomes transmuted into an energy that can move the world. It becomes changed into Ojas, just as heat or light is changed into electricity. Energy takes another form. If an aspirant has controlled anger completely, half of his Sadhana is over. Control of anger means control of lust also. All vices, evil qualities and wrong actions take their origin in anger. If anger is controlled, all bad qualities die by themselves. He who has controlled anger cannot do any wrong or evil actions. He is always just. An easily irritable man is always unjust. He is swayed by impulses and emotions. Too much loss of semen is the chief cause for irritability and anger. The root-cause for anger lies in egoism. Through Vichara egoism should be removed. Then only one can control anger completely to the very root. Through development of the opposite virtues such as Kshama, love, Santi, Karuna and friendship it can be controlled to some extent. The force can be reduced. Jnana only completely fries all Samskaras. But practice of Mauna is of great help in controlling anger. It is very difficult to say when a man will be thrown into a state of fury. All on a sudden he gets a terrible fit of anger for trifling matters. When the anger assumes a grave form, it becomes difficult to control. It should be controlled when it assumes the form of a small ripple in the subconscious mind. One should watch the mind carefully, whenever there is a sign of irritability. Then it becomes very easy.

When a man is very furious, he loses all control. Anger

gains strength by repetition. If it is checked, man gains strength of will gradually. An aspirant should direct all his attention towards the conquest of this powerful enemy. Sattvic food, Japa, meditation, prayer, Satsanga, Vichara, service, Kirtan, Brahmacharya, Pranayama—all will pave a long way in eradicating this dire malady. A combined method should be adopted in its removal. When a man abuses you, try to keep quiet. Bear the insult. You will gain strength. Check the impulses and emotions to begin with. Whenever there is likelihood of a burst of anger during conversation or debate, stop your speech. Always try to speak sweet, soft words (Madhura and Mridu). The words must be soft and the arguments hard: but if the words are hard, it will bring discord. If you find it difficult to control anger, leave the place at once and take a brisk walk. Drink some cold water immediately. Chant OM loudly for 10 minutes and then repeat OM SANTI mentally for 10 minutes. Smoking, meat-eating and drinking of liquors make the heart very irritable. Therefore they should be completely abandoned. Tobacco brings diseases of heart. It gives rise to "tobacco-heart" which gets easily irritated.

Be careful in the selection of companions. Talk little. Mix little. Plunge yourself into spiritual Sadhana. Think that the world is a long dream; that the world is Mithya. This will prevent anger. Make Vichara: "What is abuse? What do I gain by getting angry? It is only wasting of energy and time. I am not the body. The Atman is the same in all." This will completely remove anger. Anger spoils the blood. It throws various poisons into the blood.

Instances are recorded of women who have killed their children by nursing them with breast-milk when they were in a fit of anger. In the light of modern psychology all diseases take their origin in anger. Rheumatism, heart-diseases and nervous diseases are due to anger. The whole nervous system is completely shattered by one fit of anger. It takes months before it is restored to normal equilibrium.

34. Tamas or Inertia

A microscopic minority only are fit for whole-timed meditation. People like Sadasiva Brahman and Sri Sankara only can spend the whole time in meditation. Many Sadhus who take to Nivritti Marga have become completely Tamasic. Tamas is mistaken for Sattva. This is a great blunder. One can evolve beautifully by doing Karma Yoga in the world if he knows how to spend his time profitably. A householder should seek the advice of Sannyasins and Mahatmas from time to time, draw a daily routine and adhere to it strictly amidst worldly activities. Rajas can be converted into Sattva. Intense Rajas takes a Sattvic turn. It is impossible to convert Tamas all on a sudden into Sattva. Tamas should be first turned into Rajas. Young Sadhus who take to Nivritti Marga do not stick to routine. They do not hear the words of elders. They do not obey the orders of the Guru. They want absolute independence from the very beginning. They lead a happy-go-lucky life. There is no one to check. They have their own ways. They do not know how to regulate the energy and how to chalk out a daily programme.

They aimlessly wander about from place to place. They become Tamasic within six months. They sit half an hour in some Asana and imagine that they are having Samadhi. They think they are realised souls. If an aspirant who has taken to Nivritti Marga finds that he is not evolving, he is not improving in meditation, he is going into Tamasic state, he should at once take up some kind of service for some years and work vigorously. He should combine work along with meditation. This is wisdom. This is prudence. This is sagacity. Then he should go in for seclusion. One should use his commonsense all throughout his Sadhana. It is very difficult to go out of Tamasic state. A Sadhaka should be very cautious. When Tamas tries to overtake him, he should immediately do some sort of brisk work. He can run in the open air, draw water from well, etc. He should drive it off by some intelligent means or others.

35. Greed

First comes Kama (desire). Then comes anger. Then comes greed. Then comes Moha. Kama is very powerful. So prominence is given to it. There is intimate connection between Kama and Krodha. Similarly there is close relationship between greed and Moha. A greedy man has got great Moha for his money. His mind is always on the moneybox and the bunch of keys he has tied to his waist-cord. Money is his very blood and life. He lives to collect money. He is a gatekeeper only for his money. The enjoyer is his prodigal son. Money-lenders are the favourable tools of our friend, greed. He has taken his stronghold in their minds. These are the Shylocks of the present day. They suck the blood of poor people by taking enormous interest (25%, 50% and even 100% at times). Cruel-hearted people! They pretend to show that they are of charitable disposition by doing acts such as opening of Kshetras, building temples etc.

Such acts cannot neutralise their abominable sins and merciless acts. Many poor families are ruined by these people. They do not think that the bungalows and palaces in which they live are built out of the blood of these poor people. Greed has destroyed their intellect and made them absolutely blind. They have eyes but they see not. Greed always makes the mind restless. A man of one lakh of rupees plans to get 10 lakhs. A millionaire schemes to become a billionaire. Greed is insatiable. There is no end for it. Greed assumes various subtle forms. A man thirsts for name and fame and applause. This is greed. A sub-judge thirsts for becoming a High Court judge. A third-class magistrate thirsts for becoming a first-class magistrate with full powers. This is also greed. A Sadhu thirsts for getting physical Siddhis. This is another form of greed. A Sadhu thirsts for opening several Ashrams in different centres. This is also greed. A greedy man is absolutely unfit for the spiritual path. Destroy greed of all sorts by Vichara, devotion, meditation, Japa, Dhyana, Santosh, integrity, honesty, disinterestedness and enjoy peace.

36. Moha

Here comes another great obstacle which troubled even Sri Sankara. He had to attend the sick-bed and funeral rites of his mother, though he was a Sannyasin. A great sage, Pattinathu Swami of South India sings when his mother died: "There was fire at first in Tripura Samhara. Then there was fire in Lanka by Hanuman. Now the death of my beloved mother has caused burning the fire in my stomach and heart. Let me also apply fire to this corpse of my mother." Moha is infatuated love for one's own body, wife, children, father, mother, brothers, sisters and property. Moha, like greed, takes various subtle forms. The mind gets attached to one name and form or other. If it is detached from one name and form, it clings tenaciously to another name and form.

Look at the Moha of monkeys. If the baby-monkey dies, the mother-monkey will carry the dead body for two or three months. Such is the power of Moha! Mysterious is Moha! If the father receives a telegram that his only son is dead, he gets immediately a shock and faints. Sometimes he dies also. This is the power of Moha. The whole world runs through Moha. It is through Moha one is bound to the wheel of Samsara. One gets pain through Moha. Moha creates attachment. Moha is a kind of powerful liquor that brings intoxication in the twinkling of an eye. Even Sannyasins get Moha for their Ashrams and disciples. Moha should be eradicated by Viveka, Vairagya, Vichara, Atma-Chintan, devotion, seclusion, study of Vedantic literature etc. Moha can only be removed *in toto* by renunciation and Sannyasa and Self-realisation.

You never weep when millions of people die in a war. But you weep bitterly when your wife dies. Why? Because you have Moha for her. Moha creates the idea of "mine-ness." Therefore you say: "My wife, my son, my horse, my home." This is bondage. This is death. Moha creates infatuated love for sensual objects. Moha produces delusion and perverted intellect. Through the force of Moha, you mistake the unreal, dirty body for the real, pure Atman; you take the unreal world as a solid reality. These are the functions of Moha. Moha is a strong weapon of Maya.

37. Hatred

This is the deadliest foe of an aspirant. It is an inveterate enemy. It is an old-standing associate of the Jiva. Ghrina, contempt, prejudice, sneering, taunting, teasing, ridiculing, mocking, frowning, showing wry face are all forms of hatred. Hatred bubbles out again and again. It is insatiable like lust or greed. It may temporarily subside for sometime, and may again burst out with redoubled force. If the father dislikes a man, his sons and daughters also begin to hate that man without any rhyme or reason whatsoever, although that man has not done them any wrong or injustice. Such is the force of hatred. If any one even remembers the figure of a man who has done him some serious injury some forty years ago, at once hatred creeps into his mind immediately and his face shows clear signs of enmity and hatred.

Hatred develops by repetition of hatred-Vritti. Hatred ceases not by hatred but ceases by love only. Hatred needs prolonged and intense treatment as its branches ramify in various directions in the subconscious mind. It lurks in different corners. Constant selfless service combined with meditation for a period of twelve years is necessary. An Englishman hates an Irishman and an Irishman hates an

Englishman. A Catholic hates a Protestant and a Protestant hates a Catholic. This is religious hatred. There is communal hatred. One man hates another man at first sight without any reason. This is Svabhavic. Pure love is unknown in this world amongst worldly people. Selfishness, jealousy, greed and lust are retinues of hatred. In Kali-Yuga the force of hatred is augmented.

A son hates his father and sues him in the court. The wife divorces her husband. Where is the Pativrata Dharma of Hindu ladies? Has it disappeared from the soil of India? In India marriage is a sacrament. It is a sacred act. It is not a regular contract. The husband holds the hands of his wife, both look at Arundhati star and take a solemn pledge before the holy fire. The husband says: "I shall be as chaste as Rama and promise to live with you peacefully, procreating healthy, intelligent offspring. I shall love you till I die. I will never look at the face of another lady. I will be true to you. I shall never separate myself from you." The wife in return says: "I shall be unto you like Radha unto Krishna, like Sita unto Rama. I shall serve thee till the end of my life in sincerity. Thou art my very life – Thou art my Prana Vallabha – I shall realise God by serving thee as God." Look at the horrible state of present-day affairs! This deplorable state of affairs is due to so-called modern civilisation and modern education. Pativrata Dharma has gone. Ladies have become independent. They forsake their husbands and do whatever they like. Culture does not consist in husband and wife walking on Mount Road and Marina Beach holding their hands or placing their hands on the shoulders. This is not real freedom. This is vile imitation. This is unfit for Hindu ladies. This fashionable habit will destroy the feminine grace and modesty which are their characteristics and which adorn them.

Pure unselfish love should be cultivated. One should have fear in God. Solomon says: "Fear of the Lord is the beginning of wisdom." Service with Atma Bhava can remove hatred completely and bring in Advaitic realisation of oneness of life. Ghrina, prejudice, contempt, etc., will completely vanish by selfless service. Vedanta in daily life when put into actual practice can eradicate all sorts of hatred. There is one Self hidden in all beings. Then why do you hate others? Why do you frown at others? Why do you treat others with contempt? Why do you divide and separate? Realise the unity of life and consciousness. Feel Atman everywhere. Rejoice and radiate love and peace everywhere.

38. Valediction

O my dear aspirants! I send you the thought-currents of Peace from the peaceful atmosphere of the sacred Himalayas, the Abode of Rishis.

Peace is absolute serenity and tranquillity, wherein all the mental modifications, Sankalpas, thoughts, imaginations, whims, fancies, moods, impulses, emotions, instincts, etc., cease entirely and the individual soul rests in his own native, pristine glory in an unruffled state. It is not of course the temporary state of mental quietude which worldly people speak of in common parlance when they retire for a short time in a solitary bungalow in a forest for a little rest, when they are tired after a long journey. Peace is Turiya state or the fourth condition of superconsciousness. Peace is realm of infinite bliss, eternal life and eternal sun-shine, where the three kinds of Taapas viz., Adhidaivika (pain caused by gods as thunder, etc.; supernatural); Adhyatmika (pain caused from self within as headache; naturo-intrinsic suffering); and Adhibhautika (pain caused by the Bhutas as scorpion-sting, snake-bite, etc.; naturo-extrinsic suffering). Cares, worries and anxieties and fear which torment the soul here, dare not enter, where all distinctions of caste, creed and colour vanish altogether in the one embrace of Divine Life and where desires, cravings find their full satiety. Peace is eternal life, in the pure spiritual consciousness, Atman, Brahman or Highest Self.

Peace is within. Search Peace within the chambers of your heart through one-pointed concentration and meditation. If you do not find Peace there, you will not find it anywhere else. Remember, dear friends, that the goal of life, the *summum bonum* of existence is the attainment of Peace and not the achievement of power, name, fame and wealth. God is Santi-Svarupa (embodiment of Peace). Srutis emphatically declare: *"Ayam Atma Santo* — This Atman (Self) is Silence."* Desire is the greatest enemy of peace. Desire causes distraction of various sorts. There is no peace for him who has no concentration. There can be no happiness for the unpeaceful. In that Supreme Peace all pains, sorrows, miseries and tribulations vanish forever.

Give up all desires, cravings, longings, egoism and "mine-ness." You will get Peace. The Peace of the Eternal lies near those who know themselves, who are disjoined from desire and passion, subdued in nature, of subdued thoughts. The man who is endowed with supreme faith and has mastery over his senses, gets Supreme Peace quickly.

Dear brothers! Children of Immortality! Plod on. Push on. Do not look backward. Forget the past. Forget the body and the world. But forget not the centre. Forget not the source. A glorious, brilliant future is awaiting you. Purify. Serve. Love. Give. Live in Om. Feel always and everywhere the Indwelling, all-pervading Presence. Realise the Self. Rest in the magnanimous ocean of Peace, in the stupendous sea of stillness. Drink the nectar of Immortality. May the Indwelling Presence be your Centre, Ideal and Goal. May Joy, Bliss, Immortality, Peace, Glory and Splendour abide with you forever.

Dear brothers! I have placed before you in detail all obstacles that stand in the way of God-realisation and have suggested various, effective methods to remove these obstacles. Stand up now like an undaunted spiritual solider in the Adhyatmic battlefield. Become a spiritual hero of great intrepidity and unique chivalry. Get over the obstacles fearlessly one by one and manifest divine glory, splendour, purity and sanctity. Wait patiently with a calm and serene mind for results. Do not be hasty, rash and impetuous. Allow proper time for regeneration and renovation. *Nil desperandum* – never despair. Wear the Vairagya-coat of arms. Wield the shield of Viveka. Hold the banner of faith. March boldly and cheerfully with the band of BHUM BHUM; OM OM OM; RAMA RAMA RAMA; SHYAM SHYAM SHYAM. Stop not till you drink the elixir of immortality to your heart's content. Stop not, dear Sadhakas, till you enter the immortal realms of eternal sunshine, undecaying beauty, unfading ecstasy, supreme bliss, infinite joy, unalloyed felicity and unbroken peace. This is your final destination. You can take eternal rest now. This is your goal. This is your highest aim and purpose of life. Rest now in everlasting peace, friends! Good-bye unto you all. Cheer yourselves. Share this rare panacea with your brothers. Elevate them. This noble and stupendous selfless work is awaiting you now in the Grand Plan. Fulfil the Divine Will and become a Buddha of undying fame. Salutations unto you all!

Santi Mantra

Om Poornamadah Poornamidam
Poornat Poornamudachyate;
Poornasya Poornamaadaya
Poornamevaavasishyate.

Om Santih! Santih! Santih!

The whole (Brahman) is all that is invisible. The whole (Brahman) is all that is visible. The whole (Hiranyagarbha) was born out of the whole (Brahman). When the whole (the Universe) is absorbed into the whole (Brahman) the whole alone (Brahman) remains.

Om Peace! Peace! Peace!

Chapter VI

SAMADHI OR COSMIC CONSCIOUSNESS

1. Message of Prem

Prem is the flower of flowers. It is the rarest of all flowers. It is cultivated in the hearts of devotees. Prem or Bhakti is intense love or highest form of devotion to God. It is supreme attachment to the Lotus-Feet of the Lord. It springs from the bottom of the devotee's heart. There is not a bit of effort. There is a genuine, natural, spontaneous longing to meet God in the heart. Just as fish cannot live without water, just as the sun-flower cannot live without the sun, just as the chaste wife cannot live without her husband, so also a true Bhakta cannot live without God even for a moment.

Bhakti or Prem is of the nature of nectar. It gives freedom to the devotee and makes him perfect and fully satisfied. It takes him to the Lotus-Feet of the Lord.

For all beings a human birth is difficult to obtain, more so a male body. There are three things which are indeed rare and are due to the Grace of the Lord viz., human birth, the longing for liberation and the protecting care of a perfected sage. The man who, having by virtuous actions in previous births, obtained a human birth with a male body and good intellect to boot is foolish enough not to exert for Self-realisation. He verily commits suicide, for he kills himself by clinging to things unreal.

There is no hope of immortality by means of riches. Such indeed is the emphatic declaration of the Sruti: *"Na karmana na prajaya dhanena tyagenaike amritatvam-anasuh* — Neither by rituals, nor by progeny, nor by riches, but by renunciation alone one can attain immortality."* Mere giving up of objects will not constitute real renunciation.

Dear friends, remember this point well. True Tyaga consists in renouncing egoism, mine-ness, selfishness, Moha, Deha-Abhimana, desires and cravings.

Even the greatest of persons will in course of time become the lowest of the low. Countless kings, earls, barons, emperors and millionaires have come and gone. Where are those distinguished poets, intellectual geniuses, reputed scientists with boasted intellects? Where are Shakespeare, Kalidas, Byron, Newton, Kant, Plato and Faraday?

In youth you are enveloped with total ignorance, in adult age you are entangled in the meshes of women, in old age you groan under the burden of Samsara and debility. You eventually die and pass away from the scene. Being thus always occupied, when will you, dear brothers, find time to devote yourself to the commission of virtuous deeds, Nishkama Karma, Bhajan, Satsanga, Kirtan and meditation?

Why should you realise Atman? Because Self-realisation gives you freedom from the Samsaric wheel of birth and death and bestows on you supreme peace, illimitable Ananda and unalloyed felicity. Hear the emphatic declaration of the Srutis: "This Atman (Self) which is free from sin, undecaying, undying, free from sorrow, hunger and thirst, with true desires and true resolves, that is what is to be sought after and which one must wish to understand. One who has sought after this Self and understands It, obtains all worlds and all desires." "The Infinite (the great) is Bliss. There is no bliss in what is small. The Infinite alone is Bliss. But one should wish to understand the Infinite." — Chhandogya Upanishad.

Religion must educate and develop the whole man — his heart, his head and his hand. Then only he will have real perfection. There must be integral development. One-sided development is not commendable. You must have the head of Sankara, the heart of Buddha and the hand of Janaka. Vedanta without devotion is quite dry.

Pure love is divine Prem. It is the spontaneous outpouring of affection and devotion from the bottom of the heart of a sincere devotee towards God. The only Sara-vastu in the world is Love or Prem. It is eternal and undecaying. Physical love is passion or Moha. Universal Love is Divine Love. Cosmic Love, Visva Prem, Universal Love are all synonymous terms. God is Love. Love is God. Selfishness, greed, egoism, vanity, pride, jealousy and anger contract the heart and stand in the way of developing Universal Love.

Who of us is really anxious to know the truth about God or Divine Love? We are more ready to ask ourselves: "How much money you have got in the Bank? Who said that against me? Do you know who am I? How are your wife and children doing?" and questions of this sort, than questions like: "Who am I? What is this Samsara? What is freedom? Whence have I come? Whither shall I go? Who is Isvara? What are the attributes of God? What is our relationship to God? How to attain Moksha? What is the Svaroopa of Moksha?" How many of you, sisters and brothers, ask questions of this nature?

Sravanam kirtanam Vishnoh-smaranam paadasevanam;
Archanam vandanam dasyam sakhyam-atmanivedanam.

"Hearing the Name of the Lord, singing (His) praises, remembering (Him), serving His Lotus Feet, worshipping Him, bowing before Him, attending on Him, loving Him as a Friend, and surrender of the self completely to Him—these are the nine ways of developing devotion."

Sri Vishnoh Sravane Parikshidabhavad Vaiyasikah Kirtane
Prahladah Smarane Tadanghribhajane Lakshmih
                                        Prithuh Poojane;
Akrurastvabhivandane Kapipatir Dasye cha Sakhyerjunah
Sarvasyatmanivedane Balirabhat Krishnaptirevampara.

"In hearing was Parikshit; in Kirtan was Vaiyasika (Sukadev, son of Vyasa); in Smarana was Prahlada; in serving the Feet of the Lord was Lakshmi; in worshipping was Prithu; in prostrating, Akrura; in serving, the Lord of the monkeys (Hanuman); in loving Him as a Friend, Arjuna; and in surrendering completely to Him was Bali. Thus the highest attainment of Lord Krishna is to be had."

Just as taking of food brings Tushti (satisfaction), Pushti (nourishment to the body) and cessation of hunger, so also Bhakti brings Vairagya and Jnana.

Have Avyabhicharini Bhakti. It is undivided love. The devotee loves God and God alone. His mind is ever fixed at the Lotus-Feet of the Lord. His whole mind, heart and soul are given to God. This is Avyabhicharini Bhakti.

No development of Prem or Bhakti is possible without right conduct (Sadachara). Just as a disease can be cured by medicine as well as dietetic adjustment, so also realisation of God can be had by devotion and Sadachara. Bhakti is the medicine. Sadachara represents dietetic adjustment or Pathya.

What is Sadachara then? To speak the truth, to practise Ahimsa, not to hurt the feelings of others in thought, word and deed, not to speak harsh words to anyone, not to show any anger towards anybody, not to abuse others or speak ill of others and to see God in all living beings is Sadachara. If you abuse anyone, if you hurt the feelings of others, really you are abusing yourself and hurting the feelings of God only. Himsa (injuring) is a deadly enemy of Bhakti and Jnana. It separates and divides. It stands in the way of realising unity or oneness of Self.

You injure another man on account of ignorance. If you always bear in mind that you see God in every man and animal and that God is seated in the hearts of all living beings, you will not injure anyone. You begin to injure others the moment you forget to see God in others.

Keep a spiritual diary. Note down in the diary when you become angry towards others, when you hurt the feelings of others and so on. This is very important.

Even for a quarter of a second, the time taken for the eyelids to close and open, if your mind does not run away from the Lotus-Feet of the Lord (if your devotion is, in other words, like Taila Dhara) at all times, you will have the whole wealth of all the three worlds at your disposal. The Lord gives you a word of assurance to this effect. He follows such a devotee wherever he goes. He wears the dust of his feet as His Tilaka on His forehead.

Some say that Bhakti should be cultivated in old age when one retires from service and gets pension. This is a serious mistake. Is there any guarantee that you will live to such an old age to discharge your higher responsibility? Has God given you a written document to this effect? Make hay while the sun shines. Winnow the corn while the wind blows. Sow the spiritual seeds when you are young. In old age you will have no strength of body and mind to do rigorous Sadhana.

Kamala and Krishna had no children. They were building castles in the air one night when they were sleeping on a raised bedstead. Kamala asked the husband: "How will you manage for the sleeping place of our son, if I get a child?" Krishna replied: "I will make room on this very wooden cot itself." He moved some inches from his wife. She again asked: "What will you do if I beget a second son?" "I will make room on this very cot itself." He moved actually a few inches further to the edge of the cot. Kamala again asked: "My dear husband, what will you do if I get a third son?" The husband said: "I will make room for him on this very cot." While he was moving to the very end of the cot he tumbled down and fractured his left leg.

In the morning Krishna's neighbour came and asked him: "Krishna what is the matter with your leg?" Krishna replied: "I broke my leg on account of my false son."

Such is the case with the people of this world. They suffer on account of Mithya Abhimana (false identification),

Mithya Ahamkara (false egoism) and Mithya Sambandha (false relationship through body).

That from which this universe has evolved, That in which this universe subsists and That in which this universe involves should be understood as Brahman, Atman or God or Supreme Being.

That in which there is neither East nor West, neither light nor darkness should be understood as Brahman.

The highest end of human existence than gaining which there is no greater gain, than whose bliss there is no greater bliss, than knowing which there is no higher knowledge — that should be understood as Svaroopa or Brahman or God.

A drunkard is not one who drinks liquors, but one who is intoxicated with the pride of wealth, power, position, rank, intelligence and false learning from books and passion. A blind man is not one who is not able to see with these physical eyes, but one who is not able to perceive the One Imperishable Essence "Avinasi Vastu" that is seated equally in all these beings through the inner eye of intuition or Divya Chakshus. A dead man is not one whose Pranas have departed from his physical body, but one who spends his life in eating, drinking and sleeping only and who is not doing worship of God for his liberation. A cobbler is not one who manufactures shoes but one who talks of body and its relations and who has Charma Drishti and *not* Atma Drishti.

There are two ways for attaining God-Consciousness. They are the Pravritti Marga and Nivritti Marga. Pravritti Marga is the path of action or Karma Yoga. Nivritti Marga is the path of renunciation or Jnana Yoga.

Three things are indispensably requisite for attaining Moksha. They are: (1) Guru-Bhakti, devotion towards the spiritual preceptor, (2) Jijnasa, a keen longing for liberation and (3) Satsanga, association with Bhaktas, Sadhus,

Mahatmas and Yogins. He alone who is endowed with these three requisites can cross the ocean of Samsara.

Mark here the importance of Bhakti Yoga

Purushah sa parah Partha bhaktyaa labhyastvananyayaa;
Yasyantahsthani bhutani yena sarvamidam tatam.

"He, the Highest Spirit, O Partha, may be reached by unswerving devotion to Him alone, in Whom all beings abide, by Whom all this is pervaded." (Gita: VIII-22.)

Bhaktya tvananyaya sakya ahamevamvidhorjuna;
Jnatum drashtum cha tattvena praveshtum cha Parantapa.

"But by devotion to Me alone I may thus be perceived, Arjuna, and known and seen in essence, and entered, O Parantapa." (Gita: XI-54.)

Mayyavesya mano ye mam nityayukta upasate;
Sraddhaya parayopetaste me yuktatama matah.

"Those who, fixing their mind on Me, worship Me, ever steadfast and endowed with supreme faith, are the best in Yoga in My opinion." (Gita: XII-2.)

Yoginamapi sarvesham madgatenantaratmana;
Sraddhavan bhajate yo mam sa me yuktatamo matah.

"And among all the Yogins, he who, full of faith, with the inner self abiding in Me, worships Me, he is considered by Me to be the most completely harmonised." (Gita: VI-47.)

Let me say a word on practical Sadhana. The Sastras are endless; there is much to be known; time is short, obstacles are many; That which is the Essence should be grasped, just as the swan does in the case of milk mixed with water.

O Nectar's sons! Wake up. Open your eyes. Grasp the Essence (God). Remember the pains of Samsara. Remember death. Remember the saints. Remember God. Sing His names: *"Hare Rama Hare Rama, Rama Rama Hare Hare; Hare Krishna Hare Krishna, Krishna Krishna Hare Hare."* Cultivate Bhakti. Develop the nine modes of devotion (Nava Vidha Bhakti). Serve Bhagavatas. Feel His Indwelling Presence. everywhere. Have Darshan of Sri Krishna in this very birth, nay this very second. Become a glorious Bhagavata, a Jivanmukta and radiate joy, bliss and peace all around and everywhere. Friends! Let me remind you once more. Forget not even for a second that Flute-Player of Vrindavana, thy Immortal Friend, thy joy, thy solace in life. Repeat always His Mantra 'Om Namo Bhagavate Vaasudevaya.' May the blessings of Sri Krishna be upon us all!

2. Samadhi

The four kinds of Mukti and the Bhava Samadhi of Bhaktas, the lower Samadhis of a Raja Yogi (viz., Savitaraka, Nirvitarka, Savichara, Nirvichara, Saananda, Sasmita, Ritambhara Prajna etc.,) and the lower Savikalpa Samadhis (viz., Sabdanuvid, Dhrisyanuvid) of a Vedantin all lead to the experience of cosmic consciousness. The ways of approach may be different but the fruit is the same. The experiences are common. Intuition, revelation, inspiration, ecstasy are synonymous terms.

Wordsworth in his poem "Tintern Abbey" describes Samadhi as follows:—

"..........That blessed mood,
In which the burthen of the mystery,
In which the heavy and the weary weight
Of all this unintelligible world,
Is lightened:—that serene and blessed mood
In which the affections gently lead us on,
Until, the breath of this corporeal frame
And even the motion of our human blood
Almost suspended, we are laid asleep
In body, and become a living soul:
While with an eye made quiet by the power

Of harmony, and the deep power of joy,
We see into the life of things"

The state of the cosmic consciousness is grand and sublime. It induces awe, supreme joy and highest, unalloyed felicity, free from pain, sorrow and fear. This state of cosmic consciousness is below the absolute consciousness or Nirguna-Brahmic Consciousness wherein the seer, sight and the things seen, or the knower, knowable and knowledge, or the subject and object become one. In cosmic consciousness there is yet the seer and the seen. It is doubtlessly a very subtle experience. It is divine experience. It is revelation of the Karana Jagat wherein the types are realised. Brahmic Consciousness is the experience of Maha-Karana wherein there is neither time, space nor causation. It is unconditioned, ineffable state. Srutis describe it negatively. *Neti, Neti* — not this, not this. "*Yato vacho nivartante aprapya manasa saha anandam brahmano vidvan nabibheti kadachana* — The mind and speech return back from it baffled as they are not able to grasp and describe it; the wise who knows the Brahman which is bliss, is not afraid of anything at any time."

Sri Sankara, Dattatreya, Vama Dev, Jada Bharata, Mansoor, Shams Tabriez, Madalasa, Yajnavalkya had the experience of supercosmic consciousness whereas Rama Das, Tulasi Das, Kabir, Hafiz, Tukaram, Mira, Gauranga, Madhva, Ramanuja, Lord Jesus, Lord Buddha had experience of cosmic consciousness. The pure Brahmic Consciousness is to be felt by the Sadhaka. It cannot be described in words. The language is imperfect. The cosmic consciousness is the experience of Brahma-Loka. It is the consciousness of Brahma or Hiranyagarbha. The Yogi acquires all Divine Aisvaryas. He who experiences cosmic consciousness attains many kinds of Siddhis, which are described in Bhagavata and Raja Yoga of Patanjali Maharshi.

Arjuna, Sanjaya, Yasoda had this experience of cosmic consciousness. Yasoda saw the whole Virat in the mouth of Bala-Krishna. Gita (XI) describes this state of consciousness through the mouth of Arjuna in these words: "Thy mighty form, with many mouths and eyes, long-armed, with thighs and feet innumerable, vast-bosomed, set with many fearful teeth, radiant, Thou touchest heaven, rainbow hued, with opened mouths and shining mouths and shining vast-orbed eyes on every side, all-swallowing, fiery-tongued, Thou lickest up mankind devouring all. Into Thy gaping mouths, they hurrying rush, tremendous-toothed and terrible to see. Some caught within the gaps between Thy teeth, are seen, their heads to powder crushed and ground."

In the West also people have to recognise the truth about cosmic consciousness when one rises above body-consciousness. Some have also tasted and experienced this state. In France, Professor Bergson is preaching about intuition, which transcends reason but does not contradict it. Bucke describes cosmic consciousness as follows: "Cosmic consciousness is a third form, which is as far above self-consciousness as is that above simple consciousness. It is Supraconceptual. The cosmic consciousness as its name implies, is the life and order of the universe. Along with the consciousness of the cosmos there occurs an intellectual enlightenment, which alone would place the individual on a new plane of existence. To this is added a state of moral exaltation, an indescribable feeling of elation and joyousness and a quickening of the moral sense, which is fully as striking and more important, both to the race and the individual, than is the enhanced intellectual power. With these comes what may be called a sense of immortality, a consciousness of eternal life, not a conviction that he shall have it, but the consciousness that he has it already." The eye celestial usually comes to a Yogi (Mystic) who has advanced much in Mysticism. But it is not possible for everyone to get this celestial eye, as each and everyone cannot be a Mystic. Sri Krishna therefore said to Arjuna, "In the Form in which you have seen Me, I cannot be seen even by means of Vedas, by austerities, by gifts or by sacrifices." (Gita: II-53.)

He who gets the experience of supracosmic consciousness has the feeling of Apta-Kama (one who has obtained all that he desires). He feels: "There is nothing more to be known by me."

The Jivahood has gone now. The little 'I' has melted. The differentiating mind that splits up has vanished. All barriers, all sense of duality, differences, separateness have disappeared. There is no idea of time and space. There is only eternity. The Jiva has realised his identity with Brahman. The ideas of caste, creed and colour have gone now. When he becomes a Brahma-Varishtha, when he enters the seventh-stage of Jnana or Turiyatita, even the slight body-consciousness which was in a state of Samskara or mental retentum disappears. He has to be fed by spectators. The world completely disappears for him. He experiences the state described by Ajati-Vadin or the utterance of Srutis "Na cha nana asti kinchana—there is no such thing as diversity."

The world is a mental creation. It is mere impression only. There is no world during sleep. You may argue that the world exists for the waking man. Yes, quite true. If there is mind, there is world. What is mind then? It is a bundle of impressions, ideas, habits. The two currents, Raga-Dvesha, keep up the life of the mind. If these two currents are destroyed, there is death for the mind. It is called Manonasa. That Yogi who has achieved Manonasa cannot perceive the world. If you can consciously destroy the mind through Samadhi, this world disappears. Just as you see the rope only when the Bhranti (illusion) of snake has vanished, so also you see Brahman only when the Bhranti of world and body has disappeared by knowledge of the Self.

My scientists and students of science may not believe me. Do this practice now. Shut yourself up in a room for a week. Cut off all connections. Do not read newspapers. Observe perfect Mauna (silence) also. Then feel how far the impressions of the world remain in your mind. You will feel that the world is a dream. If you practise for a long time, you will realise the truth of my statement. The world is a solid reality for a man of passion and greed, for a sensualist who has gross mind. For a Yogi of cosmic consciousness, it dwindles into an airy nothing.

Cosmic consciousness is the fruit of Chaitanya Samadhi, where the Yogi feels perfect 'awareness', super-sensuous plane of knowledge and intuition. He feels his existence "*Aham Asmi* – I exist", whereas the Jada-Samadhi of a Hatha Yogi cannot bring in this superconscious state. It is something like deep sleep. There is no supersensuous divine knowledge in this state. The breathing stops completely. The Prana is fixed up somewhere in the Muladhara Chakra. Even if you cut his leg, he will not feel any pain. There will be no bleeding. But the Samskaras and Vasanas are not burnt here. Whereas in Brahmic Consciousness, the Vasanas and Samskaras are fried *in toto*. There is Alambana (support for the mind), there is Triputi (triad: knower, knowable, knowledge). There are subtle Samskaras in Savikalpa Samadhi or lower Samadhi. In Nirvikalpa Samadhi, there is neither Alambana nor Triputi nor Samskara. The Jada-Samadhi cannot give liberation. One can enter into Jada-Samadhi without any moral perfection, whereas cosmic consciousness can never be had without ethical perfection. Note this point very carefully.

Absolute fearlessness, desirelessness, thoughtlessness, I-lessness, mine-lessness, angerlessness, Brahmic aura in the face, freedom from Harsha (elation) and Soka (grief) are some of the signs that indicate that the man has reached the state of superconsciouness. He is also always in a state of perfect bliss. You can never see anger, depression, cheerlessness, sorrow in his face. You will find elevation, joy and peace in his presence.

Just as a drunken man is not conscious whether he has cloth on his body or not, when it is in a state of dropping down on the ground, so also the Yogi who is experiencing supracosmic consciousness is not conscious of his body. A Jivanmukta who is in the fourth Bhumika will have slight consciousness of his body in the form of a Samskara or mental retentum.

Just as a man doubts whether his old rotten shoe is clinging to his foot or not when he is sometimes absent-minded, so also the Jivanmukta doubts whether his body is hanging like an old rotten shoe or not. That Sannyasi or an Avadhoota who fully rests in Brahman and has no idea at all of the slightest difference between a male and female, is entitled to throw off his Kowpeen altogether. That Kowpeen also will drop by itself.

He who is naked should not live in an Ashram, a town, or a village. He should roam about unknown, not caring for good or bad and cast off his body as a slough on a dunghill or dilapidated house. So says Narada-Parivrajaka Upanishad. To live naked in an Ashram, but to have all sorts of comforts, to have disciples and to take interest in the development of the Ashram does not look nice. It does not appeal to some sections of people at least. That Sannyasin or Mahatma who wants or keeps something for his body in an Ashram can wear also a small cloth along with his Kowpeen. This will not go against his realisation or Jivanmukti. Physical nudity alone will not constitute real Tyaga. Some persons study the description of a Jnani in the seventh Bhumika in Vivekachudamani or Yoga Vasishtha and try to imitate this external state without having any internal development or attainment of that highest state of consciousness. This is a mistake. This is hypocrisy. Some Sannyasins falsely assume the state of Brahma Varishtha. They like to be fed by young ladies.

In Uttarkashi in the Himalayas a young man heard the Katha of Yoga Vasishtha from Swami Deva Giri wherein there was a description of a Jnani of seventh state of Jnana. This young man gave up at once food for 15 days, began to pass motions and urine in his room and imagined that he was in the seventh stage of Jnana. An intelligent neighbour applied a plant called *Bitchu-Katta* to his body which produced severe pain like scorpion-sting. He yelled out like anything and came back to his senses. He went to the Kshetra as usual for taking alms. Is this not hypocrisy? His internal mental state has not reached the highest zenith of Brahmic consciousness. It remained in a raw, crude, unpolished state, though he externally put on the state of Paramahamsa who dwells in the absolute consciousness.

You will find in Kumbha Mela at Haridwar batches of Naga Sadhus, young boys marching in procession in a nude state. Are these boys Jitendriya Yogins? Is this not hypocrisy? Hypocrisy takes various forms. One should fully understand the subtle ways and workings of the mind. Mind is Maya.

If you take camphor or Haritaki or Nux Vomica seed for some time, you will lose your power of erection in the generative organ. This does not mean that you are a Jitendriya Yogi. There are some expert old men who give a twist to the spermatic cord and thereby paralyse the nerve-erigens that cause erection of the organ. The mind remains in the same state. Passion is the same. Real Sannyasa is internal, mental nudity. The mind is absolutely free from Vasanas and Samskaras. This is the real Avadhoota state.

You cannot find the symptoms and signs of cosmic

consciousness in these pseudo-Samadhists who have recently cropped up in these days and who have shut themselves up in underground rooms. If you take the seeds of *Apamarga* (*Nayurivi* in Tamil), you will be free from hunger and thirst. The use of the Apamarga seeds for destroying hunger and thirst is as follows: These seeds have seven subtle skins or outer husks. Dry them in the sun and rub them on the hands. Take ⅛th of a seer of this seed. Make Kheer of this seed with milk and sugar and drink. Take a purgative to start with. Live on milk for two days. Take an enema also. All old faecal matter should be evacuated. You will have pleasant sensations and feelings of joy. There will be neither hunger nor thirst. There are two varieties of Apamarga seeds. The red one is better.

There is another plant or grass that is obtainable on the way to Kailas. It grows on rocks. You will have to pluck this before sunrise. You can be free from hunger for six months. The pseudo-Samadhists use these seeds and roots. When they come out of the room they are the same persons with worldly Vasanas and Samskaras. They are talkative and Rajasic.

Yogi Ramacharaka writes about cosmic consciousness in his book Raja Yoga as follows: "There is a stage still higher than this last mentioned, but it has come to but very few of the race. Reports of it come from all times, races, countries. It has been called 'Cosmic Consciousness' and is described as an awareness of the Oneness of Life — that is, a consciousness that the Universe is filled with one Life, an actual perception and 'awareness' that the Universe is full of life, motion and mind, and that there is no such thing as Blind Force or Dead Matter, but that all is alive, vibrating and intelligent. That is, of course, that the Real Universe, which is the Essence or Background of the Universe of Matter, Energy and Mind, is as they describe. In fact, the description of those who have had glimpses of this state

PRACTICE OF BHAKTI YOGA

would indicate that they see the Universe as All-Mind – that all is Mind at the last. This form of consciousness has been experienced by men here and there – only a few – in moments of 'Illumination,' the period lasting but a very short space of time, then fading away, leaving but a memory. In the moment of 'Illumination', there came to those experiencing it a sense of 'in-touchness' with Universal Knowledge and Life, impossible to describe, accompanied by a joy beyond understanding.

"Regarding this last, 'Cosmic Consciousness' we would state that it means more than an intellectual conviction, belief or realisation of the facts as stated, for an actual vision and consciousness of these things came in the moment of illumination. Some others report that they have a deep abiding sense of reality of the facts described by the report of the Illumined, but have not experienced the 'vision' or ecstasy referred to. These last people seem to have with them always the same mental state as that possessed by those who had the 'vision' and passed out of it, carrying with them the remembrance and feeling, but not the actual consciousness attained at the moment. They agree upon the essential particulars of the reports. Dr. Maurice Bucke, now passed out of this plane of life, wrote a book entitled 'Cosmic Consciousness' in which he describes a number of these cases, including his own, Walt Whitman's and others, and in which he holds that this stage of consciousness is before the race and will gradually come to it in the future. He holds that the manifestation of it which has come to some few of the race, as above stated, is but the first beams of the sun which are flashing upon us and which are but prophesies of the appearance of the great body of light itself.

"We shall not here consider at length the reports of certain great religious personages of the past, who have left records that in moments of great spiritual exaltation they became conscious of 'being in the presence of the Absolute' or perhaps within the radius of 'the light of Its countenance.' We have great respect for these reports and have every reason for believing many of them authentic, notwithstanding the conflicting reports that have been handed down to us by those experiencing them. These reports are conflicting because of the fact that the minds of those who had these glimpses of consciousness were not prepared or trained to fully understand the nature of the phenomena. They found themselves in the spiritual presence of something of awful grandeur and spiritual rank and were completely dazed and bewildered at the sight. They did not understand the nature of the Absolute and when they had sufficiently recovered they reported that they had been in the 'presence of God,' the word 'God' meaning their particular conception of Deity — that is, the one appearing as Deity in their own particular religious creed or school. They saw nothing to cause them to identify this something with their particular conception of Deity, except that they thought that 'it must be God' and knowing no other God except their own particular conception, they naturally identified the Something with 'God' as they conceived Him to be. And their reports naturally were along these lines.

"Thus the reports of all religions are filled with accounts of the so-called miraculous occurrences. The Catholic saint reports that he 'saw the light of God's countenance,' and the non-Catholic reports likewise regarding God as he knows Him. The Mohammedan reports that he caught a glimpse of the face of Allah and the Buddhist tells us that he saw Buddha under the Tree. The Brahmin has seen the face of Brahma, and the various Hindu sects have men who give similar reports regarding their own particular deities. The Persians have given similar reports and even the ancient Egyptians have left records of similar occurrences. These conflicting reports have led to the belief, on the part of

PRACTICE OF BHAKTI YOGA

those who did not understand the nature of the phenomenon, that these things were 'all imagination' and fancy, if indeed not rank falsehood and imposture. But the Yogis know better than this. They know that underneath all these varying reports there is a common ground of truth, which will be apparent to anyone investigating the matter. They know that all of these reports (except a few based upon fraudulent imitations of the real phenomenon) are based upon truth and are but the bewildered reports of the various observers. They know that these people were temporarily lifted above the ordinary plane of consciousness and were made aware of the existence of a Being or Beings higher than mortal. It does not follow that they saw 'God' or the Absolute, for there are many beings of high spiritual growth and development that would appear to the ordinary mortal as a very God. The Catholic doctrine of Angels and Archangels is corroborated by those among the Yogis who have been 'behind the veil' and they give us reports of the 'Devas' and other advanced Beings. So the Yogi accepts these reports of the various mystics, saints and inspired ones, and accounts for them all by laws perfectly natural to the students of the Yoga philosophy, but which appear as supernatural to those who have not studied along these lines.

"But we cannot speak further of this phase of the subject in this lesson, for a full discussion of it would lead us far away from the phase of the general subject before us. But we wish to be understood as saying that there are certain centres in the mental being of man from which may come light regarding the existence of the Absolute and higher order of Beings. In fact, from these centres comes to man that part of his mental 'feelings' that he calls 'the religious instinct or intuition.' Man does not arrive at that underlying consciousness of 'Something Beyond' by means of his Intellect — it is the glimmer of light coming from the higher centres of the Self. He notices these gleams of light, but not understanding them, he proceeds to erect elaborate theological and creedal structures to account for them, the work of the Intellect, however, always lacking that 'feeling' that the intuition itself possesses. True religion, no matter under what name it may masquerade, comes from the 'heart' and is not comforted or satisfied with these Intellectual explanations, and hence comes that unrest and craving for satisfaction which comes to man when the light begins to break through.

"Miss Laurie Pratt of America writes about an experience in cosmic consciousness in 'The Hindu Mind' as follows: 'The Hindus have written much on cosmic consciousness but in the West this subject is much less known. However, those who have read Doctor Bucke's 'Cosmic Consciousness' and Edward Carpenter's 'Towards Democracy' know that these authors believe that cosmic consciousness is a natural faculty of man, and that a future race of men on this earth will be born with this faculty well developed and not merely latent as it is now. Bucke's theory is that just as man advanced from the state of simple consciousness, which he shared with the animal kingdom, into a state of Self-consciousness peculiar to man alone and marked by the development of language, so he must inevitably come into a higher state of consciousness, distinguished by a cosmic or universal understanding.

"Bucke maintains that the increasing number of people who have attained some degree of cosmic consciousness in the past few centuries is proof that these persons constitute the vanguard or forerunners of the new race. Among those in the West whom Bucke believes to have had the cosmic sense more or less well developed (in recent centuries) are St. John of the Cross, Francis Bacon, Jacob Boehme, Blaise Pascal, Spinosa, Swedenborg, William Wordsworth, Alexander Pushkin, Honore de Balzac, Emerson, Tennyson,

Thoreau, Walt Whitman and Edward Carpenter. He also mentions Ramakrishna as a Hindu example.

"Besides these famous men, it is doubtlessly true that many hundreds of men and women in each century, unknown to fame, have been exalted to some degree of cosmic consciousness. There is no doubt in my mind that the message brought to America by Hindu teachers in recent years has been the means by which hundreds and perhaps thousands of Americans have achieved, through the meditation practices taught them, a glimpse of divine consciousness. Some few students have gone further, and attained very high illumination. Here we have an example of how the cosmic sense is being developed in larger and larger numbers paving the way for the great race of the future.

"One Paragraph from Bucke's books is well worth quoting here: 'In contact with the flux of Cosmic Consciousness all religions known and named today will be melted down. The human soul will be revolutionised. Religion will absolutely dominate the race. It will not depend on tradition. It will be believed and disbelieved. It will not be a part of life, belonging to certain hours, times and occasions. It will not be in sacred books nor in the mouths of priests. It will not dwell in churches, meetings, forms and days. Its life will not be in prayers, hymns nor discourses. It will not depend on special revelations, on the words of gods who came down to teach, nor on any Bible or Bibles. It will have no mission to save men from their sins nor to secure them entrance to heaven. It will not teach a future immortality nor future glories, for immortality and all glory will exist in the here and now.

"The evidence of immortality will live in every heart as sight in every eye. Doubts of God and of eternal life will be as impossible as is now doubt of existence; the evidence of each will be the same. Religion will govern every minute of every day of all life. Churches, priests, forms, creeds, prayers, all agents, all intermediaries between the individual man and God will be permanently replaced by direct unmistakable interaction. Sin will no longer exist nor will salvation be desired. Men will not worry about death or a future, about the kingdom of heaven, about what may come with and after the cessation of the life of the present body. Each soul will feel and know itself to be immortal, will feel and know that the entire universe with all its good and with all its beauty is for it and belongs to it forever. The world peopled by men possessing Cosmic Consciousness will be as far removed from the world of today as this is from the world as it was before the advent of self-consciousness. This new race is in the act of being born from us and in the near future it will occupy and possess the earth.

A Definite Way to Contact God

"The fact that there is a technique such as Yoga practices, whereby Cosmic Consciousness can be attained is in itself proof that higher sense is indeed an inherent faculty of all men, needing but the necessary training to call it forth. Most people believe that divine Knowledge comes to only a few chosen people, and that the average man can approach no nearer to God than his 'faith' will take him. Realisation that there is a definite way to contact God, a technique usable by all men in all circumstances, has come with such a liberating shock to students of Hindu spiritual science that they feel they have undergone a new birth.

"I have one such case in mind. An American man who, as soon as he had heard the Yogoda Message brought to America by Swami Yogananda of India was swept up into Cosmic Consciousness. This student was possessed of intense religious faith and aspiration. Though well read in the sacred scriptures of the world, especially those of the Hindus, he knew that this intellectual knowledge was barren and stony; it did not feed the soul-hunger within him. He did not wish merely to read about spiritual food, but to taste it. Under the even tenor of his days there yawned a black abyss of despair — despair that he was worthy of any direct contact with God, since no such experience was given him. He finally came to doubt not God, but the possibility that he would ever be able to have more than an intellectual comprehension of Him. This conviction struck at the roots of his life and made it seem a worthless and meaningless thing.

"Into this dark night of his soul came a dazzling light brought by the teacher from India. The student felt the heavy weight of despair lifting from his heart. Returning to his home one night from the last of the public lectures, he was conscious of a great peace within himself. He felt that in some deep fundamental way he had become a different person. An impulse urged him to look into a mirror in his room, that he might see the new man. There he saw not his own face, but the face of the Hindu teacher whose lecture he had attended that evening.

"The flood-gate of joy broke in his soul; he was inundated with waves of indescribable ecstasy. Words that had been merely words to him before — bliss, immortality, eternity, truth, divine love — became, in the twinkling of an eye, the core of his being, the essence of his life, the only possible reality. Realisation that these deep, everlasting founts of joy existed in every heart, that this immortal life underlay all the mortality of humanity, that this eternal, all-inclusive love enveloped and supported and guided every particle, every atom of creation burst upon him with a surety and divine certainty that caused his whole being to pour forth in a flood of praise and gratitude.

"He knew, not with his mind alone, but with his heart and soul, with every cell and molecule of his body. The sublime splendour and joy of this discovery were so vast that he felt that centuries, millenniums, countless aeons of suffering were as nothing, as less than nothing, if by such means that bliss could be obtained. Sin, sorrow, death — these were but words now, words without meaning, words swallowed up by joy as minnows by the seven seas.

Physiological Changes

"He was aware, during this first period of illumination and during the months which followed, of a number of physiological changes within himself. The most striking was what seemed a rearrangement of molecule structure in his brain or the opening up of new cell-territory there. Ceaselessly, day and night, he was conscious of this work going on. It seemed as though a kind of electrical drill was boring out new cellular thought-channels. This phenomenon is strong proof of Bucke's theory that cosmic consciousness is a natural faculty of man, for it gives evidence that the brain-cells which are connected with this faculty are already present in man, although inactive or non-functioning in the majority of human beings at the present time.

"Another important change was felt in his spinal column. The whole spine seemed turned into iron for several months, so that, when he sat to meditate on God, he felt anchored forever, able to sit in one place eternally without motion or consciousness of any bodily function. At times an influx of superhuman strength invaded him and he felt that he was carrying the whole universe on his shoulders. The elixir of life, the nectar of immortality, he felt flowing in his veins as an actual, tangible force. It seemed like a quicksilver or a sort of electrical, fluid light throughout his body.

The 'Everlasting Arms'

"During the months of his illumination, he felt no need of food or sleep. But he conformed his outward life to the pattern of his household, and ate and slept when his family did. All food seemed pure spirit to him, and in sleep he was pillowed on the 'Everlasting arms', awakening to a joy past all words, past all powers of description.

"He had previously suffered from heavy colds and had been a constant smoker; now his body was purged of sickness, and desire for cigarettes was wiped completely from his consciousness. His family and friends were aware of a great change in his appearance and manner; his face shone with a radiant light; his eyes were pools of joy. Strangers spoke to him irresistibly drawn by a strange sympathy; on the streetcar, children would come over to sit on his lap, asking him to visit them.

"The whole universe was to him bathed in a sea of love; he said to himself many times: 'Now at last I know what love is! This is God's love, shaming the noblest human affection. Eternal love, unconquerable love, all-satisfying love!' He knew beyond all possibility or thought of doubt that love creates and sustains the universe, and that all created things human or subhuman, were destined to discover this Love, this immortal bliss that is the very essence of life. He felt his mind expand, his understanding reach out, endlessly widening, growing, touching everything in the Universe, binding all things, all thoughts to himself. He was 'centre everywhere, circumference nowhere.'

The Atom-Dance of Nature

"The air that he breathed was friendly, intimate, conscious of life. He felt that all the world was 'home' to him, that he could never feel strange of alien to any place again; that the mountains, the sea, the distant lands which he had never seen, would be as much his own as the home of his boyhood. Everywhere he looked, he saw the 'atom-dance' of nature; the air was filled with myriad moving pinpricks of light.

"During these months, he went about his daily duties as usual, but with a hitherto unknown efficiency and speed. He was a student at college during this period, and passed all his examinations without looking at a textbook. His mind was bathed in a sea of Knowledge. Typed papers flew off his machine, complete without error in a fourth of his customary time. Fatigue was unknown to him; his work seemed like child's play, happy and careless. Conversing in person or over the telephone on any business, his inward joy covered every action and circumstance with a cosmic significance, for to him this telephone, this table, this voice was God, God manifesting Himself in another of His fascinating disguise.

Unutterable Gratitude

"In the midst of his work, he would suddenly be freshly overwhelmed by the goodness of God who had given him this incredible, unspeakable happiness. His breath would stop completely at such times; the awe which he felt would be accompanied by an absolute stillness within and without. Time and space were swallowed up, gone without trace like all unreality. Underlying all his consciousness was a sense of immeasurable and unutterable gratitude; a longing for others to know the joy which lay within them; but most of all, a divine knowledge, past all human comprehension, that all was well with the world, that everything was leading to the goal of Cosmic Consciousness, immortal bliss.

"He can well imagine, with Doctor Bucke that a race of men possessing as a normal and permanent faculty this sense of Cosmic Consciousness would soon turn the earth into a Paradise, a planet fit for Christs and Buddhas, and a polestar for the wheeling universe."

In the Upanishads he who has experience in Cosmic Consciousness is called 'Sarva-Vit' i.e., one who knows everything in detail. May we all attain the state of Cosmic Consciousness, our birthright, centre, ideal and goal.

3. Upadesamritam

1. Enquire "Who am I?" and realise the Self.

2. Make friendship with anyone after studying him very carefully.

3. After you have made friendship with anyone, never break it till the end of life.

4. Don't do wrong actions to gain something.

5. Don't speak harsh words.

6. Desire fervently to do righteous deeds.

7. Do always virtuous actions.

8. Control anger by forgiveness, patience and Vichara.

9. Don't prevent anyone from doing charity.

10. Parents are visible gods on earth.

11. Therefore respect, serve and protect your parents.

12. Don't harm others.

13. Hear the wise words of great souls and follow them.

14. Don't rob the wealth of others.

15. Do those actions that are pronounced to be right by the Sastras.

16. Remove Ajnana by getting Atma-Jnana.

17. Be in the company of sages.

18. Don't make friendship with childish persons.

19. Move with the world tactfully. Adapt.

20. Don't believe your enemies.

21. Follow the instructions of sages and the Sastras.

22. Give up bad company.

23. Don't eat much.

24. Don't talk much before great souls.

25. Don't be partial.

26. Become a Sattvic, noble man.

27. Tread the path of Truth or Moksha.

28. When you talk, don't omit anything.

29. Take some notes and talk freely.

30. Do daily Svadhyaya (study of religious books).

31. Avoid unnecessary discussions.

32. Don't brag or self-glorify.

33. Control desires.

34. Don't exaggerate or concoct or twist when you talk.

35. Begging is deplorable; begging is practical death.

36. Persevere. Be patient.

37. *Nil desperandum* (never despair).

38. Be grateful to that man who has helped you.

39. Learn when you are young.

40. Don't sleep too much (sleep maximum six hours).

41. Protect creatures or dumb animals.

42. Don't kill.

43. Become a vegetarian.

44. Feed another and then eat.

45. Share what you have with others.

46. Don't perform mean acts.

47. Develop Udarata (nobility or large heart).

48. Develop mercy and cosmic love.

49. Don't gamble.

50. Develop Sattvic virtues.

51. Don't speak anything that will provoke another's anger.

52. Whatever work you do, do it thoroughly.

53. Protect those who take shelter under you.

54. Till the fields and eat.

55. Take care of your health.

56. Observe the laws of hygiene and health.

57. Don't speak words despicable to wise men.

58. Walk with determination in the path of Righteousness.

59. Pray and meditate between 4 to 6 a.m. and 8 to 9 p.m.

60. Don't visit the houses of prostitutes.

61. Don't go to law courts.

62. Don't get discouraged under any circumstance whatsoever.

63. Talk distinctly with force and emphasis.

64. Speak truth only always.

65. Don't indulge in idle talk.

66. Don't do any action harmful to any one.

67. Think thrice before you do any action.

68. Don't eat too many sweetmeats.

69. Don't indulge in the use of intoxicants and liquors.

70. Take care of your property.

71. Don't attend cinemas.

72. Give up fashion.

73. Lead a simple, pious life.

74. Don't follow the evil advice of your wife.

75. Don't fight.

76. Don't blaspheme.

77. Develop far-sightedness.

78. Don't do sinful actions.

79. Do daily charity.

80. Worship God.

81. Keep daily memorandum note-book for jotting down.

82. Keep a daily spiritual diary.

83. Have a definite aim and ideal in life.

84. Discipline the Indriyas.

85. Take daily exercise.

86. Control breath.

87. Do selfless service in society.

88. Cultivate Sraddha and Bhakti.

89. Relieve the pains of others.

90. Give up pride, hypocrisy and cunningness.
91. Don't talk about your possessions.
92. Praise others always.
93. Talk by directly looking at another's face.
94. Observe Mauna daily for 2 hours.
95. Preserve Veerya.
96. Serve Mahatmas with devotion.
97. The world is unreal.
98. Give up back-biting and fault-finding.
99. Lead a life of contentment.
100. Control mind.
101. Seek happiness within.
102. Give up attachment, "I-ness" and "mine-ness".
103. Treat respect and honour as dung and poison.
104. Remember God at all times.
105. See God in all faces and objects.
106. Learn to discriminate.
107. Get knowledge of Self.
108. Rest in your Satchidananda Svaroopa.

Go through these instructions carefully with one-pointed mind daily in the morning and live in the spirit of these instructions. This contains the essence of all Sadhana, the essence of four Vedas. Here is an inexhaustible spiritual wealth. Here is a spiritual treasure, which no dacoits can plunder. The unemployment problem is solved now. The miseries of the world are removed now. You will have a glorious and brilliant life, which is ineffable. You will have neither wants nor desires, neither torments nor anxieties, neither worries nor fear. You will attain immortality and everlasting bliss if you strictly adhere to these instructions. Become a practical Yogi. This is what I expect of you. This is the spiritual fee. This is the remuneration for the spiritual doctor who takes care not only of your physical body but of your mind and soul also. Dive deep and enjoy the spiritual bliss. Farewell Friends! Peace be with you all!

Epilogue

Na dhanam na jnanam sundarim
Kavitam va jagadeesa kamaye
Mama janmani janmaneeshvare
Bavatat bhaktirahaitukee tvayi

"I crave not for money, nor for wisdom, nor for a beautiful woman, nor for poetic genius, O Lord of the world; in every birth of mine may Ahaituki Bhakti (spontaneous devotion), grow in me towards Thee, O Lord."

These are the words of Sri Chaitanya Mahaprabhu. Repeat this mentally at all times with meaning. This will produce in you true devotion, Vairagya to sensual objects and perfect self-surrender.

Dear friends, I have to point out to you that *"Anantasastram bahu veditavyam, Svalpascha kalo bahavascha vighnah, Yat sarabhutam tadupasitavyam, Hamso yatha ksheeramivambumisram.* The Sastras are endless; there is much to be known; time is short, obstacles are many; that which is essence should be grasped, just as the swan does in the case of milk mixed with water."

That essence is Prem. Prem is the only Sara-vastu in this world. Drink this essence. Taste this honey of devotion. Drink this nectar of Immortality and attain the everlasting abode of peace and immortality which was attained by Tukaram, Tulasidas, Ramdas, Mira, Kabir, Prahlada and Dhruva of yore.

May the fire of devotion grow brighter in you all. May Lord Krishna bestow on you spiritual strength to control the Indriyas and the restless mind! May the blessings of Bhagavatas be upon you!

Chapter VII

BHAKTI SUTRAS OF NARADA

1.The Nature of Divine Love

Salutation to Para Brahman and Rishi Narada!

अथातो भक्तिं व्याख्यास्यामः ॥१

Athaato bhaktim vyakhyasyamah. (1)

Now, we will explain Bhakti.

Notes and Commentary

Atha means now. It is something used in the sense of sequence. It is a word that is used when a subject is begun, to invoke the Divine blessing. *Sutra* means an aphorism or terse saying impregnated with deep significance. Just as flowers and pearls are arranged or studded on a thread, so also philosophical ideas´ are studded or spread or arranged in the aphorism. Rishis always have expressed their ideas in the form of laconic Sutras. That is the beauty in the writings of Rishis or seers. That is the sign of God-realisation. The six *Darsanas* or schools of philosophy are embodied in the form of Sutras only. Without a commentary it is difficult for laymen to understand these Sutras.

Bhakti is defined in the following Sutra. Those who have understood the magnitude of human sufferings in this sense-universe and those who have realised that this world is unreal, impermanent, illusory, perishable, full of troubles, difficulties, miseries, pain, sorrow and tribulation and those who desire to free themselves from the round of births and deaths with its concomitant evils of old age, diseases, etc., should know what Bhakti is, how to develop Bhakti, who is God or Lord or Isvara, the relationship between God and

man and the methods to realise God, or to approach Him or
to attain God-Consciousness.

2. Definition of Bhakti

सा त्वस्मिन् परमप्रेमरूपा ॥२

Saa tvasmin paramapremaroopaa. (2)

It is of the form of Supreme Love towards God.

Notes and Commentary

The term *Bhakti* comes from the root "Bhaj", which
means "to be attached to God." *Bhajan,* worship, *Bhakti,
Anurag, Prem, Priti* are synonymous terms. Bhakti is love for
love's sake. The devotee wants God and God alone. There
is no selfish expectation here. There is no fear also.
Therefore it is called *"Parama-prema-rupaa."* Is the son
afraid of his father, who is a Sessions Judge? Is the wife
afraid of her husband? So also a devotee entertains not the
least fear of God. The fear of retribution vanishes in him.
He feels, believes, conceives and imagines that his *Ishtam* is
an Ocean of Love or Prem.

अमृतस्वरूपा च ॥३

Amritasvaroopa cha. (3)

And it is of the nature of Nectar.

Notes and Commentary

God, Immortality (Amritam), peace (Santi), Absolute,
Infinite (Ananda), Intelligence, Consciousness (Chit),
Eternity, Bliss (Ananda), Nirvana, Freedom (Mukti),
Perfection (Siddhi), are synonymous terms.

Devotion gives Immortality. Bhakti is an embodiment of
Amritam or nectar. Nitya Sukha (eternal bliss), Immortality,
Parama Santi (supreme peace), Nitya Tripti (eternal
satisfaction), Akhanda Sukha (unbroken joy) can be had
only in God. That is the reason why aspirants attempt for
God-realisation. Worldly pleasure is not constant. He who

smiles and laughs for five minutes weeps bitterly for hours together. No man in this world is perfectly happy. A multimillionaire is full of cares, worries, anxieties and fear. He is afraid of enemies. He is guarded by sepoys. He has to take injections for getting sleep, as he is always worried. He is worse than a prisoner. Rockfeller, the richest man in the world, who could pave a road of several miles with golden sheets expressed to a priest who went to behold his glory and opulence: "O reverend priest! I am the most miserable man in the world. I can't eat anything; my stomach, kidneys and liver are filled with germs and diseases. I am always restless". Maitreyi puts a question to her husband: "O my Lord! Can the wealth of the three worlds give me immortality?" Yajnavalkya replied: "Certainly not, my beloved." Yama also says to Nachiketas: "Wealthy people, on account of delusion and pride, lose their memory, intellect and understanding, and go round and round in this impermanent and unhappy world and come again and again in my clutches. Wealth and woman are my two snares to entrap the worldly-minded persons whose minds are filled with lust and greed. You are above these things. You have shunned all my temptations. You have selected the Sreyo-Marga".

This is a world of diversity. Intellects are different. Faces are different. Religions are different. Sounds are different. Faiths are different. Colours are different. Faculties are different. Tastes and temperaments are different. But one thing is common in all. Every one of us wants Nitya Sukha (eternal happiness), infinite Knowledge, Immortality, freedom and independence. These things can be obtained by God-realisation alone.

3. Fruits of Bhakti

यल्लब्ध्वा पुमान् सिद्धो भवति, अमृतो भवति, तृप्तो भवति ॥४

PRACTICE OF BHAKTI YOGA

Yallabdhva puman siddho bhavati, amrito bhavati,
tripto bhavati. (4)

By attaining which man becomes perfect, immortal and fully contented.

Notes and Commentary

These are the fruits of Bhakti. Sutras 4, 5 and 6 describe the fruits of Bhakti. All weaknesses and *Doshas* (faults) vanish. People put a question: "How can we love God whom we have not seen?" Remain in the company of Bhaktas; hear the Lilas of Bhagavan, His Aisvaryas (Divine powers) or Vibhutis, His Madhurya (grace and beauty); serve Bhaktas; sing His Name daily and do Japa of His Mantra; stay for one year in Ayodhya, Vrindavana, Chitrakuta, Rishikesh or Pandharpur. You will develop love for God.

यत्राप्य न किञ्चिद्वाञ्छति, न शोचति, न द्वेष्टि,
न रमते, नोत्साही भवति ॥५॥

Yat prapya na kinchid vanchati, na sochati, na dveshti,
na ramate, notsaahee bhavati. (5)

By obtaining which he does not desire anything, neither grieves nor hates anything, does not indulge in sensual pleasures, nor becomes zealous (in endeavours for self-advancement or self-aggrandisement).

Notes and Commentary

Why does desire manifest? On account of Aidya or ignorance or imperfection or lack of bliss. When one gets Darshan of God, all desires are burnt up. When the boy Dhruva had Darshan of Lord Hari, the desire to obtain kingdom that prompted him to worship, disappeared. Devotion is a fire like *Jnanagni* (fire of wisdom) that burns up all mundane desires.

How can a trace of earthly desire remain when the devotee attains God, the embodiment of bliss? Darshan of God comes in various ways viz., in dreams, in physical form with four hands, with conch, mace, discus and lotus-flower in the hands, in the form of cosmic consciousness (Visvarupa Darshan) which Arjuna had, in the form of Hiranyagarbha consciousness or full knowledge of Brahma-loka, etc. Note how Arjuna expresses his experiences of cosmic consciousness: "Nor source, nor midst, nor end; infinite force, unnumbered arms, the sun and moon Thine eyes; I see Thy face, as sacrificial fire, blazing, its splendour burneth up the worlds." God sometimes gives Darshan to encourage His devotees by coming down in Vimana (or celestial car). Akasa Vani, dazzling lights in space or sky are some other encouragements which God gives to push His devotees on the path vigorously and rapidly. The devotee should not stop his Sadhana on account of false *Tushti* (satisfaction) when he gets His Darshan. He should ever rest in God. He should have perfect *Nishtha* in God always (Svaroopa-sthiti). He should not leave off his practices till he merges himself in the Lord — *Maha-Bhava* or *Tanmaya* State (Parama Prem).

The devotee who realises God is freed from grief also. Can darkness remain in the presence of light? How can sorrow manifest when one is immersed in the Ocean of Bliss and Prem? Grief is a mental creation. It manifests when the mind is attached to body and illusory connections. When the mind is obliterated, when there is Self-absorption and self-effacement by merging in the bosom of God, how can grief approach the devotee? Absolutely impossible. The devotee does not hate anything. Hatred is due to ignorance. How can the devotee hate anybody when he sees Lord Hari in everything? He feels that the world is manifestation of the Lord and all movements and actions are His Lilas. He has no *Ghrina* or dislike for faecal matter, dirt, Chandala, scavenger, cobbler, beggar, prostitute, thief, etc. He says: "I see everywhere my sweet Lord. It is Hari who is playing the part of prostitute, thief, dacoit, scavenger". He has an all-embracing, all-inclusive, exalted mental state. This cannot be adequately described in words. It has to be felt. Mira, Gouranga, Hafiz, Tulasi Das, Kabir, Ram Das all enjoyed this state. Tulasi Das says: *"Shiyaram maya sab jaga jane, karahu pranam jory juge pani* — Know everything as Siyaram, Sita and Rama, and with folded hands do prostrations to all, to everything."

In Purusha Sukta you will find a description of the Purusha: "The Purusha has one thousand heads, one thousand eyes, one thousand feet." There is an echo of these ideas in the Gita (XIII-13): "With hands and feet everywhere, with eyes, heads and mouths everywhere, with ears everywhere, He exists in the worlds enveloping all". Lord Krishna gives advice to Uddhava and prescribes an easy way for reaching Him. "Know, Uddhava, that Brahmin, Chandala, ass, dog, king, beggar are all My forms. When you meet any object, do prostration and feel My presence". Nama Dev said to the dog: "O Vittala, my dear in the form of dog, do not run away with the dry bread. It will affect your soft throat. Pray, let me apply ghee to the bread". He ran with ghee in a cup to the dog. Sri Ramakrishna Paramahamsa prostrated before an outcaste girl: "O Mother Kaali! I see Thee in this girl." Pavhari Baba prostrated before a thief with a bag of utensils: "O thief Narayan! Pray, accept these things, I never knew that thief Narayan was in my cottage". Eknath, a Maharashtra Bhakta gave his ring voluntarily to a thief when he entered the house: "O thief! Take this ring also. Your *kartavya* (duty) is to steal the things. Thou art Vittala (Krishna). Keep up this *Lila*." Have you understood the sublime state of these exalted Bhaktas who have a new angle of vision? A day will come to you also. Exert. Struggle. Pray. Worship. Meditate. Plunge yourself in Bhajan with zeal, earnestness and fervour.

Give up this unquenchable thirst for sensual pleasure, woman, money and worldly prosperity which is the greatest obstacle in the path of devotion and turn your mind towards God. Here is an inexhaustible and imperishable spiritual wealth which no dacoit can rob and a Divine Bliss which is not mixed with fear or pain.

यज्ज्ञात्वा मत्तो भवति, स्तब्धो भवति, आत्मारामो भवति ॥६

Yajjnatva matto bhavati, stabdho bhavati,
atmaramo bhavati. (6)

By knowing which he becomes ecstatic (with overjoy), quiet, and happy in his own Self.

Notes and Commentary

When one is happy in his own Self, then alone he becomes independent. If one depends for his happiness on perishable objects, he begins to weep when the centre of his pleasure is withdrawn. The husband weeps when his wife or son dies, when the bank in which he has deposited his money fails. Objects that are conditioned in time, space and causation are *vinasi,* perishable. They cannot give, therefore, eternal happiness to human beings. So in the Gita, Bhagavan Sri Krishna says: "The enjoyments that are born of contacts are only generators of pain, for they have a beginning and an end, O Kaunteya! The wise man does not rejoice in them." (Gita: V-22.) "That happiness which arises from the contact of the sense-organs with the objects, which is at first like nectar, and in the end like poison—*Agre amritopamam pariname vishamiva*" (Gita: XVIII-38.) "With the self unattached to external contacts he finds happiness in the Self; with the self engaged in the meditation of Brahman he attains to the endless happiness." (Gita: V-21.) "The man who rejoices only in the Self, who is satisfied with the Self and who is content in the Self alone, for him verily there is nothing to do." (Gita: III-17.) Nothing can shake a man who rejoices in the Self *(Atmarati)*; who is satisfied in the Self *(Atma Tripti);* and who is contented in the Self *(Atma Santoshi);* and who plays in the Self *(Atma Kreeda).*

It is *Vasana* (subtle desire) that draws a man outside towards external objects. *Avidya* (ignorance) has got two forces, the *Avarana* or veiling power, the Sakti that screens the man from his real Sat-chit-ananda Svaroopa behind, and the *Vikshepa Sakti* that makes the mind and senses outgoing. The restlessness of the mind is due to desire and Vikshepa Sakti. Avidya clouds the understanding and produces intoxication, destroys the intellect and makes the intellect perverted, stony and barren. Therefore man always thinks that he can get pleasure in external objects, mistakes the body, children and wife as Atman and takes the unreal world as real. When lust manifests, the intellect becomes blind and the most intelligent man becomes an easy prey to passion. A worldly-minded man vainly searches for his happiness in outside perishable objects. The idea that he should dive deep into the chambers of his heart by collecting all the dissipated rays of the mind, and by withdrawing the out-going senses to meditate on God never strikes him. He never believes in devotion, concentration and meditation. He cannot imagine a pure, unalloyed happiness that is independent of external objects, although he enjoys the bliss of the Self daily at night. He foolishly thinks: "If I have a bungalow in Mussoorie for summer, if I have a car, if I have my own cow for good milk, if I have a son, if I have a garden, I will be happy." The tendency of the mind is such that it tries to seek happiness outside in perishable objects. This is due to the force of Avidya.

But the devotee gets the grace of the Lord. His intellect is calm and tranquil. All the outgoing energies become transmuted into spiritual energy. He gets help and strength from *Mantra-Sakti, Sadhana Sakti* and *Upasana Sakti*. Sattva flows from the feet of the Lord towards his mind. All desires melt away. The Vikshepa Sakti is destroyed. He has the firm, unshakable conviction that the real happiness is in God. His mind is always inward. He has *Antarmukha Vritti*.

The senses do not wander about. They get absorbed in the mind and the mind gets absorbed in God. He is ever peaceful. He enjoys the happiness within. He delights in the bliss of God. He therefore stands adamantine even amidst grave troubles and calamities. So Rishi Narada uses the expressions *"Stabdho bhavati"* (the devotee becomes serene) and *"Atmaramo bhavati"* (happy in the bliss of the Self).

The devotee gets divine intoxication. Lord Gouranga was so much intoxicated with the divine nectar of Prem that sometimes he did not know when it was daybreak and when it was night. Mira, though a young Rani, danced in the streets amidst males and men of inferior class on account of this intoxication of Krishna-prem. Sri Ramakrishna Paramahamsa remained in the thick jungle for four days without taking any food when he was under this divine intoxication. Words can hardly describe the nature of this divine intoxication. One has to feel it himself. Even if there is a mild intoxication, it will give immense strength to the devotee to face the difficulties in the battle of life. Therefore Narada says: *"matto bhavati."*

4. Renunciation

सा न कामयमाना निरोधरूपत्वात् ॥७

Saa na kamayamana nirodharupatvat (7)

It is not moved by desire, because of its nature being manifested in the form of control (of desires).

Notes and Commentary

Desire is an enemy of peace. Desire is an enemy of devotion. Without renunciation (Tyaga) Bhakti can never be cultivated in the heart. *Vishaya-asakti* (attachment to sensual enjoyments) is the obstacle in developing devotion. Energy leaks out. No improvement is seen in spiritual Sadhana. The devotee always complains: "I have not realised anything in the path of devotion. My mind remains in the same state. It always wanders about wildly in the sensual grooves. I am restless. What is to be done?" Desire is very powerful. It assumes various subtle forms. Desire is Maya's weapon to hurl down the Jivas into the mire of Samsara. There is no end for desires. It is unconquerable. Enjoyment does not bring satisfaction of a desire. Just as fire is increased by pouring ghee over it, so also desire is strengthened by *Bhoga*. Have you not studied the life of Raja Yayati in Mahabharata? He borrowed the youthful state from his son and enjoyed for thousands of years and cried out in the end: "Alas! My passion has not gone. There is no satiety. My heart is still burning with lust." Bhartrihari weeps bitterly: "I have renounced the world, wife and kingdom. I live on leaves and water. I do penance. Yet lust is troubling me." Such is the potency of desire.

That is the reason why Lord Krishna says in the Gita (III-39, 40, 41, 43 & II-55): "Enveloped is wisdom by this constant enemy of the wise in the form of desire, which is insatiable as a flame. The senses, the mind and the reason are said to be its seat; by these, enveloping wisdom, it bewilders the dweller in the body. Therefore, O best of the Bharatas, mastering first the senses do thou slay this thing of sin, destructive of wisdom and knowledge. Thus understanding Him as greater than the Reason, restraining the self by the Self, slay thou, O mighty-armed, the enemy in the form of desire, difficult to overcome. When a man abandoneth, O Partha, all the desires of the heart, and is satisfied in the Self, by the Self, then is he called stable in mind."

First annihilate *Asakti;* then the *Kamana* (longing) will die by itself. Eventually preference also will be destroyed. When the attraction towards external objects ceases, then there yet remains the internal craving which is called *Trishna* (thirsting for objects). This is the most dangerous enemy of devotion. When the attraction towards objects, external as well as internal, ceases without any veil, then it is termed *Mukta* (free from) *Trishna*. The mere thought of longing that such and such a thing should come to oneself is *Trishna*. It is this strong chain of *Trishna* that you should unshackle yourself from, if you want to grow in Bhakti. Cut off the *Trishna-Tantu* (the thread of sense-hankering) by the sword of Vairagya. This is "Nirodha" or control of desire.

निरोधस्तु लोकवेदव्यापारन्यासः ॥८

Nirodhastu lokavedavyaparanyasah. (8)

On the other hand, Nirodha (control of desires) means the resignation to the Lord of all worldly and scriptural observances.

Notes and Commentary

A worldly-minded man cannot work without expectation of fruits of his works. He reaps the fruits by going to heaven. He comes back again to this Mrityu-loka when the virtuous works are exhausted. He again does good and evil Karmas. Thus he is caught up in the never-ending wheel of Samsara or *Avagamana-Chakra*. Rishis, Seers and the Vedas therefore advise that the works should be performed without expectation of fruits and should be consecrated to the Lord as *Isvararpana*. Then the heart is purified and Bhakti develops. That is the reason why Lord Krishna advises Arjuna: "Whatever thou doest, whatever thou eatest, whatsoever thou offerest, whatsoever thou givest, whatsoever thou doest of austerity, O Kaunteya! do thou that as an offering unto Me." (Gita: IX-27.) Patanjali Maharshi, the exponent of Raja Yoga philosophy, also says: *"Ishvara-pranidhanadva* — Success is speedy in Yogic practice and attainment of Samadhi by surrendering the fruits of works at the feet of the Lord as an offering." Ishvara-pranidhana is an important item in his Kriya-Yoga and Niyama.

Egoism, ambition and Vasanas are obstacles in the way of

self-surrender. Subtle hidden Vasanas will try to come to the surface of the mind. Desires, which are suppressed for some time, will again manifest with redoubled force, if the aspirant is not careful, if there is some waning in his Vairagya and spiritual practice, and if he mixes with worldly-minded people. Generally the aspirant consciously or unconsciously, wittingly or unwittingly keeps up some desires for his gratification. He does not wish to part completely with his desires. Therefore the self-surrender does not become perfect and unreserved. So the grace of the Lord does not descend. Even if there is an atom of desire or egoism, there is no possibility of Divine Grace. Mira says: "I have given up my mind, my heart, my soul, my Chitta, my intellect, my all to my beloved Giridhar Gopal." This is complete self-surrender. Mark the word 'my all'. The Lord becomes a slave of a Bhakta only when he has made absolute, ungrudging, self-surrender. He is very cruel and puts His devotee to severe tests and trials. Only when Surdas poked his eyes with the thorns and remained without food and water in the thick jungle, Lord Krishna appeared before him with sweetmeats and water. He did not hear the words of Draupadi, so long as she kept up her own strength and traces of egoism. When she cried aloud with perfect sincerity and total resignation: "O Dwarakanath, O my beloved! Come to my rescue." Then He ran to the scene, she had abundant clothes, and her modesty was saved. *Nyasa* means renunciation. This brings *Nirodha* (control) of mind. It is renunciation of the fruits of works. Renunciation of egoism is *Sarva-Tyaga* (renunciation of all). All desires, selfishness, Raga, Dvesha, body-idea, Deha-abhimana, are hanging on egoism. Egoism is the pivot on which all these are centred. Kill egoism. Then the surrender becomes complete. Even if there is a tinge or grain of egoism, the Lord will not reveal Himself.

तस्मिन्ननन्यता तद्विरोधिषूदासीनता च ॥९

Tasminnananyata tadvirodhishoodaseenata cha. (9)

(Nirodha also means) concentrated (or single-minded) devotion to the Lord and indifference to all that is antagonistic to Him.

Notes and Commentary

"Ananyata" is single-minded devotion unto the Lord. The child thinks of the mother and mother alone. A passionate husband thinks of his wife and wife alone. A greedy money-lender thinks of his money and money alone. Even so the devotee should entertain in his heart the picture of his *Ishtam* and *Ishtam* alone. Then he can have *Darshan* of God easily. Lord Krishna says to Arjuna: "I am easily attainable by that ever-steadfast Yogi who constantly and daily remembers Me (for a long time), not thinking of anything else (with a single mind or one-pointed mind), O Partha!" (Gita: VIII-14.)

The single-minded devotion can only manifest by constant and protracted practice in a quiet room, and *Vairagya*. Whenever the wavering and unsteady mind runs out, curb it, draw it and fix it again and again at the face or lotus feet of the Lord. It takes some time for the collection of scattered rays of the mind, and for establishing new habits in the mind. One should not be discouraged in the beginning. Patience, perseverance, attention, faith, strong will, fortitude, power of endurance are needed. These virtues should be cultivated. Satsanga, dietetic adjustment, milk and fruits, fasting, control of sleep, reduction in the hours of sleep, sometimes seclusion, observance of Mauna, Brahmacharya should be resorted to. The mind is naturally prone to love of ease, gluttony, laziness, seeking of comforts, gossiping, worldly talks, sight seeing etc. It should be gradually trained, tamed and disciplined by suitable methods. It is like a spoiled, indulgent child. It must be sometimes coaxed, while at other times, if it is unruly and disobedient, it must be threatened and whipped. Fasting is whipping. Mauna is whipping.

Udaseenata is indifference to sensual enjoyments and sensual objects. Objects are enemies of God. Sons, wife, property, cattle, house, friends, relatives are the enemies of God. You must cherish perfect indifference to these objects. You must destroy ruthlessly Moha for these objects and develop the state of *Nirabhimanata* (without 'mine-ness'). Moha is infatuated love towards body, children, father, mother and wife. Attachment to the body is deep-rooted. You must not think of the body and its wants too much. Thoughts of body, thoughts of food, thoughts of wife and children make you forget God. You cannot have thoughts of God if you have thoughts of *Anatma* things (non-sentient objects).

There is supreme joy and bliss in Udaseenata. You will find in the Mundaka Upanishad: "Two birds, inseparable companions, dwell upon one and the same tree. One of them eats the sweet fruit; the other looks on without eating. On the same tree, the Jiva immersed in worldliness and bewildered grieves on account of helplessness. But when he sees the other, the Lord, who is adored by all, and His glory, then his grief passes away." Here one bird is the Jiva, the other bird is the Lord. The tree is this body. Udaseenata destroys all sorts of attachments and desires. Attachment is death. Udaseenata is eternal life. Lord Krishna says: "An *Udaseena* (indifferent man) is dear to Me." (Gita: XII-16.) Just as the spectators of a cricket or football match enjoy the game nicely, so also an Udaseena who is quite unconcerned with the world enjoys as a witness of this world-drama and passes beyond grief. In the Gita (XIII-9) you will find: "Unattachment, absence of self-identification with son, wife or home and constant balance of mind in wished for and unwished for events — this is declared to be the Wisdom."

Remember, dear readers! that Udaseenata is not physical nudity. It is not the living on Neem leaves or cow's dung or groundnut. Performance of foolish kinds of austerities (Moodha Tapas) does not constitute Udaseenata. Lord Krishna says (Gita: XVII-5, 6): "Those men who practise terrific austerities not enjoined by the scriptures, given to hypocrisy and egoism, impelled by the force of lust and attachment, senseless, torturing all the elements in the body and Me also, Who dwell in the body, – know thou these to be of demoniacal resolves."

Udaseenata is purely a mental state. Queen Chudala was a perfect Udaseena though she reigned over a dominion; but her husband was attached to his begging bowl and walking-stick though he lived in a forest. A man may be attached to his Kowpeen or a fountain-pen even, whereas a king like Janaka may be a perfect Udaseena though he is amidst luxuries and opulence. Worldly people attach much importance to external show only. This is a great pity. This is their horrible mistake. A man may be nude and yet his mind may be full of desires. Some hypocrites pretend to be Virakta Sadhus to exploit the householders. Householders should use their discrimination always. Udaseena Vritti comes from *Mithya Drishti* and *Dosha Drishti* in objects and from discrimination between the real and the unreal.

अन्याश्रयाणां त्यागोऽनन्यता ॥१०

Anyasrayanam tyago'nanyata. (10)

Single-heartedness means the abandoning of all other supports.

Notes and Commentary

Here is a definition of *Ananyata* – mind is clinging to persons, objects or places with leechlike tenacity. Wherever there is a little sensual pleasure, the mind is attached there, through Raga. All the pleasure-centres should be destroyed. Then alone the mind can be turned towards God with one-pointed concentration. The mind is always jumping like a monkey. Now it thinks of sweetmeats or fruits. Then it thinks of cinema-show for feasting the eyes. Then it wants to hear some melodious music. Then it wants to talk something with some friends. Just as a Chinaman is drawn hither and thither by his five wives, so also the mind is tossed hither and thither by the five Indriyas. It is always restless.

Through Vairagya and discrimination all these pleasure-centres should be destroyed. Then through constant, steady Abhyasa of Japa and Dhyana, it should be turned towards God. The struggle is doubtless, keen and hard. How difficult it will be to send up the waters of the Ganga above towards Badri Narayan! Still more difficult it will be for taking the mental energy towards God. It is easy to direct the mental energy towards sensual objects. It is but natural. It is the nature of the mind to run by itself towards objects without the least exertion. It is its *Svabhava*. Lord Krishna says: "With the mind not moving towards any other thing, made steadfast by the method of habitual meditation, and constantly meditating, one goes to the Supreme Person, the Resplendent, O Partha." (Gita: VIII-8.) "Fix thy mind on Me only, thy intellect in Me, (then) thou shalt no doubt live in Me alone hereafter. If thou art unable to fix thy mind steadily on Me, then by the Yoga of constant practice *(Abhyasa Yoga)* do thou seek to reach Me, O Dhananjaya." (Gita: XII-8, 9.) In the practice of concentration one should have the same patience and perseverance as that of the bird which tried to empty the ocean with its beak or blade of grass. Arjuna aimed at the bird above by seeing the reflection of the bird in the water. The arrow-maker was so much absorbed in his work that he did not notice the huge crowd of the Raja and his retinue. Such must be the nature of concentration on God in the Adhyatmic battlefield. Just as the bird that is tied to a post flutters about hither and thither and eventually rests on the post, so also the mind that wanders about here and there in sensual objects finally rests in God, through the practice of one-pointed concentration and devotion.

लोके वेदेषु तदनुकूलाचरणं तद्विरोधिषूदासीनता ॥११

Loke vedeshu tadanukulacharanam
tadvirodhishu-udaseenata. (11)

By indifference to all that is antagonistic to Him means the performance of those social and scriptural rituals and ceremonies that are congenial to Him.

Notes and Commentary

Lord Krishna says: "If also thou art not equal to constant practice, be intent on My service; performing actions for My sake, thou shalt attain perfection." (XII-10.) "Acts of sacrifice, gift and charity should not be relinquished, but should be performed; sacrifice, gift, and also austerity are the purifiers of the intelligence." (XVIII-5.)

These rituals purify the heart and prepare the ground of Antahkarana for the growth of devotion. These actions should be performed without attachment and without expectation of fruit. The sacrifice which is offered by men without desire for fruit as enjoined by the ordinances, under the firm belief that sacrifice is a duty, that is pure. The three kinds of austerity viz., physical, verbal, and mental Tapas prescribed in the Seventeenth Chapter of the Gita purify the heart rapidly. They are:

1. *Physical:* Worship given to the gods, to the twice-born, to the teachers and to the wise, purity, straight-forwardness, continence and harmlessness, are called the austerity of the body.

2. *Verbal:* Speeche causing no annoyance, truthful and beneficial, the practice of the study of the scriptures are called the austerity of speech.

3. *Mental:* Mental happiness, equilibrium, silence,

self-control, purity of nature, this is called the austerity of the mind.

This threefold austerity, performed by men with the utmost faith, without desire for fruit, harmonised, is said to be pure.

Without purification of the mind, there is no hope of cultivating Bhakti in the heart.

Agnihotra, Vaisvadeva, Brahma Yajna, Sandhyavandana in the three periods of time, Pancha Maha Yajnas — all are best calculated to purify the Chitta. They should be performed daily without any break. Observance of Chandrayana Vrata and Krichhra Vrata destroy sins effectively. They serve the purpose of Prayaschitta for expiating sin. The more the mind-mirror is cleansed, the better it is. Though these ceremonies are not necessary for an advanced Bhakta, yet they are very essential for neophytes.

Sraddha, Tarpan, observances and gifts on the occasion of eclipses should not be neglected. Consult the code of Manu or Yajnavalkya Smriti and you will get abundant information on this subject. Various kinds of Prayaschitta destroy various kinds of sin. If you find it difficult to consult the scriptures, consult Pundits and Acharyas and they will guide you. If you do not observe these rituals, you will be subject to Pratyavaya Dosha, the sin of omission. Jaimini lays great stress on Karmas (Agnihotra etc.)

Pradosha Vrata, Ekadasi Vrata are observances that propitiate Lord Siva and Lord Hari respectively. They should also be observed rigidly.

भवतु निश्चयदार्ढ्यादूर्ध्वं शास्त्ररक्षणम् ॥१२

Bhavatu nischayadardhyadurdhvam sastrarakshanam. (12)

Let there be strict adherence to the injunctions of the Sastras till a firm conviction in God is attained (also till profound devotion is fully developed).

Notes and Commentary

That is the reason why Lord Krishna says: "The ignorant, the faithless, the doubting self goes to destruction; there is neither this world nor the other, nor happiness for the doubting self." (Gita: IV-40.) "Therefore, let the scriptures be the authority in determining what ought to be done and what ought not to be done. Having known what is said in the ordinance of the scriptures, thou shouldst act here in this world." (Gita: XVI-24.)

The mind should not be allowed to have its own ways. He who follows the injunctions of the Sastras will evolve quickly. He will have no uneasiness in mind. He will have satisfaction. He will feel that he is in the right path and progressing rapidly in spirituality. He will feel the nearness of God. He will have peace of mind.

Scriptures are infallible. Vedas have come out from the mouth of God. They are revelations. They are traditionally handed down from Rishis and seers to their disciples in succession (Parampara). So long as there is world, there are scriptures and teachers to guide the people in the path of Truth and Righteousness. The number of teachers may be few in the iron age but they do exist. Books are not eternal. But the ideas in the Vedas are eternal.

It does not require much wisdom and reasoning to have a firm conviction in the existence of God. I do not know why these rationalists, socialists and materialistic scientists are unnecessarily racking their brains, fighting and doubting. It is really a great pity! It is their stiff egoism that makes them deny the existence of God. Whether they accept His existence or not, He is shining from eternity to eternity. The sun is always there whether the owls accept the existence of the sun or not. There are gross impurities in their minds which screen and cloud their understanding. There are sins in their Antahkarana which make their intellects perverted. They will have to wait for some time for grasping the Truth.

Just as a young plant is fenced in the beginning and protected, so also a neophyte in the path of devotion should be well-protected. If he mixes with atheists, he will lose his faith in God quickly. He must be always in the company of Sadhus, Mahatmas and Bhaktas. Their company is an iron fortress for him. If the injunctions of the Sastras are rigidly followed, nothing can shake one's convictions. Just as a nail is driven deep into a plank by frequent hammerings, so also the Samskaras and convictions become very deep by observing strictly the sacred laws of the scriptures. This is the meaning of this Sutra.

अन्यथा पातित्याशङ्क्या ॥१३

Anyatha patityasankayaa (13)

Otherwise, there is a danger of a fall (of going astray from the right path).

Notes and Commentary

Maya is very powerful. Mysterious is the power of Moha and desire! That is the reason why Lord Krishna says (Gita: II-60 & 67): "The turbulent senses, O Arjuna, do violently carry away the mind of a wise man, though he be striving. For the mind, which follows in the wake of the wandering senses, carries away his discrimination, as the wind (carries away) a boat on the waters."

You are all aware how the Rishi Visvamitra of great Tapas became a victim of the influence of the celestial nymph. Even Lord Buddha had to face Mara. This world is full of temptations. There is fear of fall at every moment. A beginner, a tyro is unable to resist temptation. He falls a prey to its influence quite readily. The Sadhaka must be very, very careful. He should observe the injunctions of the Sastras. They pave a long way in keeping him from falling. He should not test his spiritual strength at the very outset when he had made a little progress only. Reaction may set in. The Indriyas will revolt. The mind will become furious.

He will become a victim to passion. Even at the present moment, such instances of Yoga-Bhrashtas are not lacking. When one is put to test he fails. Jaimini was tried by his Guru, Sri Vedavyasa. He failed in his Brahmacharya. Physical control alone will not suffice. No evil thoughts should arise in the mind. There must not be any unholy thrill or unholy vibration in the mind even. This is the highest standard of purity. The Gita (III-6) says: "He who, restraining the organs of action, sits thinking of the sense-objects in mind, he of deluded understanding is called a hypocrite."

Some foolish young Sadhakas do some Sadhana for four or five years in Himalayan caves, see some dazzling lights during meditation, hear some Anahata sounds in the ears and think they are realised souls. They enter the world quickly for preaching, and mix with the householders freely and get hopeless downfall rapidly. What you have gained by rigid Sadhana in twelve years, will be lost in twelve seconds if you mix promiscuously with householders and if you do not take proper precautions. You should never come out to the plains till you attain *Bhuma* or *Brahmi-Sthiti,* till you become a full-blown Yogi or Jnani.

Therefore adhere to the injunctions of the Sastras till you develop supreme devotion. The observances will drop by themselves when you are established in highest devotion.

लोकोऽपि तावदेव किन्तु
भोजनादिव्यापारस्त्वाशरीरधारणावधि ॥१४

Loko'pi tavadeva kintu bhojanadi-vyaparastva-sarira-
dharanaavadhi. (14)

Till a deep conviction (in God) is attained, (also till deep devotion is gained), social customs and usages are also to be observed only to the same extent (as Sastric injunctions). But, eating, drinking, dressing, etc., should be continued as long as there is a body.

(Sutras 12, 13, 14 deal with the observances.)

Notes and Commentary

The customary injunctions also should be followed like the scriptural injunctions. They are also helpful to the aspirant in the beginning. When he is fully established in supreme devotion and piety, he can safely dispense with the scriptural, as well as, customary injunctions. They will drop themselves when he advances in purity and devotion. But on the contrary, eating and drinking will continue as long as he lives.

5. Different Definitions of Bhakti

तल्लक्षणानि वाच्यन्ते नानामतभेदात् ॥१५

Tallakshanani vachyante nana-mata-bhedat. (15)

The marks of devotion are now described according to various views.

Notes and Commentary

Lakshana means mark, characteristic, or sign. All devotees unanimously agree in the essential characteristics of devotion. But some give prominence to certain indications, while others to certain other marks. That is all. There cannot be any fundamental difference in the essence. *Nanamatabhedat* means according to various opinions.

पूजादिष्वनुराग इति पाराशर्यः ॥१६

Pujadishvanuraga iti Paarasaryah. (16)

Intense attachment in the worship of the Lord and like performances is the characteristic of devotion, according to the son of Parasara (Bhagavan Vyasa).

Notes and Commentary

Puja is worship of God. *Anuraga* is intense attachment. Prahlada says: "O Hari! May not the ceaseless flow of love and attachment leave my heart, while I am constantly meditating upon Thee." (Vishnu Purana I-20-19.) Devotion cometh and goeth in the beginning. When it is fully ripe, the devotee has intense attachment to the lotus-feet of the Lord. Even for the infinitesimal part of a second his mind does not stir from the point or *Lakshya*: This is *Anuraga*.

कथादिष्विति गर्गः ॥१७

Kathadishviti Gargah. (17)

According to Acharya Garga, attachment to the hearing of praises and greatness of the Lord is the mark of devotion.

Notes and Commentary

Here is a difference of opinion. It is the hearing of praises and greatness of the Lord that inspires a man to take to the spiritual path. Parikshit realised God through hearing Srimad Bhagavata from the sacred mouth of Sri Suka Dev. Man gets several knocks and blows in the daily battle of life. He gets failures and disappointments. This world becomes a hot furnace to him. He approaches the Bhagavatas and hears the praises of God. Then the mind gradually is turned towards God. The mind of the rogue Ratnakar was turned towards God after meeting Narada.

आत्मरत्यविरोधेनेति शाण्डिल्यः ॥१८

Atmaratyavirodheneti Sandilyah. (18)

Maharshi Sandilya is of the opinion that the sign of devotion is a constant feeling of Bliss in the Self.

Notes and Commentary

God is an embodiment of Bliss. The devotee who always dwells in God must enjoy the Bliss of God. There is always divine aura and bloom in his face. The eyes sparkle and glitter with Divine effulgence. Those who surround the devotee experience the bliss, because he radiates joy all around (vide Sutra 6). If a devotee is always morose and unhappy, if his countenance is cheerless, if he is peevish, there is surely some error in his Sadhana. He is not enjoying the Bliss of the Self. Ananda is a very important sign of devotion. It is a fundamental sign of a Jivanmukta too.

नारदस्तु तदर्पिताखिलाचारता तद्विस्मरणे परमव्याकुलतेति ॥१९

Naradastu tadarpita-akhilacharata tad-vismarane parama-vyakulateti. (19)

But Devarshi Narada then is of opinion, however, that the sign of devotion is surrendering all actions to God and feeling severe grief in forgetting Him.

Notes and Commentary

The devotee gets *parama-vyakulata* when he forgets his Beloved. Lord Gouranga, Mira and the Gopis of Vrindavana exhibited this sign. This is *Viraha-agni* (pain from separation of the Lord). This feeling can hardly be described in words. It has to be felt. It breaks the heart of the devotee. This Sutra does not in any way contradict Sutra 18. An advanced Bhakta who always rests in God has no *Viraha*. He is always in divine bliss.

अस्त्येवमेवम् ॥२०

Astyevamevam. (20)

There are such and such instances.

The next Sutra will illustrate the view of Narada.

यथा व्रजगोपिकानाम् ॥२१

Yatha Vrajagopikanam. (21)

Just as it was shown by the Gopis, the cow-maids of Vraja or Vrindavana.

Notes and Commentary

The Gopis surrendered all their actions at the Lotus-Feet of Lord Krishna. They experienced acute agony even if they missed His presence even for a second. When they heard the sweet, melodious flute of their Beloved, they left their houses while milking the cows. With minds absorbed in

Krishna they rushed forth to where their Lover was, without taking notice of each other. Some did not wait to see the boiling of the milk. Some did not take down boiled wheat from the oven. Some were giving food to others, some were giving milk to their own children. Some were serving their husbands and some were taking their own food. But they all left their work half-finished. They gave up their household duties, with clothes and ornaments all in disorder; they hurriedly went to Krishna. When Krishna disappeared they asked the trees if they had seen their Lover. They enquired of the creepers, the earth and the deer.

तत्रापि न माहात्म्यज्ञानविस्मृत्यपवादः ॥२२

Tatrapi na mahatmya-jnana-vismriti-apavadah. (22)

Even there (the love of the Gopis), there is no particular reason for forgetting the sense of greatness of the Lord.

Notes and Commentary

Why does a man undergo miseries and sufferings? Because he has forgotten God, owing to the influence of Avidya or Maya. That devotee, in whom there is descent of His grace, can never forget Him even for a second. Try to remember the Lord along with every breath, inspiratory and expiratory. Keep the Gita always in your pocket and a Japa-Maala around your neck. Repeat His Name always. Be in the company of Bhaktas. Study Bhagavata, Ramayana, or the Gita daily. Then you cannot forget Him.

Reduce your activities. Do Satya-vyavahara. Reduce your wants. Destroy the desires as they spring up in the mind. Do not try to fulfil them. Increase your Japa on Sundays. Do *anushthana* of 4 lakhs of Japa during Easter, summer and Christmas holidays. Do Akhanda Japa or Akhanda Patha of Bhagavata or Akhanda Kirtan for seven days (Saptaham). During these seven days live on milk and fruits and wear clothing washed by your own hands. Observe perfect *mauna* and celibacy. All the members of the house should follow these rules strictly. Then there is no possibility of forgetting Him. The Lord is quite close to you. Your house will be turned into Vaikuntha. The Lord says: "O Narada, I dwell not in Vaikuntha, nor in the hearts of Yogis, but I dwell there where My Bhaktas sing My name — *Na aham vasami vaikunthe yoginam hridaya na cha, madbhakta yatra gayanti tatra tishthami narada.*"

तद्विहीनं जाराणामिव ॥२३

Tadviheenam jaaranamiva. (23)

A love without it (the sense of greatness of the object loved—the Lord) is simply a passion of a woman towards her paramour.

Notes and Commentary

Passion is not love at all. It is an animal instinct. It is carnal love. It is of a beastly nature. It is shifting. If the wife loses her beauty on account of some incurable malady, she gets a divorce and the husband marries a second wife. This state of affairs is going on in the world. But Bhakti is Suddha Prem. It is divine love. It is unchanging. The devotee cherishes always the sense of majesty and magnanimity of the Lord. His Ishtam is the Lord of his very breath (Prananatha or Pranavallabha). It is this idea that keeps up his devotion, nourishes and strengthens it. If this idea of the sense of greatness of the Lord is lacking, then he has no devotion. His devotion is tantamount to the passion of a lustful husband and wife. There is no grandeur in his devotion. Remembrance of the tenth chapter of Gita wherein all the Vibhutis of God are described, will keep up the idea of the sense of greatness of God. Devotion is a sublime, sacred sentiment. It elevates the soul immediately to lofty heights of divinity. When a man comes to realise the Mahima of the Lord, all worldly desires die and all attachment and ties are broken and the man is keen and eager to have Darshan of the Lord.

नास्त्येव तस्मिंस्तत्सुखसुखित्वम् ॥२४॥

Nastyeva tasmimstat-sukha-sukhitvam. (24)

In this love of the paramours there certainly does not exist any corresponding feeling of happiness (of the other).

Notes and Commentary

In mercenary love, there cannot be any real happiness between the two, the lover and the beloved. If the husband is in a dying condition, the wife takes the bank passbook and walks to her mother's house quietly. If the husband loses his job for some time, the wife shows a wry face, speaks harsh words and does not serve him properly with any love. This is selfish love. There is no real affection from the core of the heart. Even our sisters of ill-fame show for some time abundant love, sweet smile and honeyed words towards their customers, so long as they can extract money. Can you call this love and real happiness? Just tell me frankly. There are cunningness, diplomacy, crookedness and hypocrisy here. So there are always quarrels, fighting and Asanti in the house. Husbands and wives are not really united. There is always a tug-of-war. They pull on anyhow, dragging a dreary, cheerless existence.

6. Supremacy of Devotion

सा तु कर्मज्ञानयोगेभ्योऽप्यधिकतरा ॥२५॥

Sa tu karma-jnana-yogebhyo'pyadhikatara. (25)

Bhakti is, indeed, greater than action, knowledge and Yoga.

Notes and Commentary

Arjuna puts a question to the Lord: "Those devotees who, ever steadfast, thus worship Thee and those also who worship the Imperishable and the Unmanifested—which of them is better versed in Yoga?" (Gita: XII-1.) The Lord gives the answer: "They who with mind fixed on Me ever harmonised worship Me, with faith supreme endowed, they in My opinion are best in Yoga." There again He says: "The Yogi is greater than the ascetics; he is thought to be greater than even the wise; the Yogi is greater than the men of action; therefore become thou a Yogi, O Arjuna. And among all Yogis, he who, full of faith, with the inner Self abiding in Me, adoreth Me, he is considered by Me to be the most completely harmonised." (Gita: VI-46, 47.) You will find in the eighth chapter (22) of the Gita: "He, the highest spirit, O Partha, may be reached by unswerving devotion to Him alone, in whom all beings abide, by whom all this is pervaded." Then again in XI-54 you will find: "But by devotion to Me alone I may thus be perceived, Arjuna, and known and seen in essence and entered, O Partha."

There is the keynote of devotion and surrender throughout the Gita. Bhakti-marga is easy for the vast majority of persons. God takes the form for helping the devotees. There are no pitfalls or snares in the path. The Lord is ever ready to guide the devotee. He actually takes him by His hands and embraces him in His sweet bosom of Love. He showers His grace on the devotees, as soon as He finds out that they are sincere and earnest. Success is sure in this path. Bhakti-marga is the easiest, safest, surest and quickest way for attaining the highest bliss or God-realisation. That is the reason why Narada Rishi says: "Bhakti is greater than Karma, Jnana and Yoga."

"Those who mount dizzy heights by austere practices fancying themselves liberated but being really unenlightened, because lacking in devotion to Thee, O Lotus-eyed One! fall into a chasm not having loved Thy Feet. Never so, however, Thy own, O Madhava, stray away from the path, being tied to Thee by bonds of affection and guarded by Thee, they walk fearlessly their feet on the heads of all enemies."

फलरूपत्वात् ॥२६॥

Phalarupatvat. (26)

From its being itself the form of reward.

Notes and Commentary

Devotion is higher than the others, because it is its own reward. It is devotion for devotion's sake. It is love for love's sake. Therefore Narada says *phala-rupatvat*. That is the reason why it excels others. Those who follow other paths cherish some ulterior motives in view. So they fail to attain God.

ईश्वरस्याप्यभिमानद्वेषित्वात् दैन्यप्रियत्वाच्च ॥२७॥

Isvarasyapyabhimana-dveshitvat dainya-priyatvat-cha. (27)

Also from the fact that God hates the proud and loves the humble.

Notes and Commentary

This is another reason: Humility is the greatest of all virtues. All other virtues cling to the man who is endowed with humility. Gouranga Mahaprabhu was an embodiment of meekness. He sat in the place where shoes were kept, when he wanted to have an interview with a learned Pundit. Pride is a thorn in Bhakti-marga. It destroys devotion and all other virtues. Pride is ignorance. One can win the hearts of all by humility. A Bhakta should be humbler than the blade of grass which is trodden by the feet. That man only can sing always Hari's Name. It is difficult to develop this virtue. One has to kill himself and remain like a block of stone. The stiff egoism asserts again and again.

In the Bible you will find: "Blessed are the poor in spirit, for theirs is the kingdom of heaven. Blessed are the meek, for they shall inherit the earth." Lord Jesus speaks very highly of this virtue (humility) in his sermon on the mount.

Just as fire removes the sensation of cold only of those who approach it, so also God removes the bondage of those who worship Him with earnestness and approach Him through daily prayer, right conduct and meditation.

Krishna said to Radha: "There are those who think themselves separate from Me. I rob them of their all and then when they see Me, all the ties of the world disappear. There are those, the worldly-minded, who kill the Self in them. I am cruel to them, but even to them I am kind for I confer happiness upon them in their grief. All souls are my favourites; I play many games with them till they forget all that is selfish, till they love Me for the sake of love alone, as thou now doest, O Radha."

7. Knowledge and Devotion

तस्या ज्ञानमेव साधनमित्येके ॥२८॥

Tasyaa jnanameva sadhanamityeke. (28)

Some say that knowledge (of the object loved) is a means to the attainment of devotion.

Notes and Commentary

Some say: "Even in the worldly parlance, knowledge comes first. Through knowledge of a thing, one gets love for that object. A girl gets knowledge of her would-be husband: 'He can sing well. He is beautiful. He has passed his I.A.S examination. He is now a district magistrate and so on.' Then she develops Bhava and Prem for him. A patient gets knowledge of the virtuous qualities of barley. Then he loves barley, and takes with delight barely bread. He knows it is cooling and Sattvic and so on. So also one gets Knowledge of God at first. Then he begins to love. Therefore 'Jnana' is the 'Sadhana' or means for devotion."

अन्योन्याश्रयत्वमित्यन्ते ॥२९॥

Anyonya-asrayatvam-ityante. (29)

Others say that there is a mutual dependence between devotion and knowledge.

"Anyonya-asraya" is mutual dependence. The wife is depending upon the husband for her wants, clothing, food and attendance while she is sick. The husband is depending upon his wife for his food and other kinds of service. This is mutual dependence. The king depends upon the subjects for his revenue. The subjects depend upon the king for their protection, water supply, sanitation, lighting and medical treatment. This is also a case of mutual dependence. Even so, devotion depends upon knowledge and knowledge depends upon devotion.

In the Gita (IV-39) you will find: *"Sraddhvavan labhate Jnanam* — the man who is full of faith obtaineth wisdom."

"To these, ever harmonious (worshipping in love), I give the Yoga of discrimination by which they come unto Me." (Gita: X-10.)

"By devotion he knoweth Me in essence, who and what I am; having thus known Me in essence he forthwith entereth into the Supreme." (Gita: XVIII-55.)

स्वयं फलरूपतेति ब्रह्मकुमाराः ॥३०

Svayam phalarupateti Brahmakumaraah. (30)

Love is its own reward—thus opine Brahma Kumaras (Sanaka, Sanandana, Sanatana, Sanatkumara and Narada himself— the sons of Brahma).

राजगृहभोजनादिषु तथैव दृष्टत्वात् ॥३१

Rajagriha bhojanadishu tathaiva drishtatvat. (31)

Just as is observed in the case of a royal palace, food and other things.

न तेन राजपरितोषः क्षुधाशान्तिर्वा ॥३२

Na tena rajaparitoshah kshudha-santirvaa. (32)

By it (by mere knowledge of things), a king does not find pleasure nor is there the satisfaction of hunger.

The followers of the path of devotion oppose those who hold the view that knowledge is means for attainment of devotion by the aid of the above illustration. They say: "Mere knowledge of food cannot appease hunger; so also mere knowledge cannot develop devotion."

तस्मात्सैव ग्राह्या मुमुक्षुभिः ॥३३

Tasmatsaiva grahya mumukshubhih. (33)

Therefore, the path of devotion alone should be resorted to by those who long for liberation.

The reasons for adopting the path of devotion are stated in Sutras 30, 31 and 32. In the following Sutras means for cultivating Bhakti are described.

8. How to Develop Bhakti

तस्याः साधनानि गायन्त्याचार्याः ॥३४

Tasyaah sadhanani gayanti-acharyaah. (34)

The means of attaining Bhakti are given thus by Acharyas (teachers of Bhakti).

तत्तु विषयत्यागात् संगत्यागाच्च ॥३५

Tattu vishaya-tyagat sanga-tyagat-cha. (35)

Devotion to God is attained by relinquishing all sensual pleasures and all attachments to sensual objects.

Notes and Commentary

In the Kaivalya Upanishad it is said: *"Na karmana na prajaya dhanena, tyagenaike amritatvam-anasuh* — Neither by action nor by progeny nor by riches, but by renunciation alone immortality is attained." Here are the nine means of cultivating Bhakti. Sri Rama says to Sabari: "Here (in the culture of devotion) the first means is, it has been taught, the company of the good; the second is conversation about My achievements; the third is recital of My virtues; the fourth means will be the occupation of expounding My words; the fifth is, O gentle one, constant and sincere worship of preceptor, thinking that I am he; the sixth means has been said to be virtuousness, self-restraint, observance etc., and everliving attachment to My worship; the seventh is said to be religious service with every detail, reciting the Mantra specially applicable to Me; greater adoration paid to My votaries, consciousness of Me in all beings, indifference to external objects, together with internal peace, make up the eighth; and, O lady, the ninth is the consideration of My essence. O auspicious one, devotion in the form of Love is produced in any and every one who employs this means in the shape of the ninefold (secondary or instrumental) devotion, no matter whether one be a woman or a man or gone to the inferior creation. And as soon as devotional love is produced, one feels My essence, as it were, and one who becomes accomplished by the awareness of Me, attains Me."

Lord Krishna says in the Gita: "Mindful of Me, their life hidden in Me, illumining each other, ever conversing about Me, they are content and joyful." (X-9.)

"Merge thy mind in Me, be My devotee, sacrifice to Me, prostrate thyself before Me, thou shalt come even to Me. I pledge thee My truth: thou art dear to Me." (XVIII-65.)

"United to the reason purified, controlling the self by firmness, having abandoned sound and the other objects of the senses, having laid aside passion and malice;" (XVIII-51.)

"Dwelling in solitude, abstemious, speech, body and mind subdued, constantly fixed in meditation and Yoga, taking refuge in dispassion;" (XVIII-52.)

"Having cast aside egoism, violence, arrogance, desire, wrath, covetousness, selfless and peaceful—he is fit to become the ETERNAL." (XVIII-53.)

"Becoming Brahman, serene in the Self, he neither grieveth nor desireth. The same to all beings, he obtaineth supreme devotion unto Me." (XVIII-54.)

अव्यावृत भजनात् ॥३६॥

Avyaavrita bhajanat. (36)

And from constant adoration to God.

Notes and Commentary

Worship by fits and starts will not do. It must be constant. It must be *tailadharavat* (like flow of oil). If there is break, desires will try to enter the mind. Unholy thoughts and worldly temptations will ransack the Antahkarana. Rajas and Tamas will try to overcome you. There will be resurrection of old Trishnas and Vasanas. The devotee will have to be very vigilant and cautious. That is the reason why Lord Krishna says: "*Sarveshu kaleshu mam anusmara* – At all times think of Me." (Gita: VIII-7.)

लोकेऽपि भगवद्गुणश्रवणकीर्तनात् ॥३७॥

Loke'pi bhagavad-guna-sravana-kirtanat. (37)

(Bhakti develops) even in the world from hearing and singing the virtues and attributes of God.

"*Kalau Kesava Kirtanat* – In the Kali Yuga, Salvation is attained by Kirtan or singing the praises of God." People have not got good physique and unbroken Brahmacharya to practise Hatha Yogic Kriyas such as Pranayama, Kumbhaka, Kechari Mudra etc. They lack in bold understanding, gigantic intellect and strong will to understand and practise Vedanta. The easy way is Kirtan only.

मुख्यतस्तु महत्कृपयैव भगवत्कृपालेशाद्वा ॥३८॥

Mukhyatastu mahat-kripayaiva bhagavat-kripa-lesat-vaa. (38)

But chiefly by the grace of the great ones and also by the touch (a drop) of Lord's mercy.

Notes and Commentary

Lord Krishna says: "This divine illusion of Mine, caused by the qualities, is hard to pierce; they who come to Me, they cross over this illusion." (Gita: VII-14.) In Mundaka

Upanishad and Kathopanishad you will find: "This Atman cannot be attained by discourse, nor by intelligence nor by profound study. It can be realised by him only whom It favours; him this Atman favours with its manifestation. "Bhagavat-kripa-lesat" – even a drop of the Lord's Grace is quite sufficient to free oneself from the trammels of this Samsara. It is through the Grace of the Lord alone that a man can stick to the spiritual path and can break all sorts of ties and attachments.

"Though ever performing all actions, taking refuge in Me, by My Grace he obtains the eternal indestructible abode." (Gita: XVIII-56.)

"Thinking of Me, thou shalt overcome all obstacles by My Grace; but if from egoism thou wilt not listen, thou shalt be destroyed utterly." (Gita: XVIII-58.)

"Out of pure compassion for them, dwelling within their Self, I destroy the ignorance-born darkness by the shining lamp of wisdom." (Gita: X-11.)

"Mahat-Kripa" – The grace of the great ones is also necessary. There is no difference between God and a realised Bhagavata. Both are identical. There is no hope of overhauling the old vicious Samskaras of a worldly man without the help of Satsanga of Mahatmas. Satsanga is a safe boat to take the aspirant to the other shore of fearlessness, the shore which is beyond darkness. The glory of Satsanga is vividly eulogised in Bhagavata, Ramayana and all scriptures. Books written by realised persons constitute negative Satsanga. When you study them, you are in holy communion with the authors.

Grace will descend on deserving aspirants only who are earnestly struggling in the path and who are thirsting for realisation. Nowadays people want to lead a life of ease and expect the grace of Mahatmas. They themselves do not want to do any kind of Tapas or Sadhana. They want a magic pill to put them in Samadhi at once. They want worldly comforts and realisation in one and the same cup.

Kabir, Tulasidas, Sankara and Guru Nanak have all written volumes on the glory of Satsanga with Mahatmas. Faith in God, in scriptures, attachment and devotion to God slowly develop in those who do regular Satsanga.

There is a complaint by householders nowadays that there are no good Mahatmas. This is a lame excuse. The company of Sadhus is a question of supply and demand. If there is a sincere demand, the supply will come at once. This is the inexorable law of nature. If you are really thirsty, you will find your Master at your very threshold. You lead a happy-go-lucky life; your mind is full of passion and unholy Vasanas. You do not care a bit for higher, divine life. You waste your time in idle gossiping and vain worldly talks. You have become a hopeless slave of passion, greed and name and fame. And yet you complain: "I cannot get good Satsanga." Blame yourself first. Admit your faults. Repent sincerely for your mistakes. Do Prayaschitta. Fast, pray. Cry bitterly in solitude. Make yourself a deserving Adhikhari first. Then come to me. I shall take you to the lotus-feet of blessed souls who will put you in the right path, guide you and elevate you to sublime heights. These "over-souls" or high souls are waiting to get hold of right type of aspirants. Mahatmas are in plenty. Real seekers are few. If you bring a charge: "There are no good Mahatmas," Mahatmas also bring a serious charge: "There are no real seekers after Truth."

9. Glory of the Company of the Wise

महस्तसङ्गस्तु दुर्लभोऽगम्योऽमोघश्च ॥३९॥

Mahat-sangastu durlabho-agamyo-amoghascha. (39)

The company of the great ones is, again difficult of attainment, is unapproachable and always beneficial.

Good things are always rare in this world. Musk, saffron, radium, sandalwood, learned persons, virtuous persons, heroes, philanthropists, etc., are rare. When such is the case, what to speak of saints, Yogins, Jnanins and Bhaktas! You will have to equip yourself first with the necessary qualifications of self-restraint, celibacy, calmness of mind, keen desire for liberation, humility, obedience, spirit of service etc., to make yourself fit for their company. If you get their company, the question of your salvation is solved. Sri Sankaracharya says in his Viveka-Chudamani: "Three things are rare in this world. They are (1) Human birth, (2) Desire for liberation, (3) The care of a perfected sage."

लभ्यतेऽपि तत्कृपयैव ॥४०

Labhyate-api tat-kripayaiva. (40)

The company of the Great ones is obtained by the Grace of God alone.

तस्मिंस्तज्जने भेदभावात् ।

Tasmimstajjane bhedabhavat. (41)

Because there is no difference between the Lord and His devotee.

Just as a river loses its name and form after it has entered the ocean, so also a devotee loses his individuality when he merges himself in the Lord. The mind that causes distinction is annihilated by devotion.

तदेव साध्यतां तदेव साध्यताम् ॥४२

Tadeva sadhyatam tadeva sadhyatam. (42)

Try to get love of God alone, try to get love of God alone.

10. Give Up Evil Company

दुस्सङ्गः सर्वथैव त्याज्यः ॥४३

Dussangah sarvathaiva tyajyah. (43)

Evil company should be certainly avoided by all means.

Notes and Commentary

Vilwamangal attended once the nautch-party of Chintamani. His whole Antahkarana was poisoned. He was the virtuous son of a pious Brahmin. All his good traits disappeared. He fell in love with her. He ruined his life. There are thousand and one instances like this. In Andhra Pradesh, Vemana also was spoiled by evil company in the beginning.

Novels, cinemas, sight of pairing of animals, obscene scenery, vulgar music, nude pictures, anything that excites passion are all evil companies. There is nothing more dangerous than evil company. If the wife has no religious tendencies and is of worldly nature, her company also is tantamount to evil company. That is the reason why scriptures speak very highly of solitary places in the Himalayas and on the banks of the Ganga.

कामक्रोधमोहस्मृतिभ्रंशबुद्धिनाशसर्वनाशकारणत्वात् ॥४४

Kama-krodha-moha-smritibhramsa-buddhinasa-śarvanasa-karanatvat. (44)

Because it is the cause of lust, anger, infatuation, lapse of memory, loss of intellectual power and complete destruction.

Notes and Commentary

Lord Krishna says: "Man musing on the objects of sense, conceiveth an attachment to these; from attachment ariseth desire; from desire anger cometh forth. From anger proceedeth delusion; from delusion confused memory; from confused memory the destruction of reason; from destruction of reason he perishes." (Gita: II-62, 63.) "It is desire, it is wrath, begotten by the quality of mobility; all-consuming, all-polluting; know thou this as our foe here on earth." (III-37.) "Triple is the gate of this hell, destructive of the self—lust, wrath and greed; therefore let man renounce these three." (XVI-21.) Tulasidasji says: "Wherever there is *Kama*, there is no *Rama* and wherever there is *Rama*, there is no *Kama*."

तरङ्गयिता अपीमे सङ्गत्समुद्रायन्ति ॥४५

Tarangayita apeeme sangat-samudrayanti. (45)

These evil propensities, though they are ripples at first, ultimately expand into an ocean through evil company.

Notes and Commentary

Drinking, meat-eating, hearing vulgar music, company of prostitutes, attendance of nautch-parties, theatres and cinemas excite passion and throw the victim in the hell of fire. Cinema has become a curse in India. An officer spends half of his salary in cinema and runs into debts. All have developed a bad habit for some kind of sight-seeing. They cannot remain without it. The eyes want to see some kind of lights and sensational pictures. Cinema is a very good paying business nowadays. Various sorts of half-nude pictures and obscene sights are shown on the screen. College boys and young girls are unduly thrown into a state of mental excitement. Various sorts of evils are propagated. Cinema is an enemy of devotion. It is havocing the world. It should be entirely boycotted. It does immense harm to the people. It is a great drain on the resources of man. It is a great temptation. All bad films should be thoroughly investigated and censored. Films should be passed by a religious body before they are brought on the screen. Only films which contain religious stories that are calculated to develop the moral and philosophical aspect of man may be allowed to come on the screen. A bill should be passed in the Parliament to this effect. This is a most important matter. All thoughtful men should direct their attention on this point.

It is gratifying to note that highly educated males and

females of India take part in the cinema. The college education will not do. If they want to impress the people and to do real spiritual good to the world, they should lead a life of Tapas and meditation and Brahmacharya.

11. Who Crosses Maya?

कस्तरति कस्तरति मायां ? यः सङ्गंस्त्यज्यति,
यो महानुभावं सेवते, निर्ममो भवति ॥४६॥

Kastarati kastarati mayam? Yah sangam tyajati,
yo mahanubhavam sevate, nirmamo bhavati. (46)

Who crosses, who overcomes this Maya? Only he who abandons evil company, who associates with large-hearted men and who is free from "mine-ness."

Notes and Commentary

Sri Sankara says: "*Satsangatve nissangatvam, nissangatve nirmohatvam, nirmohatve nischalatattvam, nichalatattve jivanmuktih.*" By keeping company with the Mahatmas, one becomes dispassionate. He gets Vairagya. He does not like the company of worldly men. Then he develops the state of "Nirmohatva." He becomes free from infatuation or delusion. Then his mind becomes steady and one-pointed and rests in the Svaroopa or essence. Then he attains liberation or freedom.

यो विविक्तस्थानं सेवते, यो लोकबन्धमुन्मूलयति,
निस्त्रैगुण्यो भवति, योगक्षेमं त्यजति ॥४७॥

Yo vivikta-sthanam sevate, yo loka-bandham-unmulayati,
nistraigunyo bhavati, yoga-kshemam tyajati. (47)

He who resorts to lonely places, he who roots out worldly bonds or ties, transcends the three Gunas and gives up all ideas of acquisition and preservation of property.

Notes and Commentary

The poet who liked loneliness sang: "O solitude! Where

are thy charms?" Lord Krishna lays great stress on this solitude — *"Vivikta Sevi"* (Gita: XVIII-52). *"Vivikta-desa sevitvam"* (XIII-10). Solitude has immense advantages. The mind gets one-pointedness by itself without any effort. In the world there are many distractions on all sides and a beginner finds it impossible to fix his mind on his Lakshya. One can reach a certain stage either in Yoga, Bhakti or Jnana in the world. For acquiring advanced stages, solitude is indispensably requisite. If you bring the examples of Raja Janaka and Ekanath, these are all solitary instances. Further, they were all Yoga-bhrashtas, born with a lot of spiritual Samskaras acquired through drastic Sadhana in their previous lives.

The ideas of this Sutra come in the Gita (II-45): "The Vedas deal with the three Gunas; be thou above these three qualities. O Arjuna! Free yourself from the pairs of opposites, and ever remain in the quality of Sattva, freed from (the thought of) acquisition and preservation, and be established in the Self."

यः कर्मफलं त्यजति, कर्माणि संन्यस्यति ततो निर्द्वन्द्वो भवति ॥४८

Yah karma-phalam tyajati, karmani samnyasyati
tato nirdvandvo bhavati. (48)

He who renounces the fruits of his actions, and who renounces, goes beyond the pairs of opposites (such as heat and cold, pleasure and pain).

Notes and Commentary

What you call world is not this wall or stone or tree. The world is a play kept up by these pairs of opposites, which affect the mind through the two mental currents — Raga-Dvesha, attraction and repulsion, or like and dislike. He who conquers these pairs of opposites really conquers the whole world. Heat and cold affect the body; and pleasure and pain affect the mind. He who transcends the

Dvandvas always keeps a balanced mind. This is an important sign or *linga* of a Jivanmukta.

यो वेदानपि संन्यस्यति, केवलमविच्छिन्नानुरागं लभते ॥४९

Yo vedanapi samnyasyati, kevalam-avicchinna-anuragam labhate. (49)

He who abandons even the Vedas and develops an undivided and continuous flow of love towards the Lord.

Notes and Commentary

Continuous flow of love without any break even for a second is *"avicchinna-anuragam."* Vedas can afford no interest for a man who has got this kind of incessant flow of Prem. That is the reason why the Gita (II-46) says: "All the Vedas are as useful to an enlightened Brahmin, as is a tank in a place covered all over with water."

स तरति, स तरति, स लोकांस्तारयति ॥५०

Sa tarati, sa tarati, sa lokamstarayati. (50)

(Verily) crosses (Maya), he crosses (this ocean of Samsara, all limitations); he helps mankind to cross (also).

Notes and Commentary

This world is compared to an ocean (Bhavasagara). Trishnas are the crocodiles. Vasanas are the whales or sharks. Indriyas are the rivers. The three Gunas are the waves. Raga-Dvesha are the ripples. Ignorance is the substratum. Egoism is the essence. Lord Krishna says: "Those verily who, renouncing all actions in Me, and intent on Me, worship meditating on Me, with whole-hearted Yoga, these I speedily lift up from the ocean of death and existence, O Partha! their minds being fixed on Me." (XII-6, 7.)

12. Nature of Love

अनिर्वचनीयं प्रेमस्वरूपम् ॥५१

Anirvachaneeyam prema-svaroopam. (51)

The nature of love towards God is inexpressible.

This is to be felt by the devotee himself. Even in the worldly parlance it is impossible to describe the taste of sugar-candy to one who has not eaten sugar-candy, the nature of sexual bliss to one who has not enjoyed it, and the nature of sun and sunlight to a blind man. Hence the term *'anirvachaneeyam'* is used here.

मूकास्वादनवत् ॥५२

Muka-asvaadanavat. (52)

Just as the taste of a dumb man.

प्रकाशते क्वापि पात्रे ॥५३

Prakaasate kvaapi paatre. (53)

(But) It manifests by Itself in a qualified person only.

The current of Prem or spiritual aura passes by itself from the teacher to the fit disciple. There is telepathic transference or communication between the teacher and disciple. The disciple should be a fit subject to receive the light. The seed will sprout only in a well-prepared ground. There is *Sakti-sanchar* through Sankalpa or sight by the teacher in the student.

गुणरहितं कामनारहितं प्रतिक्षणवर्धमानमविच्छिन्नं
सूक्ष्मतरमनुभवरूपम् ॥५४

Guna-rahitam kamanaa-rahitam pratikshana-vardha-maanam-avicchinnam sukshmataram-anubhavarupam. (54)

It (love) is of the form of a very, very subtle, unbroken feeling of experience that develops in volume and intensity at every moment, that is free from the three Gunas and desires.

It is very, very subtle. So the term *'sukshmataram'* is used. It always grows and increases. There is always waxing. The play of Gunas has no place here. Sensual desires cannot exist when this unbroken love operates. Whatever the mind wants can be had in God. His one attribute *Ananta* (infinity) embraces everything.

तत्राप्य तदेवावलोकयति तदेव शृणोति
तदेव भाषयति तदेव चिन्तयति ॥५५

Tat-praapya tadeva-avalokayati tadeva shrunoti tadeva bhashayati tadeva chintayati. (55)

Having once obtained that, the devotee sees only his Ishtam or Beloved, hears only about Him, talks only about Him and thinks only of Him.

13. Secondary Devotion

गौणी त्रिधा गुणभेदादार्तादिभेदाद्वा ॥५६

Gaunee tridhaa gunabhedaad-aartaadi-bhedaadva. (56)

Secondary devotion is of three kinds according to the qualities: Sattva, Rajas, and Tamas or according to the distinction of the aspirants (the suffering, the seeker for knowledge and the self-interested).

उत्तरस्मादुत्तरस्मात्पूर्वापूर्वा श्रेयाय भवति ॥५७

Uttarasmaat-uttarasmaat purva-purvaa sreyaaya bhavati. (57)

The first is better than the second and the second is better than the third in both the divisions.

14. Bhakti Easy to Practise

अन्यस्मात् सौलभ्यं भक्तौ ॥५८

Anyasmaat saulabhyam bhaktau. (58)

The method of devotion is easier than other methods (in the attainment of salvation.)

प्रमाणान्तरस्यानपेक्षत्वात् स्वयं प्रमाणत्वात् ॥५९

Pramaana-antarasya-anapekshatvaat
svayam pramaanatvaat. (59)

Because there is no need of any other evidence, as it is proof of itself.

शान्तिरूपात्परमानन्दरूपाच्च ॥६०

Saantirupaat-parama-ananda-rupaat-cha. (60)

(The path of Bhakti is easy) because it is of the nature of peace and supreme bliss.

लोकहानौ चिन्ता न कार्या निवेदितात्मलोकवेदत्वात् ॥६१

Loka-haanau chintaa na kaarya nivedita-
atmaloka-vedatvaat. (61)

One should feel no anxiety about worldly concerns, as he has consecrated himself and scriptural functions all to the Lord.

15. Bhakti and Social Customs

न तदसिद्धौ लोकव्यवहारो हेयः किन्तु
फलत्यागस्तत्साधनं च कार्यमेव ॥६२

Na tadasiddhau lokavyavaharo heyah kintu
phalatyaagastat-saadhanam cha kaaryameva. (62)

Till Bhakti is developed, no social customs and ceremonies are to be neglected, but simply their fruits. One should surely perform them. The relinquishing of the fruits should be verily practised. (Vide Sutra 11, 12, 14, 18).

स्त्रीधननास्तिकवैरिचरित्रं न श्रवणीयम् ॥६३

Stree-dhana-naastika-vairi-charitram na sravaneeyam. (63)

The seeker after Bhakti should not hear stories or description of women, riches, atheists and enemies.

Talks about women disturb the mind and excite passion. In the Narada Parivrajaka Upanishad it is said that the seeker should not look even at the picture of woman. Talks of wealthy persons will induce luxury in the aspirant. The acts of atheists will destroy the conviction of God.

अभिमानदम्भादिकं त्याज्यम् ॥६४

Abhimaana-dambhaadikam tyaajyam. (64)

Egoism, hypocrisy, etc., should be discarded.

Egoism and its attendants hypocrisy etc., are the enemies of devotion. They should be totally annihilated.

तदर्पिताखिलाचारः सन् कामक्रोधाभिमानादिकं
तस्मिन्नेव करणीयम् ॥६५

Tadarpitakhilaachaarah san kaama-krodha-abhimaana-adikam tasminneva karaneeyam. (65)

Having once surrendered all his acts to God, he (the devotee) should exhibit desire, anger, egoism etc., only to God.

त्रिरूपभङ्गपूर्वकं नित्यदास्यनित्यकान्ताभजनात्मकं वा प्रेमैव कार्यम्
प्रेमैव कार्यम् ॥६६

*Triroopabhangapurvakam nityadaasya-nityakaantaa-bhajana-atmakam va premaiva kaaryam,
premaiva kaaryam. (66)*

Love that annihilates the three-fold forms of secondary devotion due to the qualities of Sattva, Rajas and Tamas (vide Sutra 56) and makes one regard himself or herself as eternal servant or beloved of God alone is to be cultivated.

भक्ता एकान्तिनो मुख्याः ॥

Bhaktaa ekaantino mukhyaah. (67)

Devotees who have thus solely devoted themselves to God are the best (principle ones).

16. Glory of Bhaktas

कण्ठावरोधरोमाञ्चाश्रुभिः परस्परं लपमानाः
पावयन्ति कुलानि पृथिवीं च ॥६८

*Kantha-avarodha-romancha-asrubhih parasparam lapa-
maanaah paavayanti kulaani prithiveem cha. (68)*

Such devotees conversing together with a choking voice,
with hairs standing on end, and with tears flowing, purify their
families as well as the earth.

Notes and Commentary

You will find in the Gita (X-1): "Mindful of Me, their life
hidden in Me, illumining each other, ever conversing about
Me, they are content and joyful."

They get *svarabhanga* (choking of voice) when there is
ebullition of divine Prem in the heart, *pulaka* (horripulation
or standing of hair on ends) and *asrupata* (tears in the eyes).
God lives in the tears of a devotee.

तीर्थीकुर्वन्ति तीर्थानि सुकर्मीकुर्वन्ति कर्माणि
सच्छास्त्रीकुर्वन्ति शास्त्राणि ॥६९

*Teerthee-kurvanti teerthaani sukarmee-kurvanti karmani
sacchaastree-kurvanti saastraani. (69)*

They add holiness to holy places, nobleness to acts and
they elevate mere writings to the level of sacred scriptures.

Notes and Commentary

The stones on which they sat, the paths on which they
have trodden, the villages through which they have passed,
the lakes in which they have taken baths, the trees under
which they have taken their food are sanctified. Their names
are even now associated with these places and objects. Guru
Nanak's name is linked with Panjasahab, near Taxilla. His
fingers are shown in the Kund. Bodhi Tree in Gaya is
associated with Lord Buddha. Hathiaharan tank near
Sitapur is associated with Sri Rama. There are so many

Hanuman Kunds, Sita Kunds, and Lakshman Kunds in various places of pilgrimage.

तन्मयाः ॥७०

Tanmayaah (70)

In and around them they realise the presence of God everywhere and at all times.

Notes and Commentary

They have the experience that:

'Harireva Jagat-Jagadeva Harih'.
Hari is this world and the world is Hari.

'Sarvam Vishnumayam Jagat — The whole world is full of Vishnu.' This experience is described in the Gita (VII-19): "At the close of many births, the man full of wisdom cometh unto Me; 'Vaasudeva is all' sayeth he; the Mahatma, very difficult to find." This is a grand realisation. The devotee is full of divine ecstasy.

मोदन्ते पितरो नृत्यन्ति देवताः सनाथा चेयं भूर्भवति ॥७१

Modante pitaro nrutyanti devataah sanaathaa cheyam bhurbhavati. (71)

(At their devotion) their ancestors rejoice, the gods dance with joy and this earth finds in them its protectors (guardians).

17. Bhaktas Above Caste and Creed

नास्ति तेषु जातिविद्यारूपकुलधनक्रियादिभेदः ॥७२

Nasti teshu jaati-vidyaa-rupa-kula-dhana-kriya-adi-bhedah. (72)

Amongst them there exist no distinctions of caste, learning, beauty, lineage, riches, observances and the like.

Notes and Commentary

These distinctions exist when a man is petty-minded. These differences are created by the mind on account of

Avidya. They all melt away when one gets Darshan of God or Atman. Love is a great leveller. It develops equal vision (Sama Drishti). The advanced Bhakta becomes an *ativarna-ashrami*. He goes beyond Varna-ashrama. The petty rules of society and man-made laws cannot in any way bind him. He becomes absolutely free. He acts from his own viewpoint by resting on God. His will and Cosmic Will have become one. His voice is the voice of God. His words are infallible. God speaks and acts through him. The worldly people generally misunderstand him. His ways are mysterious and incomprehensible. He takes food from anybody's hands. He lives with a cobbler or barber sometimes. He dines with a scavenger. Narsi Mehta did Kirtan in the houses of cobblers and scavengers. Orthodox Brahmins excommunicated him. Narsi Mehta attended a feast. The other Brahmins ill-treated him and looked down on him with contempt. Each one of them saw a cobbler by his side. They understood the glory of Narsi Mehta and from that time onwards they began to adore him.

यतस्तदीयाः ॥७३

Yatastadeeyaah. (73)

For they all belong to Him.

Notes and Commentary

It is Lord Hari that has taken all these forms. The whole world is a manifestation of the Lord. *"Lokavattu lila kaivalyam"* — The whole world is the Lila of the Lord. God acts the part of a professor, thief, prostitute, king, beggar, saint, rogue, genius etc., in this big world-drama. He who has this understanding, will have immense peace of mind. He will entertain no pride, Ghrina, prejudice, intolerance or hatred towards anybody. One must be well-established in this Bhava. This Bhava will come and go away. Address everybody as Narayan and receive him with this Bhava. Your whole nature will be absolutely changed. It takes some time. You will have to struggle hard.

18. Instructions to Devotees

वादो नावलम्ब्यः ॥७४

Vaado naavalambyah. (74)

Vain discussion (about existence of God and His attributes) should not be undertaken.

Notes and Commentary

Vain discussions, heated debates, wrangling etc., end in hostility. When arguments fail, people take to vituperation and fighting. Discussions entail wastage of energy and time. It is only mere lingual warfare and intellectual gymnastics (Shabda-vilas and Buddhi-vilas). Nothing substantial is gained thereby. Everyone wants to show his pedantry, skill in argument etc. Such a Pundit cannot dream of getting Darshan of God. He is very far from God. But a little divine talk can be had between people who are well-united in hearts and who are free from pride, for removing doubts and exchanging of ideas. This is salutary and beneficial.

बाहुल्यावकाशत्वादनियतत्वाच्च ॥७५

Baahulya-avakaasatvaad-aniyatatvaat-cha. (75)

Because it leads to prolixity and uncertainty.

Notes and Commentary

Vain discussions will go on indefinitely for days together. Yet people will not arrive at definite, positive conclusions. They will be fighting over words, roots, conjunctions and other grammatical points. God is certainly not in Vyakarana, logic, or prosody. He is in the chambers of the heart. He is to be realised by purity and meditation and not by vain discussions. That is the reason why Lord Yama says to Nachiketas: "This Atman cannot be obtained by too much learning, or discussion or intelligence. He who gets the grace of God, who is chosen by the Lord as His favourite, gets the Darshan of Atman. He reveals to him His Nature. To him alone He manifests Himself." Therefore give up hot discussions. Be humble. Do practical Sadhana.

भक्तिशास्त्राणि मननीयानि तदुद्बोधककर्माण्यपि करणीयानि ॥७६॥

Bhakti-saastraani mananeeyaani tad-udbodhaka-karmaanyapi karaneeyani. (76)

Books on devotion should be studied with attention and the observances or acts prescribed therein (to develop devotion) should be performed.

Notes and Commentary

You must not give leniency to the mind. You must rigidly follow all the rules prescribed in the Bhakti-sastras. Then only you will evolve quickly. You must keep up daily routine and programme and follow it strictly at all costs. If you are lenient to the mind, laziness will overtake you and you will procrastinate everything. That "tomorrow" will never come. Even if you are of advanced age, think you are a college-student and follow the daily routine. The benefits of keeping up daily routine and daily spiritual diary cannot be adequately described. This is the master key for success in spiritual life.

सुखदुःखेच्छालाभादित्यक्ते काले प्रतीक्ष्यमाणे
क्षणार्द्धमपि व्यर्थं न नेयम् ॥७७॥

Sukha-duhkha-ichchaa-labhaadi-tyakte kale prateekshya-maane kshana-ardham-api vyartham na neyam. (77)

One should not waste even half a minute, as all the time one has for divine meditation is the little that remains after what is spent in experience of pleasure, pain, desire, gain etc.

Notes and Commentary

In youth you are enveloped in darkness. In adolescence you are carried away by lust and are given up to sexual pleasure. In old age you groan under the burden of Samsara. Much time goes away in sleeping, vain talk and idle gossiping. A portion is spent in disease and suffering. Where then is the time for doing virtuous actions and divine contemplation? Life is uncertain. You will be carried away by death without a moment's notice. Therefore a wise man should be very careful in spending his time profitably in meditation. Time is most precious. Every second must be utilised in the service of God, service of Bhaktas and meditation.

अहिंसासत्यशौचदयास्तिक्यादिचारित्र्याणि परिपालनीयानि ॥७८

Ahimsaa-satya-saucha-daya-astikya-adi-chaaritryani paripaalaneeyani. (78)

Virtues such as abstinence from all injury, truthfulness, purity of body and mind, compassion, faith in God and the Vedas and other excellences of character should be strictly observed.

Notes and Commentary

The principles of Yama and Niyama of Patanjali Maharshi's Raja Yoga philosophy are embodied here. These are the very foundations of Yoga. Practice of these virtues purifies the heart and prepares the Antahkarana for the reception of divine light. Compassion softens the hard heart. Truth purifies the heart. God is an embodiment of truth and he can be reached through practice of truthfulness alone. Truth alone triumphs. If one is well-established in the practice of Ahimsa in thought, word and deed, all other virtues will cling to him. Most of the vicious actions are done when one loses his temper. Brahmacharya is the highest of all virtues. No Brahmacharya, no realisation. Without faith in God, neither Sadhana nor realisation is possible. Faith is the fundamental qualification of an aspirant. It is not blind faith. It is faith based on reason.

सर्वदा सर्वभावेन निश्चिन्तितैर्भगवानेव भजनीयः ॥७९॥

Sarvadaa sarva-bhavena nischintitair-bhagavaan-eva bhajaneeyah. (79)

The Lord alone should always be worshipped whole-heartedly and with calmness of mind.

Notes and Commentary

Gita says: "*Tameva saranam gaccha sarvabhavena Bharata* — Flee unto Him for shelter with all thy being, O Bharata!" (XVIII-62.) The whole heart, mind, intellect, Chitta and soul must be given to God without any reservation. This is "*sarva-bhavena*". When you meditate, you must be free from thoughts of fear, worry or anxiety.

स कीर्त्यमानः शीघ्रमेवाविर्भवति अनुभावयति च भक्तान् ॥८०॥

Sa kirtyamaanah seeghrameva-avirbhavati anubhaavayati cha bhaktaan. (80)

Being invoked (praised), He soon manifests Himself and makes His presence felt by the Bhaktas.

Notes and Commentary

Lord Hari came out of the pillar in the form of Narasimha when Prahlada prayed with his full heart — "*Sarva-bhavena.*" Prahlada said to his father: "My Narayana is in your heart. He is in my heart. He is in this straw. He is in this pillar also." Prahlada pointed out four places. But why did Lord Narayana come out of the pillar? Because Prahlada had his full concentration with full feeling "Sarva-bhavena" in the pillar alone. He wished that Lord Hari should come out of the pillar. This was his Sat-sankalpa.

19. Bhakti: The Best Means

त्रिसत्यस्य भक्तिरेव गरीयसी भक्तिरेव गरीयसी ॥८१

Trisatyasya bhaktireva gareeyasee bhaktireva gareeyasee. (81)

In all the three periods of time i.e., past, present and future, devotion alone weighs heaviest (most glorious), devotion alone weighs heaviest (most glorious).

(Among the three truths—Jnana, Bhakti and Raja Yogas—Bhakti excels.)

(Devotion of the Lord who is existing in the three periods of time in the form of Truth is the most glorious. Bhakti alone is the most glorious.)

Repetition of the word "Gareeyasee" adds force. It glorifies Bhakti to the highest degree.

गुणमाहात्म्यासक्ति-रूपासक्ति-पूजासक्ति-स्मरणासक्ति-दास्यासक्ति-
सख्यासक्ति-कान्तासक्ति-वात्सल्यासक्त्यात्मनिवेदनासक्ति-
तन्मयतासक्ति-परमविरहासक्ति-रूपैकधाप्येकादशधा भवति ॥८२

Gunamaahaatmyaasakti-rupaasakti-pujaasakti-smarana-asakti-daasyaasakti-sakhyaasakti-kaantaasakti-vaatsalya-asakt-atmanivedanaasakti-tanmayataasakti-paramaviraha-asakti-rupa-ekadha-api-ekaadasadhaa bhavati. (82)

Devotion, though one in kind, assumes eleven-fold forms or aspects according as it manifests in the form of attachment to the attributes and greatness of God *(guna-mahatmya-asakti)*, attachment to His beauty *(rupa-asakti)*, attachment to His worship *(puja-asakti)*, attachment to His memory *(smarana-asakti)*, attachment to His service *(dasya-asakti)*, attachment to His friendship *(sakhya-asakti)*, attachment to parental affection towards Him *(vatsalya-asakti)*, attachment to Him as of a beloved wife *(kanta-asakti)*, attainment to self-dedication to Him *(atma-nivedana-asakti)*, attachment to self-absorption *(tanmaya-asakti)*, and attachment to permanent self-obliteration *(parama-viraha-asakti)*.

Notes and Commentary

The eleven modes or stages of Bhakti are described here. (This Sutra refers to various important types of Bhakti. It does not mean that there are only these eleven types. There are possibilities of as many types as there are human relationships. Even if externally they appear as different, they are all manifestations of Bhakti which in itself is only one.) The highest is Madhuryarasa or Kanta-asakti where the lover and the beloved become one. Sufists also entertain this Bhava. The Bhakta begins with Dasya Bhava, attitude of a servant like Hanuman. This is the lowest rung in the ladder of Bhakti. Then he takes up a friendly attitude towards God like Arjuna. Fear vanishes now. He claims equality with his object of worship. Then he develops a Bhava of parental affection towards God. He takes Lord Krishna as his son.

The students of the school of thought of Sri Vallabhacharya's Sampradaya entertain this Bhava. All fears and expectations vanish. There is fear of downfall in Kanta-asakti, if the devotee is not careful. He is carried away by lustful propensities. He mistakes physical sensations for devotion. Emotion is not devotion. Many unhappy, unpleasant occurrences take place in those who cherish this Bhava. A high standard of purity is required in those who take to this Bhava. This Bhava is purely mental. Dressing like a female and showing gestures like a woman is mere hypocrisy. This is not necessary in this Bhava.

20. Conclusion

इत्येवं वदन्ति जनजल्पनिर्भया एकमताः कुमारव्यासशुख-
शाण्डिल्यगर्गविष्णुकौण्डिन्यशेषोद्धवारुणिबलिहनुमद्विभीषणादयो
भक्त्याचार्याः ॥८३

Ityevam vadanti janajalpanirbhayaa ekamataah kumara-
vyaasa-suka-sandilya-garga-vishnu-kaundinya-sesha-
uddhava-aaruni-bali-hanumad-vibheeshana-aadayo
bhakti-aachaaryah. (83)

Thus the teachers of devotion—Sanatkumara, Vyasa, Suka, Sandilya, Garga, Vishnu, Kaundinya, Sesha, Uddhava, Aaruni, Bali, Hanuman, Vibhishana and others—proclaim unanimously in this strain without fear of the carping criticism of men.

Some interpret the word *Kumara* as the four Kumaras (Sanaka, Sanandana, Sanatana and Sanatkumara). Sanatkumara is the Guru of Narada and the prince among Bhaktas. Sandilya is the author of Sandilya Bhakti Sutras. Garga is the Acharya who performed the Namakarana (naming ceremony) of Sri Krishna and Balarama. Kaundinya is the son of Sandilya. The full name of Aaruni is Uddalaki Aruni.

य इदं नारदप्रोक्तं शिवानुशासनं विश्वसिति श्रद्धत्ते स भक्तिमान्भवति
स प्रेष्ठं लभते स प्रेष्ठं लभत इति ॥८४॥

Ya idam narada-proktam siva-anusaasanam visvasiti
sraddhatte sa bhaktimaan bhavati sa preshtam labhate
sa preshtam labhata iti. (84)

He who believes and has faith in this auspicious (salutaory) teaching expounded by Narada, becomes endowed with devotion and realises the most beloved (Lord), attains the most beloved (Lord).

Siva-anusaasanam is interpreted by some as 'auspicious teaching' and by some others as 'by the command of Lord Siva' (as Lord Siva is the best among Vaishnavas).

HARI OM TAT SAT

OM SANTI! SANTI! SANTIH!

Chapter VIII

INSPIRING SONGS OF SIVA

1. Shatpadi Stotra

अविनयमपनय विष्णो दमय मनः शमय विषयमृगतृष्णाम् ।
भूतदयां विस्तारय तारय संसारसागरतः ॥१ ॥

1. O Lord Vishno! Remove my immodesty and control
   my mind.
   Eradicate my desire for sensual objects.
   Make me develop mercy towards all beings.
   Help me to cross the ocean of this Samsara.

दिव्यधुनीमकरन्दे परिमलपरिभोगसच्चिदानन्दे ।
श्रीपतिपदारविन्दे भवभयखेदच्छिदे वन्दे ॥२ ॥

2. I bow to the Lotus Feet of Lord Vishnu,
   the husband of Lakshmi,
   The dispeller of despondency and fear of this world;
   Whose Glory is Sat-Chit-Ananda;
   Whose fragrance is the Ganga.

सत्यपि भेदापगमे नाथ तवाहं न मामकीनस्त्वम् ।
सामुद्रो हि तरङ्गः क्वचन समुद्रो न तारङ्गः ॥३ ॥

3. O Lord! even though there is no difference between
   me and Thee;
   I belong to Thee, not Thou to me;
   Because the waves belong to the ocean and
   not the ocean to the waves.

उद्धृतनग नगभिदनुज दनुजकुलामित्र मित्रशशिदृष्टे ।
दृष्टे भवति प्रभवति न भवति किं भवतिरस्कारः ॥४ ॥

4. O holder of Govardhan hill! The brother of Indra!

The enemy of the family of Rakshasa;
Who has the moon and the sun as eyes;
Can we not get disgust for the world, when we have
    Thy Darshan, our Lord?

मत्स्यादिभिरवतारैरेव तारवतावता सदा वसुधाम् ।
परमेश्वर परिपाल्यो भवता भवतापभीतोऽहम् ॥५॥

5. O Paramesvara! I am afflicted with the Taapa of the world.
Kindly protect me, O protector of the earth,
Who has taken the ten Avataras of fish, tortoise, etc.

दामोदर गुणमन्दिर सुन्दरवदनारविन्द गोविन्द ।
भवजलधिमथनमन्दर परमं दरमपनय त्वं मे ॥६॥

6. O Damodara! O Ocean of Virtues, O Govinda!
Who has the charming beautiful lotus-face,
Who has assumed the form of Mandara mountain
For churning the ocean of Samsara! Dispel my great fear.

नारायण करुणामय शरणं करवाणि तावकौ चरणौ ।
इति षट्पदी मदीये वदनसरोजे सदा वसतु ॥७॥

7. O Merciful Narayana! I take shelter at Thy Lotus-Feet
    in every way.
May this bee having six legs in the form of these
    six stanzas
Dwell always in my lotus face.

2. Song of Salutation

Rama Rama Rama Rama Rama – Rama Rama
                              Rama Rama,
        Rama Rama Jaya Jaya Rama
        Rama Rama Sita Rama, –

1. He who dwells in the hearts of Bhaktas,
He who destroyed Lanka Ravan,
He who ate the fruits of Sabari
To Him I give my salutations.

2. He who dwells in the Brindavana Dhama,
   He who destroyed the wicked Kamsa,
   He who ate the grains of Sudama,
   To Him I give my salutations.

3. He who dwells in the Mount of Kailas,
   He who is called as Tripurari,
   He who drank the cup of poison,
   To Him I give my salutations.

4. He who combined four parts of Nirtrogen
   With one part of Oxygen gas,
   He who divided the seasons,
   To Him I give my salutations.   (Rama Rama....)

3. Prayer Song

Rama Rama Rama Rama Rama,
Rama Rama Rama Rama Ram
Come, Come, Come, Come, O Dear Lord!
Save us, save us from the Mrityu-Samsar.
                                    (Come, Come.)

1. Art Thou not ocean of mercy and love?
   Hath Thou not saved Dhruva, Prahlad?
   Art Thou not shining in the chambers of our hearts?
   Art Thou not glittering in our sparkling eyes?
   Art Thou not beaming in the glowing faces?
   Art Thou not throbbing in the beats of our hearts?
   Art Thou not flowing along the breath in the nose?
   Art Thou not the Sakshi of our wandering minds?
   Now, then, O Lord, fill my heart with Prem, Prem, Prem,
                                    (Come, Come)

2. Am I not singing Thy Name Rama, Rama, Rama?
   Am I not chanting Thy Name OM, OM, OM?
   Am I not working, breathing and living for Thee
       in every second of my life?
   Am I not feeling Thy Presence everywhere,
   In trees and flowers, stones and chairs,

In birds and dogs, in sun, moon and stars?
Now, then, O Lord, fill my heart with Prem, Prem, Prem.

                                          (Come, Come)

4. Song of Instructions

Hare Krishna Hare Rama Radhe Govinda.
Get up at 4 a.m. Brahmamuhurta,
Get up at 4 a.m. Japo Rama Rama.
Observe Mauna daily for two hours,
Fast on Ekadasi, take milk and fruits,
Study daily one chapter of Gita,
Do regular charity — one-tenth income,
Rely on your own self, give up servants,
Do Kirtan at night, have Satsanga,
Speak the truth at all costs, preserve Veerya,
Satyam Vada, Dharmam Chara, observe Brahmacharya,
Ahimsa Paramo Dharma, love one and all,
Never hurt others' feelings, be kind to all,
Control anger by Kshama, develop Viswa Prem.

                        (Hare Krishna Hare Rama...)

5. Song of Jnana Vairagya

Sunaja Sunaja Sunaja Krishna
Nij (tu) Gitawala Jnana sunaja Krishna.
At first there is tender emotion and warm affection,
Then it grows into glowing love, burning passion.
Through Sravana and Satsanga comes admiration,
Then attraction, attachment, supreme love.
I want my dear beloved Krishna alone,
I want neither Mukti nor temporal blessings.
The world is unreal, full of miseries,
God alone is real, full of Ananda.
You are running after the unreal shadow,
You have forgotten the real substance.
You came alone (weeping), will go alone (weeping)
                              no one will follow,

Do Bhajan, do Kirtan, this will follow.
Why do you fight in vain with your brothers?
Fight with the mind and Indriyas.
Why do you weep in vain for the death of relatives,
Weep for the departure of the Lord.
The love between husband and wife is selfish love,
Brothers, sisters are united for selfish ends.
Death is ever waiting to devour you,
That 'tomorrow' will never come, open your eyes now
                                                (wake up now).
Life is short, time is fleeting, many obstacles
      (to Japa and Kirtan),
Apply yourself diligently to Yogic Sadhana.
This world is a Mela for two days,
This life is a play for two seconds,
(This body is a bubble for two seconds).
When one is in union with God, it is Samadhi,
The Yogi gets infinite bliss and knowledge.
Bhakti Yoga is crossing a river by a boat,
Jnana Yoga is crossing a river by swimming,
A Jnani gets knowledge by self-reliance,
A Bhakta gets Darshan by self-surrender.
When there is one Vritti, it is Savikalpa.
When there is Triputi-laya, it is Nirvikalpa.
When one is in fourth Bhumika, it is Jivanmukti,
When there is no body-consciousness, it is Videha Mukti.
When you are in a state of Turiya, it is Jivanmukti.
When you are in a Turiyatita, it is Videha Mukti.
When there is Aroopanasa, it is Jivanmukti,
When there is Svaroopanasa (of mind), it is Vedeha Mukti.
When Jagrat appears as Svapna, it is Jivanmukti,
When Jagrat appears as Sushupti, it is Videha Mukti.
                          (Sunaja Sunaja Sunaja Krishna...)

6. Song of Goal of Life
(Thars — Nadhur dhatom)

Ram Ram Ram — Jaya Sita Ram
    Rama Rama Rama
        (Ram Ram Ram)
Shyam Shyam Shyam — Jaya Radheshyam
        Krishna Krishna Krishna
Ram Ram Ram Ram, Rama Rama Rama Rama Rama
    Jaya Radhe Shyam
        (Rama Rama Rama)
Goal of life is Self-realisation — try try try
        (Rama Rama Rama)
    Do Bhajan Bhajan Bhajan
    Do Kirtan Kirtan Kirtan
    Do Sadhan Sadhan Sadhan
    Have Vairag Vairag Vairag
    Have Satsanga Satsanga Satsanga
Destroy the Shadripus and drink bliss, bliss, bliss,
Destroy the Shadripus,
    Kama-krodha-lobha-moha-mada-matsarya
You have become now a Jivanmukta,
You have become now a Yogindra,
You have become now a Bhagavata,
You have become now a Muni-shreshta
        (Ram Ram Ram......)

7. Shranagati Song

Rama Rama Sitaram Hey Shiyaram!   (Rama — Rama)
Satchidananda Brahmame Ananta Jyoti
Chidananda Rama Rama Santi Swaroopame
Satyam Advaita-Vastuve Jnana Swaroopame
        (Rama — Rama)
O My Lord! Give me salvation to have Karmic purgation,
O My Lord! Give me salvation to free me
    from all afflictions,
O My Lord! Give me devotion to have Thy Communion,

I am Thine! All is Thine, My Lord! Thy Will be done.

(Rama—Rama)

8. Song of Vairagya

Rama Rama Rama Rama Rama
Rama Rama Rama Rama Rama
Why do you search in vain
For pleasure outside,
Go to the fountain-source
In the subjective Atma;
Awake, arise, stop not
Till goal is reached.

(Rama Rama Rama Rama Rama)

How long you want to remain
Slave of Passion, tell me please.
Try to seek Peace within
By dispassion, practice (Vairagya and Abhyasa).

(Rama Rama Rama Rama Rama)

Are you not really fed up
With illusory objects?
Enjoy the Atmic Bliss
By Manana, Nididhyasana
Reflection, Meditation.

(Rama Rama Rama Rama Rama)

9. Song of Admonition

1. Hare Rama Hare Rama, Rama Rama Hare Hare;
   Hare Krishna Hare Krishna, Krishna Krishna Hare Hare.

2. Am I not Thou, art Thou not I? One alone is,
   therefore true,
   When the mind melts in the Silence,
   you will have Self-realisation.

3. What have you learnt, tell me frankly
   from the Bihar and Quetta Earthquakes?
   Have you got now real Vairag?
   Do you practise Japa and Kirtan?

---

4. Here is a challenge to non-believers of the
    Hindu theory of transmigration:
    Have you not heard the thrilling narratives of
    Santi Devi of her past life?

5. Can you expect real Santi if you waste your time
    in cards and cinema (cards and smoking)?
    When your throat is chocked at the time of death,
    who will help you for your salvation?

10. Song of Devotion

Rama Rama Rama Shiya Vara Rama,
Shyama Shyama Shyama Radheshyama...
Ram Ram Ram Ram, Ram Ram Ram Ram Ram Ram
Ram Ram Ram Ram, Ram Ram Ram Ram Ram Ram
Ram Ram Ram Ram, Ram Ram Ram Rama
Ram Ram Ram Ram, Ram Ram Ram Rama
    Govinda Rama, Gopala Rama,
    Janaki Rama, Kausalya Rama...
    All-wise Rama, Beloved Rama
    Merciful Rama, Ananda Rama.'

The beloved cannot be won by sweet smiles,
Whoever has won Him, has won with tears.
Shame to that rogue that does not utter Hari Hari,
Sinful are those eyes which have not seen Murali Shyam,
Though there is water in tanks, rivers and everywhere,
The Chakori bird looks for water in Svati Nakshatra,
Though there is pleasure in sensual objects,
The Bhakta looks for his joy at the
    Lotus Feet of Lord Shyam.

11. Song of Bhakti and Vairagya

Jaya Radhe, Jaya Radhe Radhe, Jaya Radhe,
                    Jaya Sri Radhe.
Jaya Krishna, Jaya Krishna Krishna, Jaya Krishna,
                    Jaya Sri Krishna.
Jaya Site, Jaya Site Site, Jaya Site Jaya Sri Site.

Jai Rama, Jaya Rama Rama, Jaya Rama, Jaya Sri Rama.
Jaya Sambho, Jaya Sambho Sambho,
Jaya Sankar Kailasapaty.
Jaya Gauri, Jaya Gauri Gauri, Jaya Sakti Jaya Parvaty.

This world is a fair, Mela for two days,
(Asar, Kshanabhangur, Svapnavat)
This life is a play for two minutes,
Therefore try to realise the Self.
(Jaya Radhe)

Mansoor and Shams Tabriez,
Sankar and Vama Dev
Madalasa and Maitreyi
Chudala and Sulabha
Had all attained the knowledge of the Self
(Jaya Radhe)

Just as logs of wood unite and separate in a river,
So also sons and fathers in this world unite and separate.
Therefore give up Moha for children, wife and property,
(Jaya Radhe)

This world is a play of the mind,
It is Sabdajala, Maya-Moha-jala,
Therefore all connections are illusory
(Jaya Radhe)

Brahma Satyam, Jagan-mithya,
Jivo Brahmaiva Kevalam (Naparah)
(Jaya Radhe)

If you have Ananya Bhakti for the Lord,
If you do unconditional self-surrender,
If you say even once from the core of your heart,
'I am Thine, my Lord, Thy Will be done',
You will have His Darshan this very second
(Jaya Radhe)

12. Song of Abhyasa

Hari Hari bol, bol Hari bol
Mukunda Madhava Govinda bol
Just as curd, pappad, achar, chutney
Goad the tongue to eat more kichidie;
So also Japa, Kirtan, Satsanga, Svadhyaya
Develop Bhakti miraculously.
Practise Yama, Niyama, Asana, Pranayama,
Pratyahara, Dharana, Dhyana, Samadhi.
Do Sravan, Kirtan, Smaran, Padasevan, Archan,
Vandan, Dasya, Sakhya, Atma-nivedan.
Have Vivek, Vairag, Sama, Dama, Titiksha,
Uparati, Sraddha, Samadhana, Mumukshutva.
Do always Sravana, Manana, Nididhyasana;
You will have quickly Self-realisation.
Satyam, Jnanam, Anantam Brahma,
Santam, Ajaram, Amritam Abhayam,   (Hari Hari bol...)

a. Bol Hari bol Hari bol, Gaura Hari bolna
   Gaura hari bolna — Gaura Hari bolna.

b. Hari Hari Hari Hari bol — Krishna Hari bolna,
   Hari Hari bolna — Krishna Hari bolna.

13. Siva Lorrie (Lullaby)

Ram Ram Ram Ram Ram, Ram Ram Ram Ram Ram
Ram Ram Ram Ram Ram, Ram Ram Ram Ram Ram
Subhase Sham tak, until break of day,
Repeat the name of the Lord, Ram Ram Ram Ram Ram.

1. This life is meant for Self-realisation,
   Do regular Sankirtan, realise the Atmic bliss
                    (Ram Ram)
   Do Nishkamya Karma Yoga, purify the heart and mind,
   Control the Indriyas, rest in your own Svaroop.
                    (Ram Ram)
   When you get knocks and blows in the battle of daily life,
   Then the mind is duly turned towards the spiritual path

(Ram Ram)
Then comes Vivek-vairag, disgust for worldly things,
Desire for liberation; have deep meditation.
(Ram Ram)
2. Twinkle, twinkle, little star, how I wonder what you are,
Up above the world so high, like a diamond in the sky.
When the blazing sun is set,
When the grass with dew is wet,
Then you show your little light,
Twinkle, twinkle, all the night.
(Ram Ram)
Hari Om Narayana, Hari Om Narayana,
Hari Om Narayana, Hari Om Narayana.
Om Namahsivaya, Om Namahsivaya,
Om Namahsivaya, Om Namahsivaya.

14. Song of Grace

1. Bhansuri bhajave Shyam madhure lataname,
Hari bolo Hari Hari, Hari bolo Hari Hari.
Radheshyama Radhe Radhe,
Radheshyama Radhe Radhe.
Sita Rama Sita Sita, Sita Rama Sita Sita,
Radha-Ramana Hari Hari, Radha-Ramana Hari Hari.
Sitapati Hari Hari, Sitapati Hari Hari.
Sambho Sankar Sambho Sambho,
Gauri Sankar Gauri Gauri.

2. O My Lord! give me Darshan, when can I see
Thy loving face?
I cannot bear the pain longer, when can I have
Thy mercy and grace?

15. The Song of Immortality

Rama Rama Rama Rama Jaya Sita Rama
Jaya Jaya Radhe Shyam.
Turn the gaze, draw the Indriyas,
Still the mind, sharpen the Intellect.

Chant Om with feeling,
O Children of Light, will you drink not,
Won't you drink not, the nectar of Immortality?
Rama Rama Rama Rama...

1. All Karmas are burnt now,
   You have become a Jivanmukta.
   That Blessed State Turiyatita
   No words can describe.
   > O Children of Light...
   > Rama Rama Rama Rama...

2. The grass is green, the rose is red,
   And the sky is blue,
   But the Atman is colourless,
   Formless and Guna-less too.
   > O Children of Light...
   > Rama Rama Rama Rama...

3. Life is short, time is fleeting
   World is full of miseries
   Cut the knot of Avidya
   And drink the Nirvanic Bliss.
   > O Children of Light...
   > Rama Rama Rama Rama...

4. Feel the Divine Presence everywhere
   See the Divine Glory all round.
   Then dive deep into the Divine Source
   And realise the Infinite Bliss.
   > O Children of Light...
   > Rama Rama Rama Rama...

5. Do Asana, Kumbhaka, Mudra,
   Shake the Kundalini,
   Then take it to Sahasrara
   Through Chakras in the Sushumna.
   > O Children of Light...
   > Rama Rama Rama Rama...

16. Song of Illusion

Sunaja Sunaja Sunaja Krishna,
Tu Gitawala Jnana Sunaja Krishna.

1. Is Bhava jalsa dukit badahu,
   Sab teje prabhu kehe saran padahu,
   Vinaya karu tap darpe kadahu,
   Harho jal isse jakkadahu,
   Mitado mitado mitado Krishna,
   Ye trividha mera taap mitado Krishna.

2. In this worldly horrible ocean,
   To row my boat there is but Thee none;
   Misleading me is great illusion,
   Without Thy Grace, the race cannot be won.
   O save me, O save me, O save Krishna,
   With me like Arjuna, behave Krishna.

17. Song of Freedom

Rama Rama Rama, Rama Rama Sita Rama
Sita Ram Radheshyam, Hare Krishna Hare Ram
Rama Rama Ram, Rama Rama Ram.
    Rama Sita Ram,   (Rama Rama Ram...)

1. Krishnaswami, Antaryami Sarva Saktiman,
   Nitya, Suddha, Siddha, Buddha, Satchidananda,
   Narayana Vaasudeva, Mukunda Murari,
   Hrishikesa Padmanabha Madhava Govinda,
   Damodara Srinivasa Madhusudana,
   Sitarama Radheshyama Sridhara Trivikrama.
                        (Rama Rama Ram...)

2. When shall I be free — when 'I' ceases to be;
   Be always self-centred and drink the Atmic Bliss.
   Remove Mala, get rid of Vikshep, destroy Avarana
   Through Karma Yoga, Upasana and Jnana Yoga.
                        (Rama Rama Ram...)

18. Song of Flute-Bearer

1. Rama Hare Siya Rama Ram,
   Rama Hare Siya Rama Ram
   Rama Hare Siya Rama Ram,
   Rama Hare Siya Rama Ram.
   Krishna Hare Radhe Shyama Shyam,
   Krishna Hare Radhe Shyama Shyam
   Krishna Hare Radhe Shyama Shyam
   Krishna Hare Radhe Shyama Shyam.
   Gauri Gauri Gange Rajeswari,
   Gauri Gauri Gange Bhuvaneswari
   Gauri Gauri Gange Maheswari,
   Gauri Gauri Gange Matheswari.
   Sri Gokul ka Rahnewala, Jaya Jaya Jaya Nandalala,
   Makhan misri khanewala, Mohan murali bansiwala.

2. Do total surrender and obtain Divine Grace,
   This is real blessed way: You will obtain supreme bliss.
   He who dwells in that Gokul, Hail Hail Hail Hail
        O Son of Nanda
   He who eats sugar-candy-butter,
        That charming flute-bearer!

19. Song of Bansuriwala

1. Darshan deejiye — Bansuriwala
   Bansuriwala, Bansuriwala,
   Bansuriwala, Bansuriwala,
   Shyam Sundar pyare Bansuriwala,
   Bansuriwala, Bansuriwala, Bansuriwala

2. The fire of the Samsara is scorching me in the extreme,
   Drench me with Thy ambrosia Nectar;
   I know Vasanakshaya, Manonas, Tattwa Jnana
        will confer Moksha,
   Let me have these through Thy Grace, Bansuriwala.
                                   (Darshan...)

---

20. Song of Prem

Thars: Sunaja

Pilade pilade pilade Krishna,
Tu prembhar pyala pilade Krishna.
Dikhaja dikhaja dikhaja Krishna,
O Madhurike Murti dikhaja Krishna.
Lagaja lagaja lagaja Krishna,
Mera Nayya ko par langaja Krishna.
Khilade Khilade Khilade Krishna,
Makkhan aur misri khilade Krishna.

21. Song of Siva Thandavam

Thars: Sunaja

Agad Bhum Agad Bhum Bhaja Damaru
Nache Sadasiva Jagat Guru
Nache Brahma NacheVishnu Nache Mahadev
Kappar leke Kaali nache, nache Adidev.

(Agad Bhum...)

22. Song of Prarthana

1. Hey Krishna Aja Bansi Baja ja,
   Hey Krishna Aja Gita Suna ja,
   Hey Krishna Aja Makkan Misri Kha ja,
   Hey Krishna Aja Lila Dikha ja.

2. O Lord Krishna come to me and play Thy Flute,
   O Lord Krishna come to me and teach me Gita,
   O Lord Krishna come to me and eat
       butter and sugar-candy,
   O Lord Krishna come to me and show me Thy Lila.

23. Song of Darshan

Ab aagaya Bansuri vala
Ab aagaya Bansuri vala
Mor Mukuta mukh Murali jake
Gale vaijayanti maala,

Ab Aagaya Bansuri vala.
(Ab Aagaya)

24. Song of Savara Bansiwala

(Rag-Bhairavi)

Savara Bhansewala, Nandlala
Gokulke rahnewala...

(Antarai)

Kabhi kabhi kahe Krishna Murari,
Kabhi kahe Natavara Girdhari...
Japa tumare Maala, Nandlala,
Gokulke rahnewala.

(Savara...)

25. Song of Real Sadhana

(Tune — Hindustani Bhairavi)
(Mettu — Suna Pyare Mohana)

1. Do real Sadhana, My dear children,
                    (Do real Sadhana...)
   Sadhana — Sadhana — Sadhana — Sadhana
                    (Do real Sadhana...)

2. To free yourself from birth and death
   And enjoy the Highest Bliss,
   I will tell you the surest way,
   Kindly hearken with greatest care
                    (Do real Sadhana...)

3. Acquire first Sadhana-Chatushtaya,
   Then proceed to the feet of Sat-Guru,
   After having Sravan and Manan,
   Then do practise Nididhyasan.
                    (Do Real Sadhana...)

4. Remove first the old, old Dehadhyas,
   By repeating Sivoham Bhavana,
   Then remove the veil, Avarana,

You will rest in your own Swaroop.
(Do Real Sadhana...)

26. Song for Developing Will

Bhajo Radhe Krishna, Bhajo Radhe Shyama.
OM OM OM OM OM OM OM OM OM OM
SOHAM SOHAM SOHAM SOHAM

1. Will is Atma-Bal, will is dynamic,
   Have a strong will and realise Atma.
   (Om Om Om Om Om)

2. Your will has become weak, through various desires,
   Destroy them to the root, by Vivek, Vairagya Tyag.
   (Om Om Om Om Om)

3. My will is powerful, I can blow up mountains,
   I can stop the ocean waves, I can command elements.
   (Om Om Om Om Om)

4. I can command Nature, I am one with Cosmic Will,
   I can dry up ocean, like Muni Agastya.
   (Om Om Om Om Om)

5. My will is pure and strong, no one can resist,
   I can influence people, I always get success.
   (Om Om Om Om Om)

6. I am hale and hearty, I am always joyful,
   I radiate joy and peace to million distant friends.
   (Om Om Om Om Om)

7. I can give Samadhi by simple gazing,
   I can do Sakti-Sanchar by mere Sankalpa
   (Om Om Om Om Om)

8. I am Yogi of Yogis; I am Emperor of Emperors,
   I am King of all Kings, Shah of all Shahs.
   (Om Om Om Om Om)

9. I can elevate aspirants by simple Master's Touch,
   I can work wonders by the power of Sat-Sankalpa.
   (Om Om Om Om Om)

10. I can heal millions from a long distance;
    This is due to will, therefore develop will.
                    (Om Om Om Om Om)

11. Give up Vasanas and think of Atma,
    This is the royal way to develop your will.
                    (Om Om Om Om Om)

12. Keep up diary, give up cares and worries,
    Do Simple Tapas and develop attention.
                    (Om Om Om Om Om)

13. Develop patience and have command of temper,
    Control the Indriyas and practise meditation.
                    (Om Om Om Om Om)

14. Have power of endurance and practise celibacy,
    All these will help you to develop your will.
                    (Om Om Om Om Om)

27. Song of a Sage

1. Bhajo Radhe Krishna, Bhajo Radhe Shyama
   Soham Soham, Sivoham Soham
   Om Om Om Om Om, Om Om Om Om Om

2. I am neither mind nor body, Immortal Self I am,
   I am witness of three states, I am Knowledge Absolute
                    (Om Om Om Om Om)

3. I am fragrance in Jessamine, beauty in flowers,
   I am coolness in the ice, flavour in coffee.
                    (Bhajo Radhe Krishna...)

4. I am greenness in the leaf, hue in the rainbow,
   I am taste-buds in the tongue, essence in Orange.
                    (Om Om Om Om Om...)

5. I am Mind of all minds, Prana of all Pranas,
   I am Soul of all souls, Self of all selves.
                    (Bhajo Radhe Krishna)

6. I am Atman in all beings, apple of all eyes,

I am Sun of all suns, Light of all lights.

         (Om Om Om Om Om...)

7. I am Pranava of all Vedas, Brahman of Upanishads,
   I am silence in forests, thunder in all clouds.

         (Bhajo Radhe Krishna...)

8. I am velocity in electrons, motion in science,
   I am effulgence in the sun, wave in the radio.

         (Om Om Om Om Om...)

9. I am support of this world, soul of this body,
   I am ears of all ears, eye of all eyes.

         (Bhajo Radhe Krishna...)

10. I am time, space, Dik and the controller,
    I am God of gods, Guru and the Director,

         (Om Om Om Om Om...)

11. I am melody in music, in *rag* and *raginis,*
    I am sound in ether, Sakti in Veerya.

         (Bhajo Radhe Krishna...)

12. I am power in electricity, Intelligence in mind,
    I am brilliance in fire, penance in ascetics.

         (Om Om Om Om Om...)

13. I am Reason in philosophers, Will in Jnanis,
    I am Prem in Bhaktas, Samadhi in Yogis.

         (Bhajo Radhe Krishna)

14. I am That I am, I am That I am,
    I am That I am, I am That I am.

         (Om Om Om Om Om...)

28. Soham Song

Do Japa of Soham Mantra
    to get over body-consciousness.
Repeat Soham Soham Soham
Practise Neti-Neti — Sruti Vakyam.
Then names and forms do vanish,

Existence alone remains behind.

(Do Japa of Soham...)

Akhanda Sat-Chit-Ananda
Vyapak Ek Rasa Paripoorna
Vyomavat Sarvavyapee
Svayam Jyoti Jnanamritam.

(Do Japa of Soham...)

Joy, Bliss, Immortality,
Here the mind takes eternal rest.
All Klesha Karmas end now,
You shine in your own Glory.

(Do Japa of Soham...)

29. Song of Vedantin

Raise the Brhamakara Vritti
Rest in Sahaja Avastha
......Brahma Jnanam......
......Glory......
Brahma Jnaname.
Enter the Samadhi through silent meditation
And get established in Brahmic consciousness,
Param...Santi...Nitya...Tripti
Sat Chit Ananda
......Moksha......
Sat Chit Ananda.
Destroy the Ahamta and Mamata
Through Vivek and Vichara.
Become Chaitanya Swaroop
......Splendour......
Chaitanya Swaroop.
Prepare the vessel through
Nishkamya Karma Yoga.
And take to the study of the
Ten classical Upanishads,
Then do Sravan...Manan...Nididhyasan

(Hearing, Reflection, Meditation)
Become Prajnana Ghana
    (Embodiment of wisdom)
      ......Atma......
      ......Ananda Ghana......
Raise the Brahmakara Vritti.

30. Song of Antaratma

Om Antaratma,
Nitya shuddha Buddha
Chidakasa Kutastha   (Om Antaratma)
Om Vyapak Svayamjyoti
Poorna Para Brahma   (Om Antaratma)
Sakshi Drashta Turiya,
Santam Sivam Adwaitam,
Amala Vimala Achala,
Avang-mano-gochara.   (Om Antaratma)
Anandamaya
Chidanandamaya
Anandamaya
Chidanandamaya   (Om Antaratma)

31. Nirugna Song

Nirgunoham, Nishkaloham
Nirmamoham Nischala
Nitya-shuddho, Nitya-buddho
Nirvikaro Nishkriya.
I am without qualities, without parts,
Without mine-ness, immovable,
Eternally pure, all-knowing,
Changeless and without action.

Nirmaloham, Kevaloham
Ekamevaadwitiyah
Bhasuroham, Bhaskaroham
Nityatruptah Chinmayah.
I am without impurity, alone,

One without a second
Self-luminous, illuminator of everything.
With eternal satisfaction and full of knolwedge.

Poornakamah Poornarupah,
Poornakalah Poornadik
Adi-madhyaanta-heeno
Janana-marana-varjitah.
I am extreme satisfaction, infinity,
Eternity, all-pervading,
Beginningless, endless and
Free from birth and death.

Sarvakarta Sarvabhokta
Sarvasakshi Soasmyaham
Sarvavayapee Madvyateeto
Nasti Kinchana Kwapyaho.
I am the doer in all, enjoyer in all.
The witness in all, the pervader in all.
There is nothing except my own Self.

32. Song of a Paramahamsa

Chidananda Chidananda Chidananda hum
Har halme almasth Sat-Chid-Ananda hum
Sivananda Sivananda Sivananda hum
Agad bhum wala Agad bhum wala Akilananda hum.
Nijanand Nijanand Nijanand hum
Har halme almasth Sat-Chid-Ananda hum.
Ajaranand Amalanand Achalananda hum
Har halme almasth Sat-Chid-Ananda hum.

(Antarai)

Nirbhaya aur Nischinta Chidananda hum
Nitya Shuddha Siddha Sat-Chid-Ananda hum
Kaivalya Kevala Kutastha Ananda hum.
(Chidananda Chidananda...)

33. Song of Brahma Vichara

Brahma Vichara Sadhana-dhara,
  Kaivalya Moksha praptayathi.
Karo Sadhan-chatushtaya, Sravan Manan
  Nididhyasan OM OM OM...
These are the Sapta-bhumikas of Jnana,
  Subhechha, Suvichar, Tanmanasi,
Sattvapatti, Asamsakti, Padarthabhavana, TURIYA

My kaun hum, kahase ayaa,
Who am I? Where from I came?
What is Brahman? What is Maya?
What is Bandha? What is Moksha?
What is Vidya? What is Avidya?
Isko vichar karna chahiye
You must make this right enquiry,

(Brahmavichara...)

34. Song of Brahma-Mayam

1. Sarvam Brahmamayam jagattu,
  Sarvam Brahmamayam...
  Sarvam Khalvidam Brahma, Neha Nanaasti Kinchana,
  All indeed is Brahman, there is no such thing as diverisity.
(Sarvam Brahma Mayam...)

2. Mata Pita Brahmam;
  Ladka ladiki Brahmam;
  Doodh dahi Brahmam;
  Chandan Vishta Brahmam;
  Garmagaram chai Brahmam;
  Thanda lemonade Brahmam. (Sarvam Brahma Mayam...)

3. Fashion, style Brahmam;
  Just and unjust Brahmam;
  Ganawala Brahmam;
  Sunnewala Brahmam;
  Harmoniumwala Brahmam;
  Tabalawala Brahmam. (Sarvam Brahma Mayam...)

35. Select Dwanis

1. Radha Krishna Shyam Murari
   Govinda Gopala Hare
   Govinda Gopala Hare

   (Antarai)

   Radha Krishna Shyam Murari,
   Gopia Vallabha Ghirwar dhari,
   Narasi Bhagatke hundi Bihari,
   Ab to aye harari wari,
   Japa mana Mohana kunj Bihari,
   Awo Awo banki Bihari,
   Aja Aja Krishna Murari.

   (Radha Krishna...)

   (Thars: Sunaja)

2. i. Sita Rama Sita Rama Sita Rama Ram
   Radhe Krishna Radhe Krishna Radhe Krishna Krishna .

   ii. Sitaram Sitaram Sitaram bol
   Radheshyam Radheshyam Radheshyam bol.

   iii. Bol Hari Bol Hari Bol Hari bol
   Sri Radhe Krishna Govinda Gopala Hari bol.

3. i. Ramaa Ramaa Ramaa Rama Rama
   Ramaa Ramaa Ramaa Rama Rama
   Radhe Radhe Radhe Radhe Radhe
   Radhe Radhe Radhe Radhe Radhe

   ii. Bhum Bhum Bhum Bhum Bhum Bhum Hara Hara
   Sankar Sankar Sankar Hara Hara.

   iii. Hari Om Hari Om Hari Om Hari Hari
   Hari Om Hari Om Hari Om Hari Hari.

4. Sri Rama Sitarama, Jaya Rama Jaya Jaya Rama.

5. Krishnananda Mukunda Murare,
   Vamana Madhava Govinda
   Govinda Govinda Govinda

6. Govinda Jaya Jaya, Gopala Jaya Jaya
   Radha Ramana Hari, Govinda Jaya Jaya.

7. Madana Mohana Bhajo Brindavanchandra Bhajo
   Radhe Govinda Bhajo Radhe Govinda Bhajo.

8. Jaya Jaya Sita Rama Ramaapati
   Jaya Jaya Radheshyam Shyam
   Jaya Jaya Sankar Kailasapathi
   Jaya Umapathi Mahadeva.

9. Sri Krishna Govinda Hare Murare
   Hey Natha Narayana Vaasudeva.

NARADIYA KIRTAN

10. Bhajaman Narayana Narayana Narayana
    Sriman Narayana Narayana Narayana
    Lakshmi Narayana Narayana Narayana
    Badri Narayana Narayana Narayana
    Hari Om Narayana Narayana Narayana.

    (Sriman Narayana...)

11. Bhum Bhum Bhum Bhum Mahadeva   (One party)
    Hara Hara Hara Hara Sadasiva   (Another party)

12. Sivaya Nama Om Sivaya Namah,
    Sivaya Nama Om Namah Sivaya.
    Siva Siva Siva Siva Sivaya Nama Om,
    Hara Hara Hara Hara Namah Sivaya,
    Siva Siva Siva Siva Sivaya Nama Om,
    Bhum Bhum Bhum Bhum Namah Sivaya.
    Siva Samba Sadasiva Samba Sadasiva
    Samba Sadasiva Samba Siva.
    Siva Siva Sankar, Hara Hara Sankar,
    Jaya Jaya Sankar Namami Sankar.

Chapter IX

LIVES OF BHAKTAS

1. Mataji Omkareshwari

(Jnani Bhaktaa)

Mataji Omkareshwari was a Sannyasini who lived for over fifteen years in Rishikesh. She came from Gujarat. She was a Jnani and a Bhakta. She knew Sanskrit well. She was trained by her own father, a Paramahamsa Sannyasin who was her real Guru. She was a fearless lady. She had lived for some time in dense jungles where human beings cannot enter. She had the beautiful way of explaining things in Vedanta with beautiful illustrations. She composed many thrilling divine songs in Gujarati. Sometimes she would take her *tambura* and do Bhajan along with her disciple Swami Atmanandaji. It would be simply grand and thrilling. She was very kind with the spirit of service deeply ingrained in her. She would serve all the Sadhus in the vicinity with Sraddha and Bhava. Love, devotion, faith, liberality, joyfulness and endurance were the prominent virtues in her. She entered into Maha Samadhi in November 1935.

2. Samarth Ramdas

Samarth Ramdas entered a garden of sugar-cane along with his disciples. One of his disciples ate a sugar-cane without asking the owner. The owner came and gave a good slap on Ramdas's cheeks. The cheeks were swollen. Ramdas did not speak a word. He left the garden quietly. He knew this was his Prarabdha. Sivaji asked Ramdas: "Guru Maharaj, what is this? I see much swelling on thy face. Kindly tell me the cause." Ramdas refused to tell. Sivaji began to insist several times. Ramdas narrated the story to him and asked Sivaji to give some lands free to the owner of the sugar-cane-garden and not to punish him in any way. Sivaji obeyed the commands of Ramdas. Look at the magnanimous heart of Saint Ramdas! He was not only a man of equal vision (Samadrishti) but a man who treated everybody alike (Samavarthi) and considered that everything was God. This is the most exalted state that can hardly be conceived of by ordinary people.

3. Pavahari Baba

You can correct a man either by punishment or by love with presents. The latter is the most powerful method. But he who adopts this method must be pure. He should do meditation and selfless service with Atma-bhav. Saints practise the second method. Pavahari Baba ran after the thief, who entered his cottage with intent to steal, and, placing a bag of vessels at his feet and prostrating before him, said: "O thief Narayan! I never knew you were in my cottage. Kindly accept this bag of vessels. This is yours." The thief was instantaneously moved by the extra-ordinary kindness and love of Pavahari Baba. He immediately became his disciple and in course of time became a wonderful saint. This is correction through love and presents. This disciple of Pavahari Baba met Swami Vivekananda in his Himalayan travels and narrated the whole story to him.

4. Raidas — The Cobbler Saint

At a time when a powerful and earnest movement for obtaining justice towards the the so-called 'untouchables' is going on in the country, it will doubtlessly be of interest to recall the name of one who, himself a cobbler, had preached four centuries ago in no uncertain words the equality of men before God. This was Saint Raidas. Namdev, Sadana, Sena, Kabir, Raidas, Kamal, Dadu, Nabhadas, Krishnadas — there is a long list of saints who, having sprung from the lower grades of society, rose to occupy a spiritual eminence therein and whose poems, such as have been preserved and handed down to us, contribute to the undying glory of the Hindi language and the Hindu religion. Next perhaps to Kabir, Raidas is the most venerated among these saints.

There is little doubt that Raidas was a cobbler by caste. The fact of his humble origin has been frequently and almost painfully reiterated in his songs. Raidas made his living by making shoes and as a cobbler he appears to have given both honest and efficient service to his customers. A considerable portion of his earnings was offered to Sadhus and holy men and he seems to have slowly risen in the estimation of his fellow citizens.

Numerous are the anecdotes and miracles related about Raidas. One of these is that a Sadhu once appeared to him and presented him with a piece of *paras* stone, the very touch of which is said to transmute iron into gold. The Sadhu even demonstrated such a transformation. Raidas would not at first accept this gift and later asked the Sadhu to slip the stone into the thatch of his cottage. When thirteen months later the Sadhu came to see Raidas again, he enquired as to what use the latter had made of the stone. Raidas told the Sadhu that he would find the stone where he had left it in the thatch. Raidas certainly lived a contented life and depended upon his own labours for his livelihood. Later on as his fame for devotion went round and he gave more and more of his time to spiritual discourses, he seems to have been induced to accept the offerings of his disciples for the satisfaction of his bare needs and, as he further advanced in age, to have given up his profession entirely. Out of the money entrusted to him by his disciples, he is said to have built a home for pilgrims and also a temple. Raidas gained the increasing veneration of his fellow citizens but a prejudice against his low caste seems to have persisted in the minds of men throughout. Raidas himself stoutly refused to accept that his low caste mattered in the eye of God and he continued to mention the names of earlier saints whose sainthood had been acknowledged in spite of their low origin.

Raidas was a pilgrim of the Bhakti-Marga or the path of devotion. To him this world is full of sorrow and suffering. The very thought of having been born caused him pain. He believed in the cycle of births and rebirths and craved for release from it. He believed that such an end can only be achieved by the mercy of God and such mercy can be had through prayer and devotion to the Supreme Being. Almost the same ideas occur in his songs again and again, He says:

This sea of existence is an endless torture,
    O Govinda! One can see no end therein.
Far, far is my home, and difficult to reach:
    Wilt Thou not give me Assurance?
Devotion to Thee is a ladder for the Saints:
    Wilt Thou not help me to climb?
It is a boat of iron, laden with stones;
    And I am without good deeds or emotions.
The desires are like waves, and infatuation Death,
    Yet my mind is after the flesh.
O Lord of the humble, listen to my prayer.
    Why does Thou delay?
Raidas is a slave at the feet of the Saints.
    Give me protection now.

Time and again is Raidas moved by the falsehood and the transience of life as it appears to thoughtless people. "Why sleepeth?" he cries out passionately, "Wake thou, O mad man. This false life thou knoweth as true."

High palace, hall and kitchens—
    and then not one hour to live!
This body is like a matted shutter made of grass:
    When the grass has been burnt up, to dust it comes.
Brother, kindred, family, and companions—all say:
    "Take him out quickly!"
The women of the house, who embraced thee in life,
    run away crying, "Ghost!"

Says Raidas: Everyone is plundered in this world.
  I have escaped saying only the Name of Rama.

Raidas's faith in the power of prayer is infinite. It is by various names that he invokes his Lord. Rama, Govinda, Hari, Murari, Mukunda—whatever name he invokes, it is always the Nirguna or the attributeless Lord that is meant. He calls upon all and sundry to join with him repeating the Name of the Lord.

Repeat, ye people, the Name of Mukunda, of Mukunda.
Without Mukunda the body wearieth.
Mukunda is the giver of redemption;
Mukunda is our father and mother.
Living repeat the Name of Mukunda.
Dying repeat the Name of Mukunda.
His servant is ever in bliss.

But the devotion, which Raidasa calls upon people to offer to the Lord, is not of the ceremonial kind. Of its futility he seems to be too well aware. The devotion, which he asks the people to offer, must result in the effacement of the self.

Such is devotion, listen, O Brother:
  When devotion is attained pride departs.
What avails the dancing and the singing?
  What avails the performance of the penances?
What avails the washing of the feet—
  If the essence is not recognised?
What avails the shaving of the head,
  What the performance of pilgrimage and fasting?
Master and slave, devotee and servant—
  these relationships avail not,
    if the Great Essence is not recognised.
Says Raidas: Devotion to Thee is a distant object—
  he who finds it is greatly fortunate.
Abandon the pride, and efface the self,
  for thou art like an ant, and eateth the pickings.

The formal offerings to the Deity are of little worth,

unless the mind be bent in devotion. How beautiful does Raidas express himself on this point!

What shall I offer Thee for worship, O Rama?
    Fruits and flowers are rare, I find not.
The milk in the cow's udder is defiled by the calf tasting.
    The 'Bhramara' hath contaminated the flower,
        and the fish the water.
The serpent entwines the sandal tree:
    Poison and nectar are to be found side by side.
In the mind is the worship: In the mind, the incense:
    In the mind I attend on Thy natural Form.
I know not Thy worship or oblation.
    Says Raidas: What shall be my fate?

Songs of great beauty and devotion could easily be multiplied. One more, however, should suffice.

How can I forsake now the utterance of Thy Name?
Thou art, O Lord, as the sandal-wood, and I am like water:
Thine odour permeates every particle of my body.
O Lord, Thou art like a dense forest,
    while I am like a peacock.
I fix my gaze on Thee, even as the Chakora
    fixes its gaze on the moon.
O Lord, Thou art like a Lamp, and I am like a wick,
    which burns out of its flame day and night.
Thou art, O Lord, like a pearl,
    and I am just a thread that strings it.
We mix together as gold mixes with borax.
Thou art the Master, O Lord, I am Thy servant.
Such is the devotion which Raidas offers Thee.

And such was Raidas, who spent his life in earnest devotion to his Lord, and may be said to have died in the faith embodied in the well-known lines:

Who cares, what one's caste or calling may be?
He who prays unto Hari, is by Hari claimed as His own.

5. Paltu Das

(The Bania Saint of Ayodhya)

Paltu Das was a sincere devotee of great repute. Rajas, Maharajas, Nawabs and Brahmin Pundits came to his cottage in a wood to pay their respects. This inflamed the hearts of the Vairagis of the place. They conspired together and set fire to his hut. It was all burnt to ashes. They thought that Paltu Das had perished. They began to rejoice. But some pilgrims from Ayodhya saw him the same night in the temple of Jagannath at Puri. Paltu Das himself mentioned in a *Doha*.

Look at the mean nature of the Vairagis who call themselves devotees of Lord Rama! Application of broad *tilaks* on the forehead, wearing of half a dozen Tulasi Maalas round the neck cannot make a man a devotee. These are all tricks to fill their stomachs. There is more jealousy amongst the present-day Sadhus than amongst householders. Householders work, earn money and do charity. They all evolve. It is only the so-called Sadhus who waste their time in idle, scandalous talks and mischief-mongering. They become Tamasic, as they have nothing to do. They do not practise regular meditation and study. They are not Sadhus in reality. They come under the category of beggars and loafers. They have simply put on coloured clothing. When the statistics is taken in the next census, these beggar Sadhus should not be reckoned as Sadhus. They should come under the heading "Beggars." These people bring disgrace to the real Sadhus and Sannyasins. Those who are doing Tapas, meditation and who are recognised as such by a board of religious people or Sadhu Sangha can alone be considered as Sadhus and Mahatmas. Their numbers will be limited. It is a grave mistake if the public say that there are 74 lakhs of Sadhus in India at the present time.

6. Charan Das

(A Bania Saint)

Charan Das was a famous Bania saint of Delhi. Banias are always greedy. They are the Shylocks of India. God lives at a long distance from them because their minds are on the money in the iron safe. But some rare spiritual gems like Charan Das came out from amongst these people also to elevate the community. Charan Das became so famous for his sanctity and miraculous powers that even the Moghul Emperor, Shahjahan was attracted towards him. One day Shahjahan sent a few baskets of filth covered with a coating of sweetmeats on the top just to test Charan Das. Charan Das knew beforehand through Divya Drishti the mentality of Shahjahan. He asked the servant who had brought the basket to remove the cover. The filth was all turned into beautiful, delicious sweetmeats of different varieties. All these were distributed amongst the people. Charan Das sent back one basket to Shahjahan as Prasad. Shahjahan was quite astonished. He felt he had never tasted sweetmeats of this kind. He at once sent for Charan Das. He paid Charan Das due respects and gave him a free plot of land. Bhakti-Sagar is a valuable book written by Charan Das. It is in Hindi. The people of U.P. like this book very much.

7. Srimati Suratkumari Devi

(Maharani Bhaktimati)

Srimati Suratkumari Devi, O.B.E., Maharani of Singahi (Khyrigarh Estate) in the district of Lakhimpur-Kheri entered into Maha-Samadhi on 26th January, 1936 at the ripe old age of 97. She was a real devotee. She was a Devi-Upasak. She was also a student of Vedanta. Being a Nepali, she ruled her estate very tactfully. She had good administrative capacity. She stood unparalleled amongst the Talukdars of U.P. She founded a Girls' School at Singahi and built a beautiful temple for Goddess Jagadamba in her estate. The Government of India conferred upon her the titles of Maharani and O.B.E for her ability and righteous administration. She was fond of company of Sadhus. Ordinary Pundits and Sannyasins could not stand before her in philosophical discussions. She loved to do Bhajan and Kirtan. For hours together she would sit at her harmonium and pour forth divine songs from the bottom of her heart. She built a solitary Ashram in the Nilkant hills, Himalayas for her spiritual Sadhana. She used to observe Mauna for months together. She was generous, noble, bold, kind, magnanimous and merciful to all. She had a strong will. She always had a cheerful, smiling countenance. In her old age she had the courage to go on a trip to Mt. Kailas. She was absolutely free from pride of being a Maharani. She used to cook food herself and serve Sadhus and sick persons with her own hands. Her face and appearance had a striking resemblance to Dr. Annie Besant. She could sit for hours together on one Asana and could do Pranayama. May her soul rest in peace!

8. Avadhoot Kesavanandaji

There is a great soul now in Rishikesh named Avadhoot Kesavanandaji. An Avadhoot is a Sannyasin who keeps no vessel or cloth. Some are naked. Some wear Kowpeen only. Kesavanandaji is a great Titikshu (one who has great power of endurance). He is about sixty-five (in 1937). He could stand for hours together in the hot sun, and remain in the waters of the Ganga for many hours in winter.

9. Sri Swami Narayanji

Swami Narayanji is another good Mahatma. He was living in Swarg Ashram sometime back. He was my neighbour. He now lives in Vrindavana. He wears a gunny-bag Kowpeen. He keeps only a time-piece and Hamsa-Danda (Asha), the Yogin's stick. He is a Bhakta of Lord Narayana. He is full of love, devotion and dispassion. Darshan of such Mahatmas inspire thousands and induces Vairagya in the minds of visitors.

10. Sri Sundarnathji

Sundarnathji was a very great Mahatma who lived a few years ago in Badri Narayan. He had no body-consciousness. He was a Sapta-Bhumika (seventh stage of Jnana) Turiyatita Jnani. He was a Yogi too. People have seen him being buried alive in snow up to his chest. Once some mischievous people burnt his leg with fire. Sundarnath said not a word. He always lived in Truth, in Brahman. What a glorious life it is to go above body-consciousness!

APPENDIX

1. Glory of Womanhood

Om! My silent adorations and prostrations to the ladies of the world, who are manifestations of my Mother Kaali!

I want to say a word on the devotional nature of Hindu ladies. In India the religion is maintained by the ladies only. There is a peculiar religious instinct in them. Hindu ladies are highly devotional. They infuse the religious spirit in the males through their daily conduct and practical life. They get up early in the morning, clean the houses, take bath, do Japa, make a small temple in their houses and keep there pictures of Lord Krishna etc., and Puja vessels. They keep the place sacred and in the evening do Arati and prayer. The atheistic male members of the house are forced to do some prayer or other through their influence on account of fear. In reality the ladies only govern the house. They are the manifestations of Sakti. They control the males.

It is said that ladies are 'Abalas' (i.e., one who is without strength). But in reality they are 'Sabalas'. They are full of strength. They hold the master-key of the Hindu Religion. They actually govern the house. They are manifestations of Mother Sakti. The element of Prakriti is predominant in them. A lady is the creatrix, generatrix and nourisher of the universe.

You will have to train your wife also. She will also have to do rigid Sadhana. Mere gossiping will not do. If she serves the husband nicely, takes care of his body with right mental attitude, and gives him the wants of the flesh, food and drink, as soon as he comes down from meditation, she can have Self-realisation in and through the form of her husband alone, like Savitri in Satyavan, Anasuya in Atri.

The husband is not entitled to do any religious rite without her presence by his side.

Yatra naryastu pujyante ramante tatra devatah,
Yatra tastu na pujyante sarvastatraphalah kriya.

(Manu Smriti, III-56.)

"Where women are honoured, there the Devas are pleased; but where they are not honoured, there no sacred rite is fruitful." Such is the glory of Hindu ladies.

That house is a miserable place, veritable hell on earth, wherein the husband moves up on spirituality and the wife pulls him down in sensual grooves and vice versa. They should be harmoniously blended or joined by the thread of the knowledge of the Self, each aspiring eagerly for attaining God-consciousness. That house is really Vaikuntha where the husband and wife lead an ideal Divine Life, singing Hari's Name, repeating His Mantra, studying Ramayana, Bhagavata, controlling the Indriyas and serving Bhaktas and Sannyasins.

The Mantra that is recited at the time of Panigrahana (marriage) in this:

Gruhnami te saubhagatvaya
Hastam maya patya jaradashtiryathasrah
Bhargo aryama savita purandhirmahyam
Tvadurgarhapatyaya devaah!

"I seize your hand so that we may have a good progeny, that you may live with me, your husband, till you become old. The One God, represented as Bharga, Aryama, Savita and Purandhi has given you to me for doing the duties of a householder."

The bridegroom addresses the bride thus:

Virasurdevakama syona sam no bhava.

"Give birth to heroes (many offsprings), and worshipping the One God bring about our happiness."

Chudala was a queen-Yogini. She had many miraculous powers. She ruled a big state in the absence of her husband Sikhidhwaja.

Sulabha was a Brahma-Vadini. She immersed herself in Atma-Vichara and Brahma Chintana. Her name comes in the Upanishads and Brahma Sutras.

Ladies by their Pati-Vrata-Sakti can do anything. They can stop the sun from rising. Savitri brought back to life her dead husband Satyavan. She fought with the God of Death actually. You are all aware of the chastity of Anasuya, wife of Atri, mother of Sri Dattatreya. She turned the Trimurties as her children by her power of chastity.

Gargi was a Jnani. Her name comes in the Brihadaranyaka Upanishad. She appeared quite nude in the court of Raja Janaka and had philosophical controversy with sage Yajnavalkya.

Madalsa was also a Jnani. She converted all her sons into Jnanins. She used to sing:

Suddhosi, buddhosi, niranjanosi,
Samsara-maya parivarjitosi.

"O Child, thou art pure, all-knowing, spotless, beyond the reach of Maya," when she was rocking the cradle of her child. The children imbibed along with the milk of the mother, the Vedantic teaching also and became sages. All ladies should follow the example of Madalsa and train their children in the path of righteousness and Truth.

In olden days Hindu ladies also led the life of celibacy, served the Rishis, meditated on Atman and obtained Brahma Jnana. They were wearing the holy thread. They engaged themselves in Brahma Vichara and Nididhyasana.

Raikva had the daughter of King Jnanasruti for his service. He was a Naishthika Brahmachari. (Vide Chhandogya Upanishad).

No doubt, it is difficult for ladies, particularly for young ladies, to pull on in the path of renunciation (Nivritti Marga). They have not got the same freedom as men have. Men can sleep and move about in any way they like. It is a great pity there is no Ashram for the lady-Sannyasins.

A mob of 10,000 persons came out to stone Mary Magdalene, the Roman prostitute. Lord Jesus addressed the mob with these words: "He that is without a sin amongst you, let him cast a stone at her." The mob was silenced at the utterance of Lord Jesus. Mary Magdalene became the next moment a saint through the grace of Lord Jesus. It is extremely difficult to say when, on whom and how the grace of God will descend. Lord Krishna says in the Gita: "They who take refuge with Me, O Partha, though of the womb of sin, women, Vaishyas, even Sudras, they also tread the highest path." Dear Devis! What reason is there then for despair? *Nil desperandum.* Be up and doing. Struggle. Exert. Practise. Plod on. March courageously. Do sincere Sadhana. The all-merciful Lord will surely crown your efforts with success. Even the vilest of us can attain salvation. Lord Krishna has given us the word of assurance.

O Vidya, would you not like to become a Mira? Mira was driven from the palace by her husband. She was very young. Did He not take care of her? When she was about to drown herself in a river according to the orders of her cruel husband, the Lord held her in His lap. Will He not do the same thing for you? Have full trust in Him and be at ease and full repose. Sing like Mira *"Mere to Giridhargopal dusaro na koi."*

One Sachi rocked the cradle of her son with the Dhwani of Hari's Name: *"Hari Hari Bol, Bol Hari Bol, Mukunda Madhava Govinda Bol,"* infused in him the honey of devotion and brought forth to the world a Gouranga who changed the mentality of the people of Bengal.

Just as the "dark, unfathomed caves of ocean bear many valuable pearls and gems of the purest ray, serene," so also amongst you all there are still many Chudalas, Sachis, Anasuyas and Sulabhas.

O Devis! Do not waste your lives in fashion and passion. Open your eyes. Walk in the path of righteousness. Preserve your Pati-Vrata-Dharma. See divinity in your husbands. Study the Gita, Upanishads, Bhagavata and Ramayana. Become good Grihastha-dharminis and Brahma-vicharinis like Sulabha and Gargi. Bring forth many Gourangas. The destiny of the world is entirely in your laps. You are holding the master-key of the world. Open the door of Elysian Bliss. Bring Vaikuntha in your home. Train your children in the spiritual path. Sow the spiritual seed when they are young.

My earnest prayer is that the ladies should sing in the early morning, as soon as they get up, Names of the Lord, Hare Ram, Govinda Ram, or Raghupathy Raghava Raja Ram. They should train their children also to sing the Names. The whole house will be charged with spiritual vibrations. Even when they cook and draw water from the wells, they should be singing in mild tone the Names of the Lord: *"Jai Sita Ram Jaya, Jaya Sitaram Jaya."* A strong habit of repeating the Names of the Lord will be formed in two months. This itself is quite sufficient for attaining God-Consciousness. Singing the Names of the Lord is a very easy way for getting Darshan of Lord in this Kali Yuga. Even when anyone dies, the habit of singing the Name of the Lord will come to the rescue.

May the Divine Flame grow brighter in you all! May the Devis shine with the effulgence of chastity! May the Devis tread the path of righteousness and attain God-Consciousness. May the Devis rejoice in their homes, leading a life of purity and divinity! May the Devis live with their husbands like Sita unto Rama! May the Devis bring forth children like Gouranga, Jnana Dev, Sadasiva Brahman, Sri Sankara! Glory, Glory unto Devis!

2. A Talk to Sannyasins

Hari Om! Adorations to Brahman! Salutations to Sri Sankara, Maha Purushas and Sannyasins! A Sannyasin is one who has renounced *(nyasa)* the Deha-Adhyasa, body-idea, selfishness, Vasanas, egoism (Abhiman). The four Kumaras of Brahma (Sri Sanaka, Sanandana, Sanatana and Sanatkumara), Sri Dattatreya and Sri Sankara are the pioneers in this path of pure Nivritti-Marga. They are the fathers for this order of Sannyasa.

The world wants economical, racial, social, political, psychological, industrial and also spiritual advancement. The spiritual side should never be ignored. That is the basis. That is the be-all and end-all. In these days leaders in the Karma-Yogic field lay stress on action alone. They have totally ignored the spiritual side of life. Even Sannyasins of various institutions are doing social service only. Some Sannyasins have scholarly erudition only and they command a little respect for sometime. They too have thrown aside the meditative side of life. They are not able to produce a real and lasting impression on the minds of the public, because they have not got the real spiritual stuff or inner Atmic strength at their back.

Spiritual men, Yogins, Jnanins and Sannyasins should appear on the platform like the comet or the second day moon of the month of November (Karthika), like Lord Jesus, for a short time, should pour forth their energy and turn out tremendous work and disappear from the field. The work of holding spiritual classes for longer times and starting Ashrams belongs to the junior Sannyasins. It will not suit the temperament of fiery spiritual giants. They will inundate the land with spiritual waters or nectar of immortality (divine knowledge) in a short time, just as the Ganga does for four months (monsoon) in the year.

No Sannyasin or householder should start an Ashram for the sake of his comfortable living. Many Sannyasins are pure in the beginning when they start an Ashram, I mean when they are poor. When they become rich, when they have got enough admirers and Bhaktas, the spirit of selfless service dwindles away, giving place to selfish motives in their hearts. The object with which they started Ashrams gets frustrated. Then it becomes a money-making institution. People have no attraction. If the head of the institution leads a life of Vairagya and absolute renunciation, the Ashram stands as a centre or nucleus of perennial peace, bliss and joy. It attracts millions of people. The world is always in need of such Ashrams with such spiritual giants as their heads.

Some young Sannyasins take a course of nux vomica seeds, swallow 120 seeds in two years, study Laghu Siddhanta Kaumudi and Nyaya for three years, imagine they have become real Siddhas, and mix freely with worldly-minded persons. This is a very grave mistake. Nux vomica produces impotency. Impotency is not establishment in Brahmacharya. They will have soon a downfall. This goes without saying. Even perfect Jnanins and full-blown Yogins should be very careful. They should avoid indiscriminate, promiscuous mixing with worldly-minded persons. The sight of pairing of fish excited a developed Rishi. The jingling sounds of the bangles of a lady, the sight of even bordered or coloured clothes causes severe excitement in the mind. They have got their own impure associations. Passion is very powerful. Mysterious is Maya. Beware, O aspirants!

It is the tongue and the palate that force the undisciplined young aspirants, Brahmacharins and Sannyasins to come in close contact with householders under the garb of doing Satsanga. O aspirants! Is it for satisfying the tongue you have left your parents, and renounced position and property and embraced Sannyasa? Or, is it for attaining Self-realisation? If it is for the former, you would have done very well by earning money in the world. Do not bring disgrace to the order of Sannyasa. If the tongue is uncontrollable, remove the *gerua* garb and go back to the world, do some work and earn money. Evolve through Karma Yoga. No control of mind is possible without control of tongue.

Satsanga has degenerated in these days. It has dwindled into some kind of mental recreation or amusement. Mere Vedantic gossiping for one hour in the evening between Sannyasins and householders with a mixture of some idle, worldly talk, some politics, some scandal-mongering and back-biting, some silly giggling, guffaw and namby-pamby sentimental out-pourings in vague platitudes is labelled as Satsanga. The minds of the Sannyasin who does Satsanga and the hearers remain in the same state even after a course of Satsanga for several years. There is no elevation and spiritual progress.

When Sadhus and Sannyasins move in the world, they should show an exemplary life of Vairagya to the householders. They should get from the householders the bare necessaries of life only. They should not mix with them very freely. They should live in a solitary place outside the village or town. They should conduct spiritual classes in a serious manner. They should not talk on worldly matters in the interval. They should not bring in too many stories that excite laughter. They should not cut jokes. There must be solemn serenity. The whole audience must be spell-bound. There must be pin-drop silence. Then only the householders will be influenced. They will feel they have got something from the Satsanga.

The moment a Sannyasin begins to ask from householders several things frequently, he loses his respect and influence. He is forced to leave the place immediately. Some shameless Sannyasins live as parasites amongst householders for months together. They are 'Kheer-Parota' birds. They are not real Sannyasins. In the coming census report the authorities should be very careful in forwarding their reports. These persons should not come under the category of Sadhus and Sannyasins. They are professional beggars in coloured garb, like the wolf in the skin of a lamb. There must be a genuine record of true Sannyasins. What is the use of swelling the number of Sadhus and showing a figure of 74 lakhs of Sadhus? You will not find more than 2000 good, cultured Sannyasins who are useful to themselves and to the country at large. A real Sadhu or Sannyasin is like a glorious sun. He shines during day and night.

Rishikesh is the only best place for Sadhus and Sannyasins. Free food, free Kutirs and free cottages are available. There is a beautiful library. Medical help can be had. You can be as free as a bird. Why do you wander then here and there? If a Sadhu or Sannyasin or an aspirant really wants to attain spiritual progress and Self-realisation, he must stick to this place without stirring out even for a day at least for a period of 12 years and must do rigorous, constant Sadhana. Change of place is not necessary. The Ganga and the Himalayas are eternally inspiring, elevating and health-giving. A change to other places is the foolish imagination of weak-willed and deluded doctors and rich people.

A Sannyasin or Sadhu can do more solid and efficient work at the very threshold of his cottage than by moving about from place to place and delivering lectures on platforms. When the flower blossoms, it does not send any invitation to the bees. The bees come by themselves. Even so, real seekers after truth will flock to the real Sannyasins at their very door. Sannyasins need not move about and advertise. In platform-lectures there is only temporary stimulation for half an hour. There are some noise, fights, quarrels, claps, "hear, hear" sounds from some corners. Only real Adhikarins will go to meet Sannyasins at their cottages. The hearts of these aspirants can be really pierced by the instructions of Sannyasins. Training of aspirants is the highest service which a Sannyasin can do. Each aspirant will become a spiritual nucleus or radiating or broadcasting centre of Joy, Peace and Knowledge. When a Sannyasin moves, his time is wasted. All sorts of people come to meet him out of curiosity. Nowadays householders do not attend to their wants. They have become extremely selfish. They show some lip-sympathy by saying: *"Swamiji Maharaj! Kuch seva bathlayiye mere layak."* This is pure humbug, hypocrisy and cunningness.

When one puts on the orange-coloured robe, he must remember that he has entered a noble order of life and that great responsibility rests on his shoulders and that he is going to become soon a religious and spiritual teacher for the world. He must try his level best to possess all the noble, divine virtues and to lead an ideal life of purity and Vairagya.

Real Sannyasins are the beacon-lights and torch-bearers of the world. Just as the lighthouse sends its light to the distant steamers in the far-off sea, so also the Sannyasins radiate their divine light to people of far off climes who are immersed in the mire of darkness and ignorance. They can move the whole world.

Glory to real Sannysins who have renounced everything, who are treading the path of Truth! Hail, hail to Sannyasins who are resting in their own Swaroop, the Brahma-Nishtas! Glory, glory to Parivrajak Acharyas, the Brahma Vidya Gurus who are disseminating the knowledge of the Self far and wide! May their blessings be upon us all!!

3. How to Develop Love

If you really want to root out hatred and develop Prem or pure love, you will have to serve that man whom your mind dislikes. You will have to serve that man who is planning to destroy you. When you hear that your bitterest enemy is sick, you will have to run immediately to his house and shampoo his legs with full Prem. You will have to attend on him day and night, just as you attend on your sick wife, son or mother. Even if inimical feelings rise in your heart, you will have to subdue them by raising frequently to opposite positive feelings of love. This is doubtlessly a trying, difficult Sadhana. But the benefits are wonderful. You will become a centre of power and energy. You will become a spiritual giant indeed. You will become an embodiment of love (Prem Murthi or Prem Vigraha.)

When you try to control anger, when somebody has injured you, you should not only check the big wave of anger, but also try to eradicate the internal burning which remains even though you do not speak harsh words or express outwardly any signs of anger in the face. This is most difficult; but it can be eradicated by continuous service and love.

Whenever your friend is annoyed with you, speak to him first with a smile and apologise sincerely with tears even though you are right. Serve him nicely with Prem. Vindictive spirit is a deadly enemy of peace, devotion, love and Jnana.

4. Glory of Mantra-writing

To
Swami Sivananda,

Madras
9-10-36.

Respected Master,

I am, sending herewith 50 Maalas of "HARE RAM" Mantra. My wife and two brothers have begun to write the same by seeing me often writing the Mantra in my leisure hours. One of my subordinates has also begun the same. When the collection becomes fairly big, I shall send the same.

The sight of the Japa Maalas which you had kindly sent, made my old mother immediately to take up doing Japa.

She has been doing the Japa "OM NAMO BHAGAVATE VAASUDEVAYA" regularly. Such is the glory of the spiritual force.

(Sd.) X.

Immortal Self,

Rishikesh,
15-10-36.

Write daily for half an hour or one hour in a clean notebook the Mantra of your Ishta Devata or SRI RAM, SRI RAM and send the notebook to me at the end of every month along with a copy of your daily spiritual diary. The writing of the Mantra develops purity and concentration. It has immense advantages. Keeping up of diary develops will-power and hastens spiritual progress and Self-realisation. It is a self-correction register. When you write letters to me write Sri Ram twelve times at the top of each letter.

Thy own self,

Swami Sivananda

5. Mysterious Self-surrender

(Sri Swami Atmananda)

Ah, mysterious are the ways of nature divine;
All faiths have tried but failed them to find;
Actions done here a standard no more.
Intentions pure have sometimes to endure
The painful reapings of some unknown past
Which human sense can hardly forecast.
A man entrenched in ambitions high,
Soaring far in the imaginative sky,
When suddenly he falls in a miserable plight
To God so pathetically he cries:
What a folly is mine! Thus unbridled to think
Unpermitted by Thee when I cannot even wink!

I am a weapon Thine, wield me as Thou wilt;
A puppet in Thy hand, drill me as Thou drillst.
Not a word to defy, not a reason to why,
I'll simply perform Thy bidding and die.
I, the little 'I' a bubble of the sea,
Appearance only in hoary antiquity.
Wilt Thou purge me to the purity of Thine?
With pains even scourge (me) to Thy divinity benign?
Diving deep in the ocean of peace,
The father and the son, in absolute bliss,
For ever are eternally one,
Inseparable indeed as the light and the sun.

6. A Soliloquy of the Lord

(Sri Swami Atmananda)

O my Lord! my love to Thee,
Let nobody come to know but he who is Thy devotee.
I entangled in earthly ties
When endangered with fall and rise
My heart at times for Thy sight so cries
Oh, Thee, when shall I see!
Split the veil of the dark so deep
Short the way, but the frightful steep
No other way excepting to weep?
I humbly question Thee.
O light and love of my maiden-heart!
For Thee have I kept this chamber apart.
To please Thee I'll sing so smart
Will Ye then sing with me?
My comrades asking You who art Thou,
You simply say "I won't say now."
Their doubt will die with my stealing brow,
Be our love then free.

7. Places for Meditation

1. *Simhachal (A.P.):* This is the next station to Waltair Jn. You can get pineapple, cocoanuts and cashew nuts in plenty here. There are many waterfalls. This place is very solitary and secluded. There are thick forests. There are educated people leading godly life. This place is quite suitable for meditation.

2. *Puri (Orissa):* You can find good places for meditation near Chakra-Tirth and on the sea-side. The sea-breeze is elevating.

3. *Ramghat (U.P):* This is on the banks of the Ganga in the Bulandshahar district. The nearest railway station is Babrala (Chandosi line). It is only three miles from Ramghat. Bhiksha can be had for Sadhus and Sannyasins. There is Kshetra where free food is given for Sadhus, Sannyasins, Vanaprasthis and Brahmacharins. Pukka Kutirs can be had. Bihari Ghat is another place equally good near Ramghat. There is the Ganga also. You can get free food and Kutirs.

4. *Karnavash:* This is a place on the banks of the Ganga near Ramghat. Free food and free Kutirs are available.

5. *Achpal:* This is a nice solitary place in Kashmir. Bhiksha can be had from the neighbouring villages. There is a nice spring and a fine garden.

6. *Bhrigu Kshetra:* This is near Anupshire in the Bulandshahar district. There are good cottages on the banks of the Ganga. Free food can be had for Sadhus and Sannyasins. There is a Kshetra.

7. *Chitrakut:* This is an ideal place for devotees of Rama. "He who does Japa of Rama Mantra here for six months living on milk and fruits, will have Darshan of Lord Rama," so says Sri Tulasidasji. It is on the banks of the Mandakini river. There are Darmashalas and good rooms.

8. *Rajpur:* This is at the foot of Mussoorie hills, eight

miles from Dehradun. This is a cool place. There are Pukka Kutirs here.

9. *Jhusi:* This is a solitary place at the junction of the Yamuna and the Ganga in Allahabd. There are good Kutirs and Dharmasalas. This is a beautiful place for divine contemplation. Just try for six months.

10. *Naimisaranya:* This is on the banks of the Gomati river. There is a railway station. There are good Kutirs and Dharmasalas. There is plenty of solitude. It is situated between Sitapur and Balamau (U.P.).

11. *Mohavan:* This is a solitary place on the banks of the Yamuna near Mathura in U.P. There are good rooms.

N.B – Householders and Vanaprasthis also can have comfortable accommodation in the above places.

8. Glossary

Aasakti—Attachment.
Abhimana—Egoism.
Abhyasa Yoga—Yoga of practice.
Adhikari—A qualified person.
Adhyatmic—Spiritual.
Adi Yajna—The first sacrifice.
Agati—Stability.
Agnihotra—Fire sacrifice.
Ahaituki Bhakti—Spontaneous devotion.
Ahaituki—Free from any sort of motive altogether.
Ahamgraha Upasana—Meditation on Nirguna.
Ahimsa—Non-injury.
Aisvarya (Vibhutis)—Divine powers.
Akasa Vani—Sound in the ethereal space.
Akhanda Japa—Unbroken repetition of God's Name.
Alasya—Laziness.
Alpam—Lower experience.
Amritam—Immortality.
Amsha Avatar—Partial incarnation.
Amsha—Portion.

Anamaya Pada—Blissful seat.
Ananta—Infinite.
Ananya Bhakti—One-pointed devotion.
Ananyata—Single-minded devotion unto the Lord.
Anatma—Non-sentient objects.
Antahkarana—Inner four-fold instrument.
Antarika—From the bottom of the heart.
Antarmukhi-vritti—Inward going tendencies of the mind.
Antaryamin—Inner Ruler.
Anuraga—Intense attachment.
Anushthana—Performance of certain religious rites
    in accordance with definite rules of the Sastras.
Anyonyaasrya—Mutual dependence.
Apara—Lower.
Apta-kama—One in whom all desires are satisfied; a Jnani.
Archana—Offerings (Generally worship with certain
    leaves and flowers).
Arta—The suffering.
Artharti—The self-interested.
Asrupata—Tears in the eyes.
Asuya—Jealousy.
Ati Varnashrami—One who is beyond the
    Varnashrama Dharma (A Paramahamsa Sannyasin).
Atma Bala—Soul-force.
Atma Nivedana Sakti—The power of self-resignation.
Atma Nivedana—complete self-surrender.
Atma Santushti—One who is contented in the Self.
Atma Vichara—Enquiry into the Self.
Atma-Jnana—Knowledge of the Self.
Atmarati—He who revels in the Self.
Atmatripti—Satisfaction in the Self.
Avadhoota—One kind of sannyasi in a nude state.
Avahana—Invoking.
Avarana—Veiling power.
Avatara—Incarnation.
Avesha Avatara—A kind of Avatara in whom the divine
    has taken possession.
Avicchinna—Unbroken.

Avidya—Ignorance.
Avyabhicharini—Single-minded devotion.
Avyakta Upasana—Worship of the unmanifested.
Avyavahita—Unmeditated devotion towards God.

Bhaktavatsala—Lover of the devotees.
Bhava—Feeling.
Bhoga—Enjoyment.
Bhuma—Unconditional Self; Infinite.
Bija—Seed.
Brahma Nishtha—One who is established in Brahman.
Brahma Varishtha—Highest type of Jnani.
Brahma Yajna—Sacrifice unto the Self.
Brahmacharya—Celibacy.
Brahmisthiti—Getting oneself established in Brahman.
Buddhi Vilas—Intellectual gymnastics; play of intellect.

Chandala—An outcaste.
Charanamrita—The washing-water of the feet of a preceptor.

Damba—Hypocrisy.
Darshan—Vision.
Dasya—Service.
Deenadayalu—Merciful towards the helpless.
Dharana—Retention; concentration.
Dhvani—Sound.
Dhyana—Meditation.
Dhyeyam—Object of worship.
Dinacharya—Daily routine.
Divya Chakshus—Divine eyes; the eye of wisdom.
Divya Drishti—Divine vision.
Divya Gandha—Super-sensual fragrance.
Dosha—Fault.
Dvandvas—Pairs of opposites.

Eka-bhakti—Undivided and whole-hearted devotion to God.

Gati—Movement.
Gauna—Secondary.
Ghrina—Dislike.
Go-shalas—Cowsheds.
Gudakesha—Conqueror of sleep.

Gunamahatmya Sakti—Attachment of the attributes and greatness of God.

Hiranyagarbha—Brahma.

Indriyas—Senses.

Irshya—Jealousy.

Isvararpana—Offering unto the Lord.

Japa—Repetition of the Name of the Lord.

Jijnasu—The seeker of Knowledge.

Jivanmukti—Liberation.

Jnanagni—Fire of wisdom.

Jnani—The wise.

Kaivalya Mukti—Absolute independence.

Kalas—Rays.

Kama—Desire.

Kamana—Longing.

Kampana—Twisting of muscles.

Kantasakti—Attachment of Him as of a beloved wife.

Kartavya—Duty.

Karuna—Mercy.

Kashaya—Hidden Vasanas.

Kevala-Jnani—A Jnani without Siddhis.

Kirtan—Singing His praise.

Kirti and Pratishtha—Name and fame.

Krama-Mukti—Progressive emancipation.

Krita-kritya—One who has done all actions.

Krodha—Anger.

Kshama—Forgiveness; patience.

Lila—Play; Sporting.

Maala—Rosary.

Madhurya—Grace and beauty.

Maha Bhava—Highest Divine ecstatic mood.

Mahima—Glory.

Mamata—Mine-ness.

Manasic Pooja—Mental worship.

Manorajya—Building castles in the air.

Mantra Sakti—Power of Mantra.

Matsarya—Jealousy; Envy.

Mauna—Silence.
Maya—Illusion.
Mithya Drishti—The vision that everything is false.
Mithyachari—Hypocrite.
Moha—Infatuated love towards children, father, wife etc.
Moodha Tapas—Foolish kinds of austerities.
Moorchha—Fainting.
Mukhya—Primary.
Mukti—Liberation or freedom.
Murti—Idol.

Natanam—Dancing.
Nava-vidha-bhakti—Nine modes of worship.
Nidra—Sleep.
Nirabhimanata—Without mine-ness.
Nirakara and Nirguna—Formless and attributeless.
Nirodha—Control of desire.
Nishkamya—Desireless.
Nishtha—One-pointed devotion.
Nitya Sukha—Eternal Bliss.
Nitya Tripti—Eternal satisfaction.
Nivritti-marga—Path of renunciation.
Niyama—Religious observances.
Nritya—Dance.
Nyasa—Renunciation.
Nyaya—Analogy.

Padasevana—Worshipping His Lotus Feet.
Pancha Maha Yajnas—The five great sacrifices.
Para Bhakti—Highest love.
Parakaya-pravesha—Entering another's body.
Parama Santi—Supreme peace.
Parama Virahasakti—Attachment to permanent self-obliteration.
Parama Gati—Highest path.
Parama Vyakulata—Feeling severe grief in forgetting Him.
Paramdhama—Supreme Abode.
Parampara—Handed down from Guru to disciple
   in succession.
Patita Pavana—Purifier of the fallen ones.
Pativrata Dharma—Observance of the vow of chastity.

Pitambara—Yellow cloth.

Pitru-worship—Worship of forefathers.

Poorna Avatara—Full incarnation with 16 rays (and with full power).

Prana pratishtha—Life-giving ceremonies.

Prananatha, Prana Vallabha—Lord of the very breath.

Prarabdha—Fructescent works.

Prasad—That which gives peace.

Pratima—Symbol.

Pratyavaya-dosha—Sin of omission.

Pravritti—Path of action.

Prayaschitta—Expiatory rites.

Prem—Pure love.

Puja—A simple form of worship.

Pujaasakti—Attachment towards His worship.

Pulaka—Horripulation or standing of hair on ends.

Purushartha—Right exertion.

Raga-Dvesha—Like and dislike.

Rasasvada—The Bliss of Savikalpa Samadhi.

Rupaasakti—Attachment towards His beauty.

Sabda Vilas—Lingual warfare; play of sound.

Sadachara—Right conduct.

Sadat—Continuous.

Sadhana Chatushtaya—Four means of salvation.

Sadhana—Any spiritual practice.

Sadhana-sakti—The power of doing spiritual practice.

Sadyo-mukti—Immediate or direct emancipation.

Saguna Brahman—Brahman with attributes.

Sakara and Saguna—With form and with attributes.

Sakhya—Friendship.

Sakhyaasakti—Attachment towards His friendship.

Sakshi—Witness.

Sakti Sanchar—Transmission of power.

Samadhi—Superconscious state.

Samadrishti—Equal vision.

Samarasa Bhakti—He who has devotion for all the aspects of Isvara.

Sameepya-mukti—State of being near Lord Vishnu.

Sampradaya—Established custom.

Samskaras—Impressions.

Sandhya—The point of junction of two periods of time.

Santi—Peace.

Sarupya-mukti—State of having the same form
   as that of Lord Vishnu.

Sarva-tyaga—Renunciation of all.

Sasvata-pada—Everlasting abode.

Satsanga—Company of the wise.

Sat-sankalpa—Pure resolve of a Jnani.

Satyam—Truth.

Satya-vyavahara—Truthful activities.

Sayujya-mukti—State of being merged in Vishnu.

Shad-ripus—Six enemies.

Shad-sampat—Six fold virtue.

Siddhi—Power, perfection.

Smarana—Remembering His Name.

Sneha—Friendship.

Soham—I am He.

Sraddha or Visvas—Faith.

Sravana—Hearing the Lila of God.

Sreyo-marga—The path of Moksha.

Sukshma—Subtle.

Sutra—Aphorism.

Svabhava—Habit.

Svadhyaya—Study of religious books.

Svarabhanga—Inability to speak; choking of voice.

Svaroopa-shtiti—Resting in Brahman.

Taila-dharavat—Like unbroken flow of oil.

Tamas—Inertia.

Tandri—Half sleep state.

Tanmaya state—Identical with That.

Tanmayaasakti—Attachment to self-absorption.

Tatashta Lakshana—Saguna Brahman.

Tattva—Truth.

Trishna-tantu—The thread of sense-hankering.

Trishna—Thirsting for objects.

Turiya-avastha—State of superconsciousness.

Tushnimbhoota—A quite state of the mind.
Tushti—Contentment.

Udaseena—Indifferent man.
Udasinata—Indifference to sensual enjoyments and sensual objects.
Upachara—Offering respect.
Upadesh(a)—Religious instruction.
Upadhis—Limiting adjuncts.
Upamasu Japa—Doing Japa in a whisper.
Upasana—Worship.
Utpatti—Creation.

Vaikhari—Verbal.
Vaikuntha—Heaven.
Vairagya—Dispassion.
Vandanam—Prostrations.
Vasana—Subtle desire.
Vatsalyaasakti—Attachment to parental affection towards Him.
Vichara—Right enquiry.
Vidya—Knowledge.
Vikshepa Sakti—Force of distraction.
Vikshepa—Tossing or oscillation of mind.
Vimana—Celestial car.
Viraha-agni—Pain from separation of Lord.
Virakta Sadhus—Dispassionate ascetics.
Visarjana—Bidding farewell to the deity.
Vishayaasakti—Attachment to sensual enjoyment.
Visva-prem—Cosmic love.
Visvaroopa-darshan—Vision of the Virat;
    Cosmic–consciousness.
Viveka—Discrimination.
Vyakarana—Grammar.
Vyakta Upasana—Worship of the manifested.

Yama—Self-restraint; The Lord of Death.
Yoga-bhrashta—One who has fallen from Yogic practices.